LEADERSHIP FOR DEVELOPMENT

LEADERSHIP FOR DEVELOPMENT:
WHAT GLOBALIZATION DEMANDS OF LEADERS FIGHTING FOR CHANGE

Edited by
Dennis A. Rondinelli and
John M. Heffron

Kumarian Press
An Imprint of Stylus Publishing

Leadership for Development:
What Globalization Demands of Leaders Fighting for Change

Published 2009 in the United States of America by Kumarian Press
22883 Quicksilver Drive, Sterling, VA 20166 USA

Copyedit by Connie Day
Proofread by Beth Richards
Index by Robert Swanson
Design and production by Rosanne Schloss, Pro Production
The text of this book is set in 11.5/15 Adobe Garamond

Printed in the USA on acid-free paper by Edwards Brothers.

∞ The paper used in this publication meets the minimum requirements of the American National Standard for Information Sciences—Permanence of Paper for Printed Library Materials, ANSI Z39.48-1984.

Library of Congress Cataloging-in-Publication Data

Leadership for development : what globalization demands of leaders fighting
   for change / edited by Dennis A. Rondinelli and John M. Heffron.
      p. cm.
   Includes bibliographical references and index.
   ISBN 978-1-56549-292-9 (pbk. : alk. paper) — ISBN 978-1-56549-293-6
   (cloth : alk. paper)
   1. Economic development. 2. Political leadership. 3. Globalization. 4. Economic
development—Case studies. 5. Political leadership—Case studies. 6. Globalization—
Case studies. I. Rondinelli, Dennis A. II. Heffron, John M.
   HD82.L3272   2009
   338.9—dc22

                                                                    2009010987

For Dennis A. Rondinelli (1943–2007), a pioneer of development scholarship and an indefatigable champion of the development rights of people everywhere.

CONTENTS

PREFACE

L eadership is the hallmark of every successful effort at international development since the late 1940s, and its absence has been the underlying cause of most development failures. This is because development, a process of change that requires the mobilization of human, financial, and physical resources, requires effective leaders who have a vision of the future and who are able, through persuasion and coalition building, to convince others of the need for change.

Although crucial in bringing about needed modifications of human and organizational behavior, leadership for economic and social development is too often either taken for granted or largely overlooked. One thing is clear, however. As globalization increases international interaction across traditional borders, and as the resources for development come increasingly from international sources, programs of foreign assistance will require public sector and private sector leaders with a more cosmopolitan outlook and with a wider range of leadership skills, attributes, and types of influence than in the past. This book focuses on the experiences of a small but representative group of men and women who, since the 1960s, have led in the creation and implementation of development and foreign assistance policies and programs in countries in North America, South America, and Asia bordering the Pacific Ocean. From these experiences it draws lessons in how individuals and organizations can exercise effective leadership on economic, social, and political issues within and across national borders.

Five fundamental research questions guide this study. First, how does global interdependence among governments and organizations in Pacific Basin nations—primarily in Asia and South America—affect approaches to and practices of leadership around important development issues? Second, how do political, business, and social leaders in the Pacific Basin exercise leadership to achieve development goals? Does it make a difference, for example, whether leaders get their advice—from experts or nonexperts, from academic or nonacademic elites—in the process of setting and pursuing development goals? Third, are transformational or transactional leadership styles more effective in bringing about development? Fourth, what differences and similarities in leadership styles, approaches, concepts, and methods within and across Asian and Latin American cultures and societies influence development decisions? Fifth, what can we learn from recent experience in these countries about the styles, traits, and attributes of successful leadership that can be used to develop future leaders in poor and underdeveloped areas of the world?

We include comparative studies of Asian and Latin American countries and provide case studies of individuals and organizations to highlight concepts and methods of leadership that have proved particularly effective in an interdependent global society, one in which leadership is required for a range of international, national, and local development policies.

This book is one of a series sponsored by the Pacific Basin Research Center at Soka University of America. The founders of Soka University of America created the Pacific Basin Research Center (PBRC) in 1991 to integrate social science research with the university's values of peace, human rights, and the dignity of life. Its purpose is to engage scholars from around the world in research focused on policies that contribute to the peaceful pursuit of human development. Over the past decade, PBRC has sponsored research published in nearly a dozen books and in numerous articles and working papers that contribute to our knowledge of international development policy. Its research has examined "great policies," policies that transcend conventional boundaries of public decision making and inspire innovation; policies promoting positive human rights; the role of social capital in human development; the impacts of globalization on national sovereignty; the challenges of nation-building in societies that have recently experienced conflict; and in a period of transition from dependency to interdependency, the changing face of globalization in the region and in the rest of the world.

PBRC's current research explores how development strategies can serve to preempt various forms of violence, including inter-ethnic rivalries, class conflict, regional secessionist movements, and struggles over natural resources. Research sponsored by PBRC seeks to illuminate how and why governments, social organizations, and private enterprises in Asian, North American, and Latin American Pacific Basin countries are responding to globalization, exercising leadership for development, and protecting and modifying cultural traditions that embody human values as development occurs.

We are grateful to all of those who contributed to the book and to those whose support made the book possible, including the good people at Kumarian Press, Jim Lance, Erica Flock, and an excellent copy editor, Connie Day. We especially appreciate the continuing encouragement of the Board of Trustees of Soka University of America, SUA President Daniel Habuki, and the founder of the university and of the Pacific Basin Research Center, Daisaku Ikeda.

—Dennis A. Rondinelli
—John M. Heffron

1

LEADERSHIP FOR DEVELOPMENT:
AN INTRODUCTION

Dennis A. Rondinelli and John M. Heffron

In the aftermath of World War II, much of Europe lay in ruins from a long and devastating bombing campaign by both Allied and Axis forces. Although the Allies won a decisive military victory, it came at a high price: the destruction of many of Europe's major cities and the economies of both winning and losing countries. At a crucial time in history, the creativity and vision of a group of American and European leaders, acting quickly and boldly to provide assistance for both short-term emergency relief and long-term economic development, put Europe back on the road to recovery. Through what later became known as the Marshall Plan, the American-led program for European recovery became the model for more than a half century of efforts by richer countries of the world to help those in poverty and distress.

At the end of World War II, the rapid recovery of Europe was not a foregone conclusion. Visionary plans developed by American leaders such as Walt W. Rostow, Will Clayton, Dean Acheson, Secretary of State George C. Marshall, and President Harry S. Truman required unusual vision and bold action to convince a war-weary American public and the United States Congress to support what many historians consider the most original and effective long-term economic development assistance program in American history.[1] American assistance for rapid and sustained economic development was essential to prevent Europe

1

from declining into deeper political fragmentation and lingering economic suffering and social disruption. Without the active leadership of a
group of people committed to these goals, the world of the 1950s and
1960s would have been a far different and more contentious one. Bold
leadership was the driving force for the momentous achievements of the
European Recovery Plan and for all of the most notable international development efforts in the following half century. And yet American leadership did not prevent the occurrence of the Cold War and its domestic
parallel in the McCarthyite witch hunts of the 1950s. Development assistance, although higher on the America agenda than ever before, played
itself out in Washington, against a backdrop of bitter anti-Communism
and its counterpart, liberal anti-anti-Communism.

LEADERSHIP'S IMPACT ON
THE DIRECTION OF DEVELOPMENT

Leadership objectives and styles have strongly shaped the post–World
War II world. Wise development strategies, coupled with far-sighted
leadership, have led some Pacific Basin countries to extraordinary growth.
Yet destructive leadership styles are often responsible for development
failures. Although the kind of bold and sweeping leadership that
marked European recovery during the late 1940s and early 1950s is now
widely recognized and celebrated, the role of leadership in economic
and social development is too often simply taken for granted or largely
overlooked.

Since the 1950s, economic and social development in Asia has depended on the emergence of leaders such as General Chen Chang, the
governor of Taiwan, whose vision launched remarkably successful programs of land reform and export-led growth on that beleaguered island
in the 1950s and 1960s; President Park Chung-Hee, who transformed
South Korea from a poor war-torn economy into an internationally competitive exporting giant during the 1960s and 1970s; Lee Kwan Yew, who
created an independent political city-state and economic powerhouse

from a poor, fragmented Malaysian and British colonial outpost in the 1970s and 1980s; and Deng Xiaoping, whose advocacy of a more market-oriented approach to economic development began the postrevolutionary process of modernizing the People's Republic of China beginning in the 1980s.

Although political leaders in Latin America have as often exploited as developed their economies and societies, visionaries frequently emerged to fight for social change. Lázaro Cárdenas, for example, first as governor of Michoacán in the 1920s and then as president of the Republic of Mexico in the 1930s, mounted an extensive campaign for political and social reform, including large-scale land redistribution. He led the movements to create modern secular schools and strengthen workers' cooperatives. Similarly, Gonzalo Sánchez de Lozada, Bolivia's president from 1993 to 1997 and again from 2002 to 2003, mobilized support for extensive economic and social reforms. As a senator from Cochabamba, as a minister of planning in the Paz Estenssoro administration, and later as president, Sánchez de Lozada liberalized a stagnant state-controlled economy, reduced hyperinflation, privatized inefficient state enterprises, created a government pension plan for elderly citizens, decentralized the government, and collaborated with another strong leader, Amalia Anaya, to modernize Bolivia's moribund education system.[2]

This pivotal role of leadership in development is not confined to any particular historical period. Contemporary leaders such as Mechai Viravaidya, founder of the Population and Community Development Association, whose imaginative leadership led to a social revolution in family planning in Thailand, and 2006 Nobel Peace Prize winner Muhammad Yunus, whose insight and persistence created the Grameen Bank in Bangladesh to extend small loans to entrepreneurs too poor to qualify for traditional bank loans, are but two examples of thousands of leaders who have brought significant and peaceful change to Asia. Erna Witoelar, the first woman minister of public works and housing in Indonesia, founded WALHI, an environmental forum and the first major indigenous environmental organization to exert pressure on the government and private industries to protect Indonesia's natural resources. She created the Indonesian Consumer Foundation and directed the Asia Pacific Philanthropy Consortium and then went on to develop the Community Recovery Program, which worked to strengthen the social safety net for the poor in the wake of the 1997 Asian financial crisis.[3]

Contemporary local leaders in Latin America have been a driving force for economic and social development. Mayor Jaime Lerner transformed his city of Curitiba, Brazil, from a poor and little-known agricultural trading center into one of the most livable cities in the world. Persistent leaders in Bogotá, Colombia—even during a period of national crisis arising from drug wars and insurgency—made that city more efficient, less congested, and far more livable for both the privileged and the poor. The transformation began in the early 1990s under the leadership of Mayor Jaime Castro and was carried on by equally strong mayors Antanas Mockus and Enrique Penalosa in the mid- and late 1990s.[4] In Haiti—a country plagued by exploitive national officials and continuing political conflict—community leaders such as Michel Chancy, a veterinarian who founded the nongovernment organization Veterimed, took the initiative to improve animal health and the productivity of poor peasant farmers and (through the "Leche Agogo" program) to help poor family farmers process and sell dairy products.[5]

Notwithstanding these cases, we must avoid falling into the trap of assuming that success requires successful leaders and that, therefore, every success in development demonstrates the importance of leadership. A much more meaningful and constructive focus is on discovering the factors that shape leadership traits, styles, and leader-follower interactions that are conducive to economic growth and alleviation of poverty in particular contexts. Traits such as courage, creativity, farsightedness, capacity to mobilize followers (and to exploit existing supplies of social capital), and empathy for the less fortunate are obviously promising characteristics, but many other leadership characteristics and relationships may or may not be associated with sound development. People in positions of political authority do not always pursue objectives that are beneficial to society or developmental for their communities and countries. Throughout history, dictatorial, corrupt, or power-hungry leaders have simply exploited the resources of their countries for their personal benefit or to reward their families, friends, or supporters. Often those who assume positions of power and authority either fail to exhibit effective leadership qualities or become what Lipman-Blumen refers to as "toxic leaders"—that is "individuals who by virtue of their destructive behaviors and their dysfunctional personal qualities or characteristics, inflict serious and enduring harm on the individuals, groups, organizations, communities and even the nations that they lead."[6] Ferdinand Marcos's support of crony capitalism and corrupt practices in the Philippines and Suharto's in Indonesia depleted their country's scarce public finances, monies that could have been used to stimulate economic development and overcome poverty, rather than channeling funds to their families and elite supporters. Pol Pot's reign of terror brought human devastation, genocide, and economic destruction to Cambodia. Augusto Pinochet's dictatorial military regime in Chile, even as it created a foundation for economic growth, imposed untold misery for those who sought democratic and participatory governance and benefits for the country's poor.

Some leaders who were more benevolent—Vicente Fox in Mexico and Fernando de la Rúa in Argentina—had good intentions but were simply unable to overcome opposition or to mobilize supporters.[7] Michael Shifter points out that the disappointment both within and outside of the country in former Mexican President Vicente Fox's leadership resulted from Fox's inability to "get things done." The Mexican president "struggled to strike deals and work effectively with a Congress still dominated by the Partido Revolucionario Institucional (PRI). Fox's cabinet and advisers are capable, but have not come together as an effective team. Still open to question is Fox's ability to articulate a clear program for the country, devise a political strategy, and instill the necessary discipline to achieve his main policy aims."[8] Thaksin Shinawatra's directive leadership style and tendency toward cronyism in making political appointments led to conflicts in Thailand that undermined his effectiveness as a legitimate leader and to his overthrow in a military coup.

LEADERSHIP AND DEVELOPMENT

We argue in this book that understanding the nature and origins of particular forms of individual and organizational leadership is important for achieving economic, social, and political changes that promote peaceful, humanistic development. Development itself is a process of change that requires leaders to mobilize human, financial, and physical resources and to transform individual and organizational behavior. The economist Michael Todaro defined development as "a multidimensional process involving the reorganization and reorientation of entire economic and social systems. In addition to improvements in incomes and output, it typically involves radical changes in institutional, social, and administrative structures, as well as in popular attitudes and, in many cases, even in customs and beliefs."[9] Development policies, in the formal sense, are a type of social innovation that requires leadership in all stages of the process, from identifying problems or recognizing opportunities for human betterment to transforming innovative ideas about problems or opportunities into action, obtaining approval or legitimacy for policy reforms, enacting policy into law or government programs, and implementing development activities.[10]

Development usually requires different types of leaders using a variety of styles and approaches at different stages of the process. As a dynamic process, development entails managing both expected and unexpected outcomes. Developmental leadership calls for a similar dynamism, a heightened sensitivity to the need for and the impact of change on people in a globalizing society. Although globalization creates new opportunities for development, it also complicates the process of change. In order to take advantage of the opportunities and to minimize the negative impacts of globalization, leaders in the public and private sectors must use methods of influence that are effective not only within their own countries but also in an international arena that both imposes constraints on development and offers resources for it. Here too, the potentially disruptive or corrosive effects of development require far-sighted leadership if change, however positive, is to be accepted at all.

From the perspective of nations providing development assistance, a crucial question is how the interactions between donors and their recipients privilege particular leaders and leadership styles. This question has been neglected in the study of the impacts of foreign assistance, which have largely focused on the volume and targets of assistance and on the economic and political commitments imposed as conditions for receiving assistance. As globalization makes international interaction across national borders more common and as the resources for development come increasingly from international sources, it may require public- and private-sector leaders to adopt new leadership traits and styles. This book explores how individuals and organizations exercise effective leadership to bring about beneficial economic, social, and political changes within and across national borders. It focuses on the leadership experience for development in the Pacific Basin—that is, in those countries in North America, South America, and Asia that border the Pacific Ocean.

We examine four fundamental research questions. First, how does global interdependence among governments and organizations in Pacific Basin nations—primarily in Asia and South America—affect approaches to and practices of leadership around important development issues? Second, how do political, business, and social leaders in the Pacific Basin exercise leadership to achieve development goals? Third, what differences and similarities in leadership styles, approaches, concepts, and methods within and across Asian, Latin American, and North American cultures and societies influence development decisions? Fourth, what lessons can be learned from recent experience with economic, social, and human development in Pacific Basin countries about the styles, traits, and attributes of leadership that could be used to develop future leaders?

We include comparative studies of leaders in Asian and Latin American countries, as well as cases of individuals and organizations that exercised leadership on important political, economic, or social development issues. We highlight effective concepts and methods of leadership in a world of interdependence and the lessons for organizations in Asia and Latin America about how to strengthen leadership for development.

CHANGING CONCEPTS OF LEADERSHIP IN PUBLIC AND PRIVATE ORGANIZATIONS

Although leaders in Asia and North and South America have always practiced diverse styles of leadership, the concepts and perceptions of effective leadership have changed over the past century. In Chapter 2, Dennis A. Rondinelli points out that Western leadership theories and practices in both the public and private sectors have changed dramatically from those based on directive, hierarchical, command-and-control approaches within single organizations to participative, consultative, and collaborative styles within and among organizational networks. Changes were driven by the increasing complexity of the issues with which public and private organizations must cope, by relentless technological innovation, and by the increasing interaction among political, business, and civil societal organizations across cultures.

Leadership is now seen less as the function of a single corporate chief executive, head of state, or organization director than as the responsibility of inter- and intra-organizational teams for vision setting, decision making, problem solving, and strategy implementation. Participatory decision making, shared leadership, and the concept of leader as "servant" are now seen as potentially more effective than highly directive command and control. All of these trends have produced changes in perceptions of ideal leadership styles, behaviors, traits, and roles within and among cultures.

Rondinelli points out that until the 1960s, concepts of leadership in Western management and public administration theories were influenced strongly by the analogy to military leadership and by the scientific management movement. Both influences fostered the perceptions that good leadership in business and public affairs was primarily directive, centralized, and exercised from the top down through a strong organizational hierarchy.

Increasing complexity in public and business organizations during the 1970s and 1980s led critics to challenge all of the assumptions underlying conventional approaches to leadership. Observers of the history of political leadership in the United States and Europe in the late 1970s drew a distinction between transactional leaders, who exert influence through the exchange of valued things, and transformational leaders, who, as James MacGregor Burns points out, seek to inspire their followers to a higher level of motivation and morality.[11] Transformational leaders formulate strong and clear visions for change and seek a fundamental metamorphosis in organizations or societies. Research on political and organizational leadership has revealed that transformational and transactional leadership styles involve very different behaviors, traits, and attributes. Yet we must always keep in mind that the merit of higher levels of "motivation and morality" depends on what basis of morality is involved. Mao Tse Tung probably regarded the execution of countless Chinese and the re-education programs of the Cultural Revolution as serving a higher good.

Leaders play a variety of roles in complex organizations, such as including representing it to the outside world, serving as liaison with external networks, monitoring information about organizational performance, disseminating information throughout the organization, initiating change, handling disturbances and settling conflicts, allocating resources, and negotiating. Researchers have documented at least five styles of leadership—directive, negotiative, consultative, participative, and delegative—each either more or less effective in different circumstances. Commanding styles may be appropriate in crises, but visionary, coaching, affiliative, democratic, and pace-setting styles can, in other circumstances, more effectively motivate, connect, empower, and harmonize followers, as well as stimulating them to achieve goals.

Current theories of leadership in a globalizing society, Rondinelli points out, recognize the need for more subtle and sophisticated traits than directive styles allow. In promoting development, the ability to integrate, coordinate, empower, and collaborate may be far more effective than commanding and controlling. Research on cross-cultural leadership indicates that even though significant differences in the effectiveness of leadership styles, approaches, and traits are evident in different cultures, people also recognize commonly valued leadership attributes across cultures.

POLITICAL LEADERSHIP, GOVERNANCE REFORM, AND ECONOMIC DEVELOPMENT

Leadership for development comes not only through visionary individuals but also through international assistance organizations, both multilateral institutions such as the World Bank and the United Nations Specialized Agencies and bilateral foreign aid programs that channel financial and technical assistance from richer to poorer countries.

The Decade for Development and Leadership in American Foreign Aid Policy

In Chapter 3, John M. Heffron traces the American legacy of international development assistance and how leaders in the administration of John F. Kennedy reconceptualized the US foreign aid program. Heffron points out that for the United States, federally assisted international development is still a relatively new concept, especially if one considers the historic place of technical assistance, in contrast to purely capital assistance, to developing countries. Indeed, it was as recently as 1949, in the wake of massive post-WWII aid programs such as the Marshall Plan, that policymakers began to consider the importance of noncapital resources rooted in knowledge and skills development. The fourth point of President Harry Truman's "Point Four Program" (first outlined in his 1949 inaugural address) introduced into development assistance policy a new mandate to share America's technical knowledge with peace-loving people throughout the world.

Heffron argues, however, that it was not until the Kennedy administration and the creation of the United States Agency for International Development (USAID) and the Peace Corps that foreign assistance began to assume its modern guise—an often complex formula of technical and labor-power support, financial aid, and host country national planning geared toward the twin ends of democracy and development. As president, Kennedy steered through Congress the Foreign Assistance Act of 1961, creating USAID in the process and personally spearheading one of its early programs in Latin America, the Alliance for Progress. He called for and promoted a "Decade for Development," taking his message to the American people, to Congress, and to the United Nations on numerous occasions before his untimely death. Kennedy's leadership and that of the talented group of people he gathered to work on foreign policy created and sustained through its founding years the Peace Corps. This body reflected the conviction that only a small force of well-trained, well-chosen, hardworking, and dedicated professionals could hope to realize the lofty goals of Truman's point four, enabling "our people," in Kennedy's own words, "to exercise more fully their responsibilities in the great common cause of world development."

Heffron examines the leadership of Kennedy and his advisors, including Walt W. Rostow, Max Millikan, Bill Moyers, Chester Bowles, Sargent Shriver, and Fowler Hamilton (USAID's first administrator) in devising a liberal international development policy within the context of the Cold War and in creating the Peace Corps to provide training and technical assistance to communities in poor countries throughout the world.

Leadership for Improved Governance

In most Asian and Latin American countries, national leaders face continuing challenges of developing democratic political systems, reforming and reinventing government, and stimulating or maintaining economic growth and social development. In Chapter 4, G. Shabbir Cheema examines how the rapid pace of globalization is stimulating profound and far-reaching changes around the world by introducing new markets, new technologies, new actors, and new rules of economic and political interaction. With increasing access to information, citizens are demanding greater accountability on the part of the executive branch of government. To cope effectively with the changes and to take advantage of opportunities provided by globalization, governments are under tremendous pressures to be not only competitive and efficient but also accountable and participatory. These demands, in turn, challenge political leaders and public officials to be highly adaptable and flexible in new leadership styles, for which traditional concepts of training and education have not necessarily prepared them.

Cheema examines the role of leadership in reinventing government in Pacific Basin countries. He identifies some of the critical issues in reinventing government to cope with the demands of the global economy and a more informed citizenry. He examines leadership characteristics and attributes required to design and implement government reforms that promote people-centered development. Based on case studies, he assesses the leadership roles in promoting innovations and good practices to revitalize governance and public administration in the Pacific Basin and argues for the need to enhance the competence of top government leaders to function effectively in a globalizing society.

Reinventing government to meet challenges of globalization and promote human development, Cheema argues, must be built on administrative and political structures and processes that are accountable and transparent, decentralized, able to manage legitimate elections and administration of justice, and capable of operating under the oversight of the parliament. He notes that, increasingly, citizens are demanding that political leaders combat exclusion, protect public goods, actively engage civil society and the private sector, use the power of information and communications technology to promote participation, and strengthen partnerships among different sectors, groups, and levels of government.

Revitalizing governance for people-centered development requires reforms that incorporate these characteristics.

The aspects of leadership that Cheema examines include hierarchical, directive, and control-oriented approaches as well as participative, collaborative, and consultative ones. He observes that different situations and problems of reinventing government in countries with different cultures and political systems have required different leadership attributes. He describes the leadership attributes of three national political leaders (Mohammad Mahathir in Malaysia, Thaksin Shinawatra in Thailand, and Vicente Fox in Mexico) and two local political and administrative leaders (Jaime Lerner in Curitiba, Brazil; and Chandrababu Naidu in Andra Pradesh, India). Not all of the leaders achieved their development goals or successfully reinvented their governments. Some, such as Thaksin Shinawatra, used command and control, applied what their critics thought were dictatorial approaches, and were relieved of power by a military coup; others, such as Vicente Fox, used more participative and consultative approaches but were simply unable to mobilize the forces required for change.

Organizational Leadership:
Japan and American Foreign Development Assistance

Programs of international assistance offer quite different types of leadership for development, depending on local political circumstances, social demographics, and cultural habits. Using Harold Lasswell's broad definition of the leader-follower relationship as the "giving and taking of orientation," William Ascher assesses and contrasts in Chapter 5 the foreign aid approaches of Japan and the United States and their implications for orienting development strategies and the behavior of actors in recipient countries. The relationships between developing countries and donor country foreign aid establishments can convey both conceptions of development and orientation toward the nature of leadership. The internal leadership structures within the Japanese and US governments also shape the foreign aid approaches and signals regarding development strategies.

Because the leadership styles displayed by foreign assistance officials have stood as role models for officials of developing nations, the inconsistencies that arise from contradictory leadership approaches help to shed light on some of the problems that developing countries continue to face. Ascher also explores another leadership issue: the relationship between the United States and Japan in their interactions in providing foreign assistance and in trying to shape the international consensus on development strategies.

Ascher contends that Japan has been very limited in the leverage that its belated Asian foreign assistance could support, as a consequence of the legacy of WWII, the need to gear development assistance to the reestablishment of trade, and the preexisting dominance of the United States and US-influenced multilateral development organizations. Japanese aid has been passive in important respects. As long as the recipient government proposed a priority list of projects and programs that could meet technical standards, the Japanese government would fund them up to the limit that the Japanese had allocated for that country. Thus it largely ignored the internal political conditions of the recipient country and the Japanese development experts' views on what kinds of projects, programs, and economic policies would be appropriate for the country.

In contrast, the past two decades have seen an elevated but largely unfulfilled Japanese ambition to lead in development strategy, with an effort to hold more important formal positions in international organizations and in intellectual leadership in advocating broad development approaches. However, the United States has imposed its geopolitical orientation on Japanese foreign assistance in numerous cases, and the role of Japan as a "thought leader" on development strategies declined with Japan's economic stagnation and the East Asian economic crisis of the late 1990s. Japanese foreign assistance has also been subject to pressure from advocacy groups, especially those promoting greater emphasis on environmental protection and alleviation of poverty, as well as in working with nonstate organizations.

Ascher argues that US foreign assistance has been compromised to a certain degree by the dominance of geopolitical objectives, by the relative stinginess of US aid (on a per capita basis), and by the contradiction between the philosophy of private sector development and the channeling of aid largely through governments. Yet US foreign aid approaches have been much more heavy-handed in imposing conditions on foreign assistance that go beyond security alliance issues, to include development strategies, economic policy, and sectoral development. Strong US "ownership" of economic development theory partly accounts for the hubris of US leadership regarding development, but so too did the enormous US bargaining power vis-à-vis many developing countries. However, this leadership has also been conveyed through alliances with like-minded technically expert officials within particular ministries of the recipient countries, often including experts trained in US universities (such as Indonesia's "Berkeley boys" and Chile's "Chicago boys"). Yet in some respects the United States also diversified its development approaches, in terms of both the vehicles of foreign assistance and the range of projects and programs.

Ascher also examines the commonalities of Japanese and US foreign aid doctrines, procedures, and institutions. These commonalities include heavy bureaucratization of foreign assistance agencies, "tied aid," preoccupation with corruption, strained relationships between the major development agencies and the more powerful agencies overseeing Japanese trade interests and US foreign relations, and the strategies for coping with the pressures from nongovernmental organizations (NGOs).

Leadership in a Crisis:
China and Japan in Comparative Perspective

The inherent strengths and weaknesses of a country's leadership are never more obvious than in times of severe economic crisis or when the country faces mounting pressures, internal and external, for systemic change and the restructuring that is usually (but not always) brought on by such stresses and strains. The differences between Chinese and

Japanese leadership—the one tested by conditions of relative economic and technological underdevelopment, the other by its rapid ascendancy and near dominance of world markets—are a good case in point. William H. Overholt in Chapter 6 offers a model of economic growth, decline, and recovery that places effective governmental leadership, not politics or particular political systems, democratic or otherwise, at the center of influence.

This is not to say that politics does not matter. However, in China's case its leaders had to set aside political considerations, including a long-standing ideological apparatus of government ownership and control of the means of production, to shore up a sagging economy in the 1990s. Leaders such as Premier Zhu Rongji, with the support of President Jiang Zemin, presided over a drastic restructuring of the economy that included not only the devolution of state enterprises to local, private, and in some cases foreign control, and with this the legitimization of free competition, but also a movement (and most important the will) to weed out and force into bankruptcy banks and other investment firms accused of corruption and mismanagement. Accountability and transparency became the watchwords of a vast reform effort that would have been impossible under revolutionary era Chinese leadership.

In Japan's case, "very strong bureaucratic management of the economy," combined with an economic policy that discouraged foreign direct investment, protected weak and faltering Japanese businesses from collapse and made a virtue of laissez-faire complacency in the face of a burgeoning financial crisis. The tribalization of the Japanese Diet into competing interest groups with a reputation for selling themselves to the highest bidder (latter-day "shoguns" who control the economic resources of Japan's key industries) has not only made a mockery of the legislature; it has made the emergence of strong and effective executive leadership practically impossible, according to Overholt. "These shoguns," he writes, "have controlled such great resources that they can overshadow prime ministers; in so doing they connect the interest groups providing the resources directly to critical decisions."

Chinese leaders, while managing a smaller economy, have managed to free themselves from the "cronyism" of the past and to take direct charge of the economic life of the nation, providing "professional management as if the country were a business conglomerate." Also, whereas Japanese leaders have tended to view international relations as so many potential entanglements, post-Marxist Chinese leaders have invited closer diplomatic relations with their neighbors, including Japan. And they have employed adaptive strategies (joining ASEAN with little or no concessions, for example) that have garnered broad international support for such critical issues in the area as energy security. Overholt concludes that by eschewing narrow political interests and by making the hard business decisions necessary to set China on a path of steady and responsible economic growth, Chinese leadership has outstripped its more complacent, half-heartedly democratic counterparts in Japan, giving the lie to the Japanese miracle of an earlier generation and laying the groundwork for more peaceful regional integration.

Political Leadership for Economic Reform

Turning to Latin America, Judith Teichman argues in Chapter 7 that although the era of globalization has not generally produced sustained growth and generalized prosperity for the region, Chile stands out as the Latin American success story by having achieved sustained high economic growth rates and substantial poverty reduction throughout the 1990s. Mexico, on the other hand, has confronted recurrent economic crises and has continued to be mired in high levels of poverty. She explores these distinct experiences with a focus on the evolution of leadership styles, strategies, and decisions from the initiation of market reform to the present. Although in the heyday of their market reform policies, Mexico (in 1985–1995) and Chile (in 1975–1988) witnessed remarkable similarities in leadership and decision-making styles, she finds that their subsequent periods of electoral democracy are characterized by important differences. Teichman contends that distinct historical features, both institutional and informal, some of them predating the market reform years, have been important in shaping leadership styles, strategies, and choices in the period of electoral democracy.

She emphasizes that *caudillismo,* a highly personal and informal source of power, has proved enormously more resilient in Mexico than in Chile. In Mexico, personal loyalty in exchange for material rewards was the glue that held the political system together until the late 1980s. In Chile, on the other hand, personalism as a means of organizing power was abandoned by members of the left-wing political leadership by the 1940s in favor of an increasingly militant left ideology. Hence, with the exception of the landholding sector and the political right, personalism had largely been replaced by programmatic political appeals in Chilean politics by the mid-1960s. Presidentialism (power highly concentrated in the hands of the presidency) was a common feature of both countries, as was the emergence of politically powerful and highly integrated landed, industrial, and financial elites.

These features, Teichman point out, despite important differences in institutional arrangements (Chile as a military regime between 1973 and 1989 and Mexico as an authoritarian single-party-dominant regime) were important in the economic reform process. In both cases, highly trained technocrats, largely specialists in economics with PhDs from well-known American universities, dominated the economic reform process, displaying key ingredients of *caudillismo* in their decision-making and leadership styles.

Chile's more successful post-1989 experience with market reform, Teichman argues, stems from a historical legacy that has shaped receptiveness among the current political leadership to the state promotion of economic growth and social justice. At the same time, the trauma of military rule produced support for economic reform measures. Whereas personalistic forms of political authority have receded in Chile, they remain resilient in Mexico, where a presidency with strong pro-market propensities remained resistant to state export-led growth. Leaders in both countries struggle with issues of equity in a region with widespread inequality and in which continued policy exclusion (despite the trappings of electoral democracy) is likely to perpetuate this disturbing reality.

LEADERSHIP FOR SOCIAL DEVELOPMENT

Many of the leaders who successfully promote development in Asia and Latin America work at local as well as national levels and focus on social as well as economic development. Social movements and the increasingly important role of nongovernment organizations and civil society groups in governance highlight the fundamental role of leadership outside of government in promoting human development.

Leadership and Nongovernmental Organizations in Asia

Ian Smillie, in Chapter 8, examines two aspects of nongovernmental organization leadership in Asia: the leadership *of* NGOs in different areas of development and the leadership *within* Asian NGOs that has helped them become prominent in their field. Smillie points out that the Asian NGO movement has grown dramatically in the last thirty years, from a limited number of welfare-type operations to tens of thousands of organizations, some of them the largest and most dynamic in their field. NGOs initiated the women's movement in Asia, especially in Muslim countries such as Indonesia and Bangladesh; they have been at the forefront of the environmental movement; they have challenged governments on a wide range of governance issues, from human rights and democracy to basic understandings of effective service delivery. Asian NGOs pioneered micro-credit, today an accepted worldwide approach to poverty reduction. They have been at the forefront of innovations in basic education, public health, and experiments in the production of generic pharmaceuticals. Smillie devotes special attention to the phenomenon in Bangladesh, where it is not without its problems, blemishes, and limitations.

He examines leadership challenges and management techniques developed by some of the more successful Asian NGOs, noting that outsiders often attribute the success of Asian NGOs to the founder-leader syndrome, which suggests that traditional Asian deference to authority, combined with large amounts of charisma, luck, ambition, and donor generosity, has made many of these NGOs what they are today. Some, including Asian observers, have argued that the long-term success of the NGO movement remains to be determined, once the first generation of leaders passes from the scene.

Smillie argues, however, that there is much more to Asian NGO management than this, noting that the context in which Asian NGOs operate is very different from that of their Northern counterparts. There is no philanthropic base (beyond *zakat* and other forms of religious tithing). Governments, laws, and regulations are often antagonistic to the very concept of the nongovernmental organization, and rapidly changing political situations—the coups, insurrections, and economic and governmental collapse that have occurred from Islamabad to Manila over the past two decades—have often placed NGOs in precarious management situations. Some have tried (or have been told) to emulate Northern management norms. But managers must balance the mission they have chosen for themselves against the expectations and concerns of their governments, as well as the expectations of donors and Northern counterparts. They must also work within the context of other national NGOs, and they must deal with the talents and limitations of their own staff. They must use an adaptive approach to leadership and management, where opportunism—often in the best sense of the word—becomes not a substitute for strategy, but the strategy itself.

Asian Leaders for Social Change and Development

Rosemary Fernholz, in Chapter 9, explores leadership for social change and development by examining four decades of experience of a foundation in the Philippines that has granted awards of recognition to leaders in Asia. The program, named for Ramon Magsaysay, a Philippine president known for his selfless service, has given more than two hundred awards to individuals for their leadership and outstanding contributions to the public good. She examines the characteristics of these leaders in the six categories for which awards are given: (1) government service—leadership from any sector of government service, (2) public service—outstanding service for the public good by a private citizen, (3) community leadership—leadership of a person or community to improve social welfare, (4) journalism, literature, and creative communication arts—leadership in the use of the media for the public good, (5) peace and international understanding—outstanding contributions to improve the foundations for peace and sustainable development, and (6) emergent leadership—outstanding work of an individual forty years or younger toward social change.

Fernholz notes that although the awards are meant to recognize outstanding accomplishments, they can go to any person "who has quietly helped others, serving selflessly and without expectation of public recognition." The awards, therefore, would highlight these leaders and their work and seek to "place living examples of exceptional service before the public." She first discusses the arrangements that brought together a national government and international donor agencies (the Philippine government, the Rockefeller Brothers Fund, and the Ford Foundation) to endow a self-sustaining award program. Then she reviews the criteria and process used to identify leaders in Asia, the evolution and an assessment of the subprogram that offers a pool of funds for awardees' own projects, and a new category to recognize emergent leadership and encourage public service among younger Asian public servants and professionals.

By 2006, there were 243 awardees from 22 countries, ranging from Afghanistan to Vietnam. Some of the awardees are prominent internationally, such as the Dalai Lama (1959 Community Leadership), Mother Teresa (1962 Peace and International Understanding), and Mechai Viravaidya (1994 Public Service). Some, however, were known only in their countries or the region. Sheila Coronel (2003 Journalism, Literature and Creative Communication Arts) fearlessly pursued investigative journalism and heads a well-respected institute that she helped found. Aniceto Lopes (2003 Emergent Leadership) made a courageous stand for justice in East Timor during a turbulent period. And Sandeep Pandey (2002 Emergent Leadership) worked tirelessly to break down caste barriers, to reduce corruption, and to promote peace in India.

Fernholz synthesizes key aspects of leadership from the examples and perceptions of the 243 awardees, focusing on selected awardees to examine key issues in leadership for development in Asia. She then analyzes leadership from the examples and perceptions of the awardees. The issues she explores are how these leaders exercise leadership to achieve developmental goals, the role of the leader's vision in her or his commitment to achieving the goals, and her or his main motivation. Fernholz also examines the extent to which leaders differ in leadership style depending on the category of leadership, the sociopolitical and cultural context of the country, and the impact of globalization, or stage of activity; how leaders work to achieve development objectives; and the commonalities or leadership traits that transcend country borders and reflect regional characteristics.

GLOBALIZATION, LEADERSHIP, AND DEVELOPMENT: EMERGING PATTERNS AND CHALLENGES

In Chapter 10, Dennis Rondinelli and John Heffron summarize and assess the findings of the chapters in this book and the implications for theories and practices of leadership for development. They return to the major research themes of the book by examining how global interdependence among governments and organizations primarily in Asia and South America affect approaches to and practices of leadership around important development issues. They then synthesize the lessons from each of the chapters about how political, business, and social leaders in Asia and Latin America exercise leadership to achieve development goals, and they address the issue of whether transformational or transactional leadership styles are more effective in bringing about change.

Rondinelli and Heffron conclude by assessing the differences and similarities among leadership styles, approaches, concepts, and methods within and across Asian and Latin American cultures and societies that influence development decisions. They summarize the lessons that can be learned from recent experience with economic, social, and human development in Pacific Basin countries about the styles, traits, and attributes of leadership that could be used by those seeking to promote development in poor communities and countries around the world.

NOTES

1. John Orme, "The Original Megapolicy: America's Marshall Plan," in John D. Montgomery and Dennis A. Rondinelli (eds.), *Great Policies: Strategic Innovations in Asia and the Pacific Basin* (Westport, CT: Praeger Publishers, 1995), 15–39.

2. Manuel E. Contreras and Maria Luisa Talavera Simoni, "The Bolivian Education Reform 1992–2002: Case Studies in Large-Scale Education Reform," *Country Studies* (Washington, World Bank, 2003).

3. Srilatha Batiwala and Aruna Rao, "Conversations with Women on Leadership and Social Transformation," 2005, accessed at www.genderatwork .org/updir/ConversationswithWomen.pdf.

4. Robert Cervero, "Progressive Transport and the Poor: Bogotá's Bold Steps Forward," *Access* 27 (Fall 2005): 24–30.

5. "Interview: Michel Chancy," *Interaction* 13 (2005) at http://www.wkkf .org.

6. Jean Lipman-Bluman, "The Allure of Toxic Leaders: Why Followers Rarely Escape Their Clutches," *Ivey Business Journal* (January-February, 2005): 1–8; quotation at 2.

7. Mariana Llanos and Ana Margheritis, "Why Do Presidents Fail? Political Leadership and the Argentine Crisis (1999–2001)," *Studies in Comparative International Development* 40, 4 (2006): 77–103.

8. Michael Shifter," Latin America's New Political Leaders: Walking on a Wire," *Current History* 102 (February 2003): 51–57; quotation at 54.

9. Michael P. Todaro, *Economic Development in the Third World*, 4th ed. (New York: Longman, 1989), 62.

10. Dennis A. Rondinelli, "Processes of Strategic Innovation: The Dynamics of Decision Making in the Evolution of Great Policies," in John D. Montgomery and Dennis A. Rondinelli (eds.), *Great Policies: Strategic Innovations in Asia and the Pacific Basin* (Westport, CT: Praeger Publishers, 1995), 223–239.

11. James MacGregor Burns, *Leadership* (New York: Harper & Row, 1978).

PART I

THE FRAMEWORK:
WHY DOES LEADERSHIP MATTER?

2

CHANGING CONCEPTS OF LEADERSHIP IN A GLOBALIZING SOCIETY

Dennis A. Rondinelli

Leadership is crucial in stimulating economic, social, and political changes that promote peaceful human development. Development is a process of social change, and thus it is driven by individuals who can mobilize the human, financial, and physical resources needed to move people and organizations away from undesirable conditions toward a more desirable state of well-being. The ability of one person to influence the thinking and behavior of others to achieve shared objectives is the essence of leadership. Development, like all forms of social progress, occurs when leaders with a vision of the future convince others of the need to take actions that will improve their lives.[1]

These concepts emerge repeatedly in studies of leadership. Robert House and Mansour Javidan defined leadership as the "ability of an individual to influence, motivate, and enable others to contribute toward the effectiveness and success of the organizations of which they are members."[2] Others define leadership as a process of social influence in which one person is able to obtain the support of others by convincing them of the mutual benefits of achieving common aims.[3] Linda Smircich and Gareth Morgan see leadership as a social process of guiding followers to understand situations and arrive at common interpretations of reality in order to move toward common goals.[4] Whatever instrumentalism these definitions may share, they also reinforce the fundamental importance of identifying an acceptable vision of the future and facilitating individual and organizational change. Yet the history of modern thought about leadership is one of vigorous debate about the most effective ways of influencing behavior, whether to enhance individual happiness or to bring about beneficial social change.

GLOBALIZATION, LEADERSHIP, AND DEVELOPMENT

The debate about the nature of leadership and its role in stimulating economic and social development has intensified with the increasing international interaction among people and organizations. Globalization has been driven, over the past half century, by increasing economic interaction among countries through more extensive trade and investment; by growing numbers of economic and political treaties, agreements, and alliances; by dramatic innovations in communications and transportation technology that allow people and organizations around the world to interact personally and through electronic means; and by the nearly instantaneous spread of knowledge and information. Globalization has brought about strong economic shifts that have benefited some people and further impoverished others.

Those concerned with promoting economic and social development or seeking either to take advantage of the potential benefits of globalization or to overcome its potential negative effects cannot ignore the impacts of globalization. Douglas Hicks correctly points out that "the vast majority of leaders confront global and globalizing realities as contextual factors that they must negotiate in their work."[5] Business leaders struggle with achieving competitive advantage in world markets; "political leaders carve out their place in the international order as a piecemeal global infrastructure develops; and leaders of civil society expand their mission to new countries and contexts."

Although globalization creates new opportunities for development, it also makes the process more complex. Burgeoning international interaction shapes not only the possibilities for development but also the ways in which it must be led and pursued. In order to take advantage of the opportunities and to minimize the negative impacts of globalization, leaders in both public and private organizations must use methods of influence that are effective not only within their own cultures and societies but also in what is rapidly becoming a global society.

Globalization and international interaction have also reshaped the concept of development, at least as it has been pursued and supported by international organizations that provide much of the financing and technical assistance for development in poorer countries.[6] In the early 1950s, development was thought of primarily as the acceleration of economic growth—that is, of finding ways to increase gross national product primarily by transforming poor countries from subsistence agricultural economies to industrial and service economies. During the 1970s, thinking about development changed from focusing almost entirely on accelerating national economic growth to promoting economic development with social equity. The focus shifted from industrial development to increasing agricultural productivity, promoting rural development, strengthening small-scale enterprise, and enhancing human development through improvements in education and health.

In the 1980s, development policies focused more strongly on reforming governments to serve their citizens more effectively, on strengthening the private sector as the engine of economic growth, on creating an investment and business climate that fostered market-oriented systems, and on technological innovation. These trends continued in the 1990s as both rich and poor countries sought to adjust to the rapid globalization of the economy and to greater international interaction among countries in economic, political, social, and technological transactions. By the end of the 1990s, however, development theorists recognized that economic growth generated by globalization did not benefit all countries and all segments of the population in any country equally. Development began to focus more strongly, especially in international assistance organizations such as the United Nations, the World Bank, and bilateral aid agencies, on poverty reduction and creating conditions that allow the poor in more countries to participate in and benefit from international economic interaction.

By the early 2000s, development theorists and assistance organizations more clearly recognized that development is more than economic growth. Amartya Sen argued that development is a process through which people achieve the freedom to choose and increase their capabilities to live the kinds of lives they value.[7]

However it has been defined, development is primarily a process of change—of moving from unsatisfactory economic, social, or physical conditions to those that people value as better. In Sen's concept, development is an expansion of human capabilities to improve their lives. Building on Sen's concepts, the first *Human Development Report* of the United Nations emphasized that people are the real wealth of nations and that development is a process of enlarging people's choices, including the choices to live a long and healthy life, to be educated, to have access to resources needed for a decent standard of living, to have political freedom, to be guaranteed human rights, and to enhance their personal self-respect.[8]

As societies are more widely and deeply influenced by political, social, economic, and technological transactions across national borders, development in any country is influenced not only by internal leaders but also by their interaction with external organizations and institutions. Globalization imposes new demands on leaders and often requires new skills, behaviors, and traits to influence those within and outside of their countries to support development goals.

EVOLUTION OF WESTERN LEADERSHIP CONCEPTS

Much of the literature on leadership comes from research and thinking about how leaders guide and manage public and private organizations in the United States. In North America, leadership theories and practices in both the public and the private sectors have changed drastically since the 1950s, from those based on directive, hierarchical, command-and-control approaches within single organizations to those based on participative, consultative, and collaborative styles within and among organizational networks. Changes in thinking were driven by the increasing complexity of modern businesses and public organizations, relentless technological innovation, and the increasing interaction among political and business organizations across national borders and cultures. Leadership is now seen not to be so much the function of a single individual as the responsibility of organizational teams for vision setting, decision making, problem solving, and strategy implementation. In a challenge to traditional notions of accountability, participatory decision making and shared leadership are now seen as potentially more effective than highly directive command and control. All of these trends have produced changes in perceptions of ideal leadership styles, behaviors, traits, and roles within and among cultures.

Leadership as Command and Control

Until the 1960s, the most influential concepts of leadership in Western management and public administration theories were derived from two fields: one based on the analogy to military leadership, the other based on the belief in scientific management. Both concepts led to the widespread perception that good business and public leadership was primarily directive or authoritarian, that decision making should be centralized in the hands of top executives or political officials, and that strategies were best implemented by command and control through a strong organizational hierarchy.

The analogy to military leadership implied that the role of corporate executives and political leaders was to control organizations through staff-line structures. Often, the analogy resulted in the prescription of an autocratic leadership style in which the leader made all the important decisions and was concerned primarily with accomplishing organizational tasks rather promoting the happiness of followers or increasing their satisfaction.[9] The leader usually did not seek or accept the participation of followers in decision making and motivated those within the organization through punishment for failing to follow orders. According to this concept of leadership, the chain of command in business and government, as in the military, was primarily one-way, running down the organizational hierarchy, through bureaucratic layers of middle management to supervisors and employees.

In the business sector, for example, when Thomas J. Watson Jr. succeeded his father as chief executive of IBM in 1956, he was dismayed to learn that "by the mid-1950s just about every big corporation had adopted this so-called staff-and-line structure. It was modeled on the military organization going back to the Prussian army in Napoleonic times." Watson noted that "in this sort of arrangement, line managers are like field commanders, their duties are to hit production targets, beat sales quotas, and capture market share."[10] Although these goals were not unworthy in themselves, they simply failed to acknowledge the role of those who were ultimately responsible for achieving them (rank-and-file workers) and relied on punishment rather than reinforcement.

The leader's function—whether in business or in government—was to set strategic goals and ensure their effective implementation, primarily through punishment for deviations from planned results. As Chester Bernard argued in his influential book *The Functions of the Executive,* the leader's role, like the military general's, was to identify those strategic factors "whose control, in the right form, at the right place and time, will establish a system or set of conditions which meet the purpose."[11]

The other influential stream of thinking during the first half of the twentieth century that reinforced the control-and-command style of leadership was scientific management. Frederick W. Taylor believed that management was largely the application of engineering principles for improving worker productivity through clearly defined and tested principles and methods.[12] His principles were embodied first in the widespread adoption of standard operating procedures during the 1930s and 1940s, and later in operations research and systems analysis. Although labor unions were suspicious of scientific management, rejecting it outright in the 1930s, management had elevated Taylor's crude time-and-motion studies to a more sophisticated rationalization of the work process that now included greater attention, for example, to the "human factor" and to human relations psychology. Nevertheless as production became at once more specialized and more mechanized, management, at least in its executive functions, found itself increasingly removed from the day-to-day operations of the shop floor and from the emotional well-being of workers. In the professional jargon of the day, Herbert Simon saw decision making as a process that he called "intelligence, design, and choice"—that is, a process of gathering information, structuring options based on assessment of production systems, and selecting optimal solutions based on statistical analysis."[13]

Both the military and the scientific analogies for political and business leadership were based, as Drucker emphasized, on two underlying assumptions that dominated prevailing theories from the 1930s to the 1970s: that there is or must be one right organizational structure and that there is or must be one right way to manage people. Leadership and management theory, Drucker contends, were also shaped by the assumptions that "1) technologies, markets, and end users are given; 2) management's scope is legally defined; 3) management is internally focused; and 4) the economy defined by national boundaries is the 'ecology' of enterprise and management."[14] Beginning in the 1960s, increasing globalization of economic, social, and political interactions shattered all of these assumptions. The effectiveness of a command-and-control style of business and political leadership, of course, had always been questioned by some scholars and practitioners, but it came under increasing scrutiny in the 1970s.

Leadership as Influence

Increasing complexity in business and public affairs during the 1970s and 1980s led scholars to question all of the assumptions underlying conventional approaches to leadership. As early as the 1940s, Abraham Maslow had concluded that people differed in their needs at different times throughout their lives and that leading them effectively required diverse incentives and leadership styles.[15] Maslow laid the foundation for human relations theorists who later attacked the assumption that there was only one right way to lead or influence people.

In the late 1940s and early 1950s, Ralph Stogdill's studies began to shift the concept of the role of good organizational leaders from setting goals and implementing them through command and control to "influencing the activities of an organized group it its efforts toward goal setting and achievement."[16] He and others noted that because leadership depends on the willingness of members of an organization or polity to follow, successful leaders in this more therapeutic culture had to learn to persuade and not just command. Stogdill argued that the traits of a good leader included capacity (intelligence, alertness, judgment), achievement, responsibility (dependability, initiative, persistence), participation (activity, sociability, adaptability) and status (socioeconomic position, popularity).[17] S. A. Kirkpatrick and E. A. Locke argued that six sets of traits differentiated leaders from nonleaders: (1) drive—achievement, ambition, energy, tenacity, and initiative; (2) desire to lead—personalized and socialized power motives; (3) honesty and integrity; (4) self-confidence and emotional stability; (5) cognitive ability—capacity to gather integrate and interpret large amounts of information and use it effectively to develop strategies for solving problems; and 6) knowledge—technical or professional expertise.[18]

In the early 1960s, McGregor explored the differences between Theory-X management, the traditional form of directive, centralized leadership, and Theory-Y management, in which the essential task "is to arrange organizational conditions and methods of operation so that people can achieve their own goals best by directing their own efforts toward organizational objectives."[19] Fiedler's research concluded that the most effective style of leadership was contingent on specific situations and conditions; in other words, the relationship between leaders and members was shaped by group atmosphere, task structure, and position power.[20]

Observing executives at work in the private sector, Mintzberg and others cast further doubt on the validity of the assumptions that organizations could be led in only one correct way or one appropriate structure. Mintzberg found that leaders play a variety of roles in complex organizations, such as representing the firm to the outside world, handling liaison with external networks, monitoring information about organizational performance, disseminating information throughout the organization, initiating change, handling disturbances and settling conflicts, allocating resources, and negotiating.[21] Bernard Bass and his associates documented at least five styles of leadership—directive, negotiative, consultative, participative, and delegative—each being either more or less effective in different circumstances.[22]

Moreover, studies concluded that effective leaders use diverse tactics to influence others to follow. Gary Yukl and J. Bruce Tracy found at least nine tactics of influence: rational persuasion, inspirational appeal, consultation, participation, ingratiation, exchange, personal appeal, coalition building, legitimization, and pressure.[23] They concluded that each of these tactics or particular combinations of them were either more or less effective, depending on the specific situation, the types of people the leaders were trying to influence, and the different types of goals they were trying to achieve.

Leadership as Transformation

Observing the history of political leadership in the United States and Europe, James MacGregor Burns, in the late 1970s, drew a distinction between transactional leaders, who exert influence through the exchange of valued things, and transformational leaders, who "engage with others in such a way that leaders and followers raise one another to higher levels of motivation and morality."[24] Transformational leaders formulate strong and clear visions for change and seek a fundamental metamorphosis in organizations or societies. He saw the work of transformational leaders as raising "the level of human conduct and ethical aspiration of both leaders and led."[25] Burns's work on political leadership and Bernard Bass's research on organizational leadership concluded that transformational and transactional leadership styles involved very different behaviors, traits, and attributes.[26]

As globalization required governments and private firms to become more agile in decision making and more innovative in addressing complex problems and opportunities, researchers in both public- and private-sector leadership studies began to observe new roles and functions that were crucial to success. Focusing on the management of innovative companies, Rosabeth Moss Kanter found little value in a purely directive style of leadership.[27] She noted that leadership in creative companies required entrepreneurship, coalition building, and bargaining and negotiation to accumulate the information, support, and resources needed to proceed with innovation. Flat, lean organizational structures were preferable to hierarchies, and in such organizations, networking and communicating were far more valued leadership traits than commanding and controlling. Charles Handy observed that leading organizations enmeshed in complex networks of relationships required influence more than authority. In such circumstances, he argued, "a leader shapes and shares a vision which gives point to the work of others."[28]

Although transactional leaders primarily use contingent or non-contingent rewards and punishments for achieving existing organizational or political objectives, transformational leaders—in seeking fundamental change—focus on (1) developing a clear vision of where an organization, community, or society should be going in the future, (2) intellectual stimulation to make people aware of the need for change and to challenge them to think about problems or needs in new ways, (3) inspirational communication to mobilize support and encourage people to see positive opportunities in changing, (4) supportive leadership in helping those whose support for change is required to take the actions needed to achieve new goals, (5) personal recognition to acknowledge the contribution of people contributing to change and reward them for their support.[29]

Leadership as Collaboration and Team Building

Increasing globalization of the economy, shifts in economic activity from manufacturing to services and from manual-labor-driven to knowledge-driven productivity, and the need for corporations and public-sector organizations to be agile in responding to global customer and citizen needs all led to wider acceptance of empowerment as an essential leadership role. Continuing globalization during the 1980s and 1990s further undermined most of those assumptions that buttressed directive leadership theories. Bennis noted that the increasing influence of technology, complexity, networking, knowledge-based productivity, customer orientation, and globalization made it virtually impossible for any single executive to know enough to direct a corporation through command and control, and by implication for one political leader to direct governments in an authoritarian manner.[30] In the high-tech, rapidly changing, global markets of the twenty-first century, Bennis argued, important work would have to be done, and organizations had to be led by "Great Teams."

Exercising leadership for development in a globalizing society requires more subtle and sophisticated traits than directive styles allow; integrating, coordinating, empowering, and collaborating become far more effective than commanding and controlling. Adler's research on international executives concluded that in order to succeed, corporations and public agencies would have to recruit and develop leaders who, in addition to other collaborative leadership traits, possessed cultural sensitivity and could learn to use diplomatic means of achieving goals, forge relationships that create respect for all parties, communicate clearly, solve cultural problems, and synergistically negotiate across cultures.[31]

Others extended the argument that successful leaders in the twenty-first century would require much more than technical expertise, intelligence, or command presence. Goleman's studies of international executives in the United States, Japan, Europe, and Latin America found many cases of failed leaders who were highly intelligent or were experts in their field. He and his colleagues attributed their failure to the lack of "emotional intelligence"—the self-awareness, self-regulation, empathy, and social skills that are essential to leading teams effectively in complex organizations.[32] They concluded that diverse leadership styles are needed under different circumstances to lead teams well. Commanding styles

may be appropriate in crises, but visionary, coaching, affiliative, democratic, and pace-setting styles can, in other circumstances, more effectively motivate, connect, empower, harmonize, and excite teams to
achieve goals. Because of their inclusion in the process, these teams are
also better situated to reevaluate goals and, should it become necessary,
to successfully manage change. This approach to leadership recognizes
that leading people and influencing them are not necessarily one and
the same. In some situations, people in leadership positions must also
be open to influence by followers. Leaders may be as much an object
of influence as they are its subject and agent.

Leadership as Service

Building on the concepts of transformational leadership, Robert Greenleaf observed another type of leader—primarily in voluntary and social
organizations, but also in the public service and sometimes in business;
these leaders used their influence and resources to improve the well-
being and achieve the objectives of those being served.[33] Greenleaf called
such people, who seek to improve the well-being of others, pursue
moral standards, and focus on the collective interests of society, "servant
leaders." Servant leaders elevate moral dialogue on issues and activities
that contribute to the betterment of their followers.

The concept of the servant leader is anchored in the belief that au-
thentic leadership emerges from a deep motivation and desire to help
others rather than from self-interest or the lust to accumulate power for
its own sake.[34] Servant leaders act as stewards, preserving and enhancing
the capacities of organizations to achieve beneficial goals, rather than
as accumulators of power to control. Servant leadership is transformational in the sense that the leader seeks to bring about beneficial change
through commitment to community building. The characteristics at
the core of servant leadership are awareness, empathy, the ability to
listen, and concern with healing. At the same time, effective servant leaders have foresight, the ability to conceptualize, and the power to persuade. Ann McGee-Cooper and Gary Looper argue that effective servant

leadership depends on the collaboration and participation of followers and on a holistic understanding of the conditions that require change, building on a shared vision, encouraging interdependence, and tolerating and learning from mistakes.[35] A good servant leader encourages creativity, questions assumptions, and remains humble.

Thus the dominant theories and practices of leadership in North America have evolved from a narrow focus on command and control to more participative, transformational, and collaborative styles and approaches. Globalization and technological advances in communications have increasingly required effective leaders in both the public and the private sectors to recognize the widespread interdependence that has come with more extensive international interaction and stronger linkages among organizations within and across national borders. In current theory, leadership depends less on charismatic individuals acting in unquestioned positions of authority and more on participation, collaboration, and team cooperation. Indeed, successful leadership skills are often seen among people who are not in the highest positions of authority, but who bring about change through what Joseph Badaracco calls "quiet leadership."[36] Quiet leaders are people throughout an organization who, with little interest in calling attention to themselves and little motivation to achieve "greatness," modestly but tenaciously identify adverse conditions or problems and act to get others to make things better.

Research indicates that humble and modest leadership may in fact be more effective than aggressive, heroic, charismatic, personalized leadership in many highly competitive organizations. Dusya Vera and Antonio Rodriguez-Lopez, examining organizations known for the humility of their top executives, point out that humble leaders tend to be more open to new ideas and to learn from others; they acknowledge their own limitations and mistakes, learn from them, ask for advice, and have a genuine desire to serve.[37] Humble leaders avoid narcissistic behavior, act with simplicity and frugality, and avoid self-complacency in order to bring about changes that sustain an organization and keep it competitive.

CROSS-CULTURAL LEADERSHIP

Effective leadership is in part defined by the culture in which it is exercised, but in a global society it is also measured by international perceptions of roles, characteristics, and traits. Differences in social, political, and cultural characteristics in Asian and Latin American countries in the Pacific Basin should produce conditions in which the efficacy of leadership concepts, methods, and approaches both converge with and differ from those thought to be important in North America. Clearly, some aspects of the evolving theories and practices of leadership in North America also appear in Asian and Latin American countries.

Political and organizational leadership in Latin America, for example, has passed through periods of *caudillismo,* in which strong male autocrats exercised power through paternalistic and authoritarian means, to more populist approaches. Yet even populist leaders in Latin America have traditionally depended on personal and paternalistic patterns of leadership and top-down processes of political mobilization.[38] Beginning in the late 1980s, many people in Latin American countries rejected militaristic dictators in favor of leaders who could produce results through more democratic and participative governance.[39] Some Asian countries have also passed through periods of royal or military dictatorships or socialist totalitarianism based on concepts of command and control to more democratic and participative styles of leadership.

Research on cross-cultural leadership indicates that although there are significant differences in the effectiveness of leadership styles, approaches, and traits among cultures, there are also commonly recognized leadership attributes across them. The more than a decade-long research project on cross-cultural leadership, GLOBE, found that the leadership dimensions valued by people in different cultures have been both converging on some dimensions and diverging on others since the early 1990s. Differences appear in the value people in different cultural groups place on various leadership traits, behaviors, and methods of influence. GLOBE researchers have found that Anglo cultures (the United States,

Canada, Australia, New Zealand, South Africa, Ireland, and the United Kingdom) endorse charismatic and value-based leadership more highly than either Latin American or East Asian cultures. Latin American cultures tend to endorse team-oriented leadership dimensions more than do Anglo and East Asian cultures. Participative leadership is valued higher in Anglo and Latin American cultures than in Asian cultures. Anglo and East Asian cultures more strongly endorse humane-oriented leadership than Latin American cultures, and autonomous leadership tends to be appreciated more in East Asia than in Latin American and Anglo cultures.[40]

Despite variations in the strength of endorsement of these leadership dimensions, the GLOBE project found that twenty-two leadership attributes (such as decisiveness and foresight) tend to be universally considered desirable and that eight leadership attributes (such as irritability and ruthlessness) tend to be universally considered undesirable. Yet many of the leadership attributes—elitist or ambitious, for example— remain culturally contingent.[41]

Convergence and divergence in leadership attributes are evident in Asia. Surveys undertaken by Robert Taormina and Christopher Selvarajah of managers and employees in organizations in Indonesia, Malaysia, the Philippines, Singapore, and Thailand found that the highest values for leadership characteristics in the Southeast Asian region were placed on consideration for others, progressive stability, strategic thinking, and trust in others, whereas status characteristics (age, gender, marital status, or years of experience) were considered less important.[42] In all five countries, "progressive stability" (being consistent in dealing with people and in making decisions, dealing calmly with tense situations, adapting to changing working conditions, being an initiator, and being knowledgeable about the work of an industry) most strongly defined leadership excellence. In Indonesia, Malaysia, and Thailand, "consideration of others" (being objective in dealing with work conflicts, considering suggestions made by employees, listening to and trying to understand the problems of employees, considering the advice of others, promoting staff welfare and development, and maintaining the self-esteem of others) was ranked as the second most frequently identified set of factors in leadership excellence. "Strategic thinking" (constantly evaluating emerging technologies, developing strategies to gain a competitive edge, focusing on maximizing productivity, having a strategic vision, keeping to work deadlines, and responding to consumers' expectations) was one of the top three sets of characteristics associated with leadership excellence in all five countries.

In most Asian countries with large ethnic Chinese populations of managers and employees, good leadership is generally influenced by Confucian values of deference to authority, paternalistic concern for followers, respect for the self-esteem of others, and harmony in interpersonal relationships. China has gone through momentous and sometimes traumatic changes in political ideology and social values, from a Confucian society to a revolutionary one, to a Communist state, and most recently to an emerging market economy, and this experience has fostered a variety of leadership styles among both business and political leaders. Research on leadership styles among chief executives of business organizations in China found six prevalent behaviors associated with good leadership: being creative and taking risks, relating and communicating, articulating a vision of the future, showing benevolence, monitoring operations, and being authoritative.[43] Based on combinations of these behaviors, managers and employees identified four leadership styles—from authoritative to "invisible" leaders—all of which were more or less effective in different organizations. All four styles were found in successful businesses.

Despite the fact that their economic and political situations differed substantially, Chinese managers in mainland China, Taiwan, and Hong Kong generally have placed strong emphasis on the importance of interpersonal relationships as a means by which effective leaders created stability and harmony in bringing about change, even in organizations that were structured into hierarchical leadership systems.[44] Managers and employees in all three countries rated rational persuasion and apprising (using factual evidence) as the most influential leadership tactics, followed by collaboration, consultation, inspiration, and ingratiation. Even among these three Chinese countries, however, subtle but important differences in leadership tactics appeared. For example, managers from Hong Kong tended to be more aggressive and to exert more pressure in dealing with their counterparts from mainland China. And Taiwanese managers tended to see inspirational influence as more effective than did their counterparts in Hong Kong and mainland China.

CONCLUSION

At the core of the concepts of both leadership and development is the process of change. Development involves social, economic, political, and physical changes that enhance the conditions under which people live and provide a better quality of life. Leaders seek to promote change in order to achieve individual, group, organizational, community, or societal goals. In an environment for leadership in a globalizing society that has become more complex, successful leaders must understand how to influence others effectively in their own cultures, but also how to change behavior and mobilize support internationally. Leaders' effectiveness is measured increasingly not only within the specific context of their own culture, but also by world standards and perceptions.

An important lesson that can be drawn from the evolution of thinking about leadership in North America—a lesson increasingly reinforced by cross-cultural research—is that just as there is no universally effective path to development, there is no universally effective style or approach to leadership. By the early 1970s, much of the research on leadership in the United States concluded, as Fiedler pointed out, that it was simply a myth "that there is one best leadership style, or that there are leaders who excel under all circumstances."[45] Fiedler concluded that the effectiveness of different leadership traits, styles, and approaches depends on culturally shaped relationships between leaders and followers, the position power of the leaders, and the leader's task structure. Different types of situations allow the successful application of different leadership traits and tactics of influence.

Effective leadership, like successful development, results from a learning process. When people learn how to promote social, economic, and political changes successfully—and to bring about those improvements through appropriate and effective means of influencing the behavior of others—the result is leadership for development.

NOTES

1. John D. Montgomery and Dennis A. Rondinelli (eds.), *Great Policies: Strategic Innovations in Asia and the Pacific Basin* (Westport, CT: Praeger Publishers, 1995).

2. Robert House and Mansour Javidan, "Overview of GLOBE," in R. House, P. Hanges, M. Javidan, P. Dorfman and V. Gupta (eds.), *Culture, Leadership and Organizations: The GLOBE Study of 62 Societies* (Thousand Oaks, CA: Sage Publications, 2004), 9–28; quotation at 15.

3. Edwin A. Locke, "Self-Interest," in R. Goethals, G. J. Sorenson, and J. M. Burns (eds.), *Encyclopedia of Leadership,* vol. 4 (Thousand Oaks, CA: Sage Publications, 2004), 1400–1406.

4. Linda Smircich and Gareth Morgan, "Leadership: The Management of Meaning," *Journal of Applied Behavioral Science* 18, 3 (1982): 257–273.

5. Douglas A. Hicks, "Globalization," in G. R. Goethals, G. J. Sorenson, and J. M. Burns (eds.), *Encyclopedia of Leadership* (Thousand Oaks, CA: Sage Publications, 2004), 570–577; quotation at 576.

6. See Arthur Lewis, *The Theory of Economic Growth* (London, Allen and Unwin, 1955); Walt W. Rostow, *The Stages of Economic Growth* (Cambridge: Cambridge University Press, 1960); Dennis A. Rondinelli, *Development Projects as Policy Experiments,* 2nd ed. (London: Rutledge, 1993).

7. A. K. Sen, *Development as Freedom* (New York: Knopf, 1999).

8. United Nations Development Programme, *Human Development Report, 1990* (New York: Oxford University Press, 1990).

9. J. Justin Gustainis, "Autocratic Leadership," in G. R. Goethals, G. J. Sorenson, and J. M. Burns (eds.), *Encyclopedia of Leadership,* vol. 1 (Thousand Oaks, CA: Sage Publications, 2004), 68–72.

10. Thomas J. Watson, Jr. "Reorganization," in Peter Krass (ed.), *The Book of Leadership Wisdom* (New York: Wiley, 1998), 427–435.

11. Chester I. Bernard, *The Functions of the Executive* (Cambridge, MA: Harvard University Press, 1938), 9.

12. Frederick W. Taylor, *Principles of Scientific Management* (New York: Harper, 1911).

13. Harry Braverman, *Labor and Monopoly Capital: The Degradation of Work in the Twentieth Century* (New York: Monthly Review Press, 1974); Herbert A. Simon, *The New Science of Management Decision* (New York: Harper & Row, 1960), 14.

14. Peter F. Drucker, *The Essential Drucker* (New York: HarperCollins, 2001), 70.

15. Abraham H. Maslow, "The Theory of Human Motivation." *Psychological Review* 50 (1943): 370–396.

16. Ralph M. Stogdill, "Leadership, Membership and Organization," *Psychological Bulletin* 47 (1950): 1–14; quotation at 3.

17. Ralph M. Stogdill, "Personal Factors Associated with Leadership: A Survey of the Literature," *The Journal of Psychology* 28 (1948): 35–71.

18. S. A. Kirkpatrick and E. A. Locke, "Leadership: Do Traits Matter?" *Academy of Management Executive* 5, 2 (1991): 48–60.

19. Douglas McGregor, *The Human Side of Enterprise* (New York: McGraw-Hill, 1960), 315.

20. Fred E. Fiedler, *A Theory of Leadership Effectiveness* (New York: McGraw-Hill, 1967).

21. Henry Mintzberg, *The Nature of Managerial Work* (New York: Harper & Row, 1973).

22. B. M. Bass, E. R. Valenzi, D. L. Farrow, and R. J. Solomon, "Management Styles Associated with Organizational Task, Personal and Integrative Contingencies," *Journal of Applied Psychology* 60 (1975): 720–729.

23. Gary Yukl and J. Bruce Tracey, "Consequences of Influence Tactics Used with Subordinates, Peers and the Boss," *Journal of Applied Psychology* 77, 4 (1992): 525–535.

24. James MacGregor Burns, *Leadership* (New York: Harper & Row, 1978), 20.

25. Ibid.

26. Bernard Bass, *Leadership and Performance Beyond Expectations* (New York: The Free Press, 1985).

27. Rosabeth M. Kanter, *The Change Masters* (New York: Simon & Schuster, 1983).

28. Charles Handy, "The Language of Leadership" in M. Syrett and C. Hogg (eds.), *Frontiers of Leadership* (Oxford: Blackwell, 1992), 7–12; quotation at 10.

29. Alannah E. Rafferty and Mark A. Griffin, "Dimensions of Transformational Leadership: Conceptual and Empirical Extensions," *The Leadership Quarterly* 15 (2004): 329–354.

30. Warren Bennis, *Organizing Genius* (Reading, MA: Addison-Wesley, 1997).

31. Nancy Adler, *International Dimensions of Organizational Behavior* (Cincinnati, OH: Southwestern Publishing Company, 1997).

32. D. Goleman, R. Boyatzis, and A. McKee, *Primal Leadership: Realizing the Power of Emotional Intelligence* (Cambridge, MA: Harvard Business School Press, 2002).

33. Robert K. Greenleaf, *Servant Leadership: A Journey into the Nature of Legitimate Power and Greatness* (New York: Paulist Press, 1977).

34. Larry C. Spears, "Practicing Servant-Leadership," *Leader to Leader* 34 (Fall 2004): 7–11.

35. Ann McGee-Cooper and Gary Looper, *The Essentials of Servant-Leadership: Principles and Practice* (Waltham, MA: Pegasus Communications, 2001).

36. Joseph Badaracco, *Leading Quietly: An Unorthodox Guide to Doing the Right Thing* (Boston, MA: HBS Press, 2002).

37. Dusya Vera and Antonio Rodriguez-Lopez, "Strategic Virtues: Humility as a Source of Competitive Advantage," *Organizational Dynamics* 33, 4 (2004): 393–408.

38. Kenneth M. Roberts, "Neoliberalism and the Transformation of Populism in Latin America: The Peruvian Case," *World Politics* 48, 1 (1996): 82–116.

39. Michael Shifter, "Latin America's New Political Leaders: Walking on a Wire," *Current History* 102 (February 2003): 51–57.

40. Peter W. Dorfman, Paul J. Hanges, and Felix C. Brodbeck, "Leadership and Cultural Variation: The Identification of Culturally Endorsed Leadership Profiles," in R. House, P. Hanges, M. Javidan, P. Dorfman, and V. Gupta (eds.), *Culture, Leadership and Organizations: The GLOBE Study of 62 Societies* (Thousand Oaks, CA: Sage Publications, 2004), 669–719.

41. Monsour Javidan, Robert J. House, and Peter W. Dorfman, "A Nontechnical Summary of GLOBE Findings," *Ibid.,* 29–50.

42. Robert J. Taormina and Christopher Selvarajah, "Perceptions of Leadership Excellence in ASEAN Nations," *Leadership* 1, 3 (2005): 299–322.

43. Anne S. Tsui, Hui Wang, Katherine Xin, Lihua Zhang, and P. P. Fu, "Let a Thousand Flowers Bloom: Variation of Leadership Styles Among Chinese CEOs," *Organizational Dynamics* 33, 1 (2004): 5–20.

44. P. P. Fu, T. K. Peng, Jeffrey C. Kennedy, and Gary Yukl, "Examining the Preferences of Influence Tactics in Chinese Societies: A Comparison of Chinese Managers in Hong Kong, Taiwan, and Mainland China," *Organizational Dynamics* 33, 1 (2004): 32–46.

45. Fred E. Fiedler, "How Do You Make Leaders More Effective? New Answers to an Old Puzzle," *Organizational Dynamics* 1, 2 (1972): 2–18, quotation at 17.

3

LEADERSHIP FOR A "DECADE OF DEVELOPMENT":
JOHN F. KENNEDY AND THE FOREIGN ASSISTANCE ACT OF 1961

John M. Heffron

The phrase "political leadership in the United States" is something of an oxymoron. And it's not because politicians are incapable of leading but because leadership itself, under the terms of the Constitution, is so highly mediated, conditioned by the divided nature of power and the resulting tendency to faction and special interest. Some argue that these conditions are natural, arising as they do from our liberties and in a representative democracy from varying, often competing conceptions of the public good. For James Madison, America's preeminent political philosopher, the solution to the clash of interests was neither its suppression nor its "adjustment" through "uniformity"—artificial responses both of which would, he believed, only exacerbate the problem. Madison's solution was twofold: the formal institutionalization of faction through an elaborate system of checks and balances, combined with its careful management (because factionalism could exert a tyranny of its own) through enlightened, republican government. Party differences notwithstanding, Madisonian considerations—of political equity, democratic control, and republican synthesis—have come to underlie much of modern American politics, as well as to define the challenge of political leadership. They give the student of presidential leadership, especially in the area of foreign aid and development where partisan differences can be so pronounced, his materials at hand.[1]

John F. Kennedy, the youngest and, by some accounts, one of the most idealistic of recent American presidents, felt acutely these restrictions—systemic in nature—on his own bid for leadership; six years of experience as a congressman and eight as a senator were apparently insufficient to blunt his disillusionment as president. Even as a freshman member of Congress "he had terrible problems with all the arcane rules and customs which prevented you from moving legislation quickly and forced you to jump a thousand hurdles before you could accomplish anything," recalled old family friend, Lem Billings. "All his life he had trouble with rules externally imposed and now here he was, back once again in an institutional setting."[2]

But Kennedy was also a pragmatist—"an idealist without illusions," in his words—who understood the nature of power and its workings in the Congress, in the courts, and in the presidency.[3] Two years into his presidency Kennedy granted a radio and television interview to representatives from the three major studios, ABC, NBC, and CBS. A question came up about his management of foreign affairs. "How do you use the Presidency, in Theodore Roosevelt's phrase 'the bully pulpit,' to move these men who are kind of barons and sovereigns in their own right up there on the Hill? Have you any way to move them toward a course of action which you think is imperative?" Kennedy's answer was typically evasive, contrasting a clear sense of the obstacles in Congress to any presidential program with notes of exasperation, fatalism, and in the end something like a sense of redemption. How he intended to bring Congress around to his policies, the heart of the question, he was unwilling to say. But bring them around, in large part, he would.[4]

Viewing the Constitution as an invitation to "delay" and defeatism ("It is very easy to defeat a bill in Congress"), the president complained to his interlocutors that everything had to go through "a committee" and "get a majority vote" first in the House and then in the Senate, where "unlimited debate" tended to favor "the opponents, even if they are a minority." Once a bill made it through both houses, a unanimous conference was required to "adjust" their inevitable differences. Failing this, it was "back to the Rules Committee, back through Congress" for yet another round of debates further bogged down by a "seniority system" that could privilege individuals, "including members of your own party," antithetical to the president's program. Kennedy's frustration must have been palpable to his viewers. Yet conflict was "inevitable," said Kennedy. Because of it, "no President's program is ever put in." This was especially true "if it is significant and affects important interests and is controversial."[5]

Kennedy's foreign aid program, which would be embodied in the Foreign Assistance Act of 1961 and its extensions, contained all of these elements. It was *significant* not only because of its breadth of purpose but also for the surpassing scope and magnitude of its ambitions. Calling for a "Decade of Development"—a "vast international effort" to close the "economic gap" between the developed and the undeveloped worlds—Kennedy presided over a reorganization of the entire apparatus of US foreign aid, streamlining and rationalizing economic assistance through a handful of new agencies, including a new Agency for International Development. It *affected important interests* by (for the first time) couching development in the language of country development and national self-help and determination, disaggregating military and economic assistance and, in the process, recasting the terms of the Cold War between the United States and its partners and the Soviet bloc.[6]

In his address to the graduating class of 1963 at American University in Washington, President Kennedy introduced publicly for the first time a vision of "world peace" and of America's role in establishing it that would not have been familiar to the bipolar world of the 1950s and 1960s. We are emphatically not seeking, he proclaimed, "a Pax Americana enforced on the world by American weapons of war . . . but peace for all men and women." In terms extraordinary for their time, he exhorted the class of 1963 (and "every thoughtful citizen who despairs of war and wishes to bring peace") to "begin by looking inward" and reexamining their own attitude toward "the Soviet Union, toward the course of the cold war and toward freedom and peace at home." He asked Americans to "direct attention to our common interests and to the means by which those differences can be solved," expressing a spirit of tolerance and cooperation almost unknown, and certainly not having issued from the presidency, since the united front against Germany in World War II. For the Wilsonian objective of American foreign policy—"to make the world safe for democracy"—Kennedy substituted his own moral equivalent, one that better reflected the needs of a pluralistic world. "And if we cannot end now our differences," he averred, "at least we can help make the world safe for diversity."[7]

Finally, Kennedy's foreign aid reforms and his method of achieving them were *controversial*. Could the United States really afford to extend something like the Marshall Plan, with its massive outlays of economic assistance to war-torn Europe, to the poor countries of Africa, Central and South America, and Central and Southeast Asia? Could it *not* afford to match the Soviet Union's own rising expenditures on foreign aid to developing nations, thereby stemming the tide of Communism in those countries? Was the Communist threat itself an exaggerated one and, in any case, the best basis for a sound, humanitarian economic assistance program such as Kennedy proposed? Could the United States count on international support for such a program or would she have to go it alone? Administratively, did the president's request for long-range funding compromise congressional oversight of foreign spending, one of its prized historical prerogatives? Was Kennedy's disdain for bureaucratic encumbrances, the formal rules and procedures within which all politicians must learn to operate, a liability in moving his reforms from thought to action? Although annual expenditures for economic development amounted in the 1960s to only one-half of 1 percent of the gross national product, no subject perhaps stirred more public controversy or greater partisan debate.[8]

For Kennedy, however, anything was acceptable but the status quo:

> The alternative [to reform] is chaos, not economy—a continuing of
> *ad hoc* crisis expenditures—a further diffusion and dilution of our ef-
> forts—a series of special cases and political loans an over-reliance on
> inflexible, hard loans through the Import-Export and World Banks,
> with fixed dollar repayment schedules that retard instead of stimulate
> economic development—a lack of confidence and effort in the under-
> developed world—and a general pyramiding of overlapping, standard-
> less, incentiveless, inefficient aid programs.[9]

Kennedy created and largely met his own criteria for what was ironically
a successful run through the congressional gauntlet. His foreign aid program was significant. It affected important interests. It was controversial.
The tipping point, he and his advisors knew, would be his leadership, his
ability, in his own words, "to gain acceptance for his point of view over
dissent, inertia, incompetence, or impatience among his own appointees
and policy officials as well as the permanent bureaucracy."[10]

Kennedy pounded away at the task for three years before his life
was cut short in November of 1963. Scattered throughout his public
papers alone, one finds sixty-three references to "foreign aid" and thirty-
three to "foreign assistance"—statements of varying length and inten-
sity in his annual State of the Union address, in special messages to
Congress, in press conferences, in radio and television broadcasts, and in
talks and speeches throughout the country at business conferences, university commencements, and numerous community associations. In nearly
three times as many years in office, Eisenhower made only forty-six and
seven such references, respectively; Truman, during his own two terms,
only sixth-three and eleven.[11]

On August 20, 1963, just three months before his death, Kennedy
held a news conference to urge House passage of the Mutual Defense
and Assistance Bill of 1963 at the funding level proposed by the administration ($4.5 billion) and supported (with a cut of $850 million)
by the Foreign Affairs Committee. He had good reason to worry. In the
end the House of Representatives would authorize only 2.8 billion, a

cut of 38 percent, or $1.7 billion less than the original request; the Senate recommended $3.3 billion. The final appropriation by Congress was $3.0 billion, a considerable (in Kennedy's words, "drastic") cutback that Kennedy probably foresaw and, in his last word on the subject on September 19, publicly excoriated. "This is no time to slacken our efforts," he warned at the August news conference. "This fight is by no means over. The struggle is not finished." The final cuts proposed by the House Appropriations Committee were a "threat to free world security." Arguing that "you cannot separate guns from roads and schools when it comes to resisting Communist subversion in under-developed areas," the president raised the specter of South Vietnam and Southeast Asia generally. Lyndon Johnson would inherit Kennedy's fears and, in the absence of economic solutions in the region, would turn to military ones that, as events were to show, proved fatal.[12]

With modernization and its associated challenges (its "explosiveness," in the words of one influential advisor) as the foreground, this chapter explores the efforts of Kennedy and his closest advisors, his "band of brothers," to create a "new look" in foreign aid policy, develop and pass their program through a doubtful Congress, and, in spite of the controversies surrounding it, persuade Americans generally of the value of long-term, foreign economic assistance.[13] Kennedy led both directly and indirectly in these efforts. At times he went directly before the Congress, the American people, and the international community to champion the proposals of his administration; at other times he worked indirectly through coalitions of the like-minded, giving the imprimatur of the presidency to the ideas and actions of otherwise more or less independent foreign policy intellectuals. In addition to providing an overview of foreign aid reformism, the chapter touches on four innovations of the Kennedy program, one institutional, and the others programmatic and conceptual in nature: the United States Agency for International Development (USAID), the Alliance for Progress, the idea of the Decade for Development, and the Peace Corps.

Kennedy's leadership in each of these areas was clear, even if the framing issues and problems defining them were not always his own.

Still the decision-making process was often opaque, even to Kennedy himself. In an introduction to his speechwriter Theodore C. Sorensen's *Decision Making in the White House,* published in 1963, Kennedy described the presidency in hindsight as "mysterious because the essence of the ultimate decision remains impenetrable to the observer—often, indeed, to the decider himself."[14] And yet, despite the "varying roles, powers, and limitations" of the office, Kennedy's leadership for social and economic development was unmistakable. He promised in an early presidential campaign speech "a man who will formulate and fight for legislative policies, not as a casual bystander to the legislative process." "In the decade that lies ahead . . . the American Presidency," he declared, "will demand more than ringing manifestoes issued from the rear of the battle. It will demand that the President place himself in the very thick of the fight."[15]

In the field of foreign policy especially, "the President alone must make the major decisions." Indeed, "if this nation is to reassert the initiative in foreign affairs," he told voters, "it must be presidential initiative. If we are to rebuild our prestige in the eyes of the world, it must be presidential prestige." His two top aides at the Department of State, Secretary Dean Rusk and Undersecretary Chester Bowles, in separate memos to the president, underscored how important it would be for Kennedy to take the fight for his economic aid program directly to Congress and to the American people. The new aid program, wrote Rusk, would require "the highest level of presidential leadership" in order "to attract the necessary support [in] the historic situation we now find ourselves." Direct and forceful leadership in the area of foreign affairs, whatever its effectiveness, was one campaign promise that Kennedy would deliver on.[16]

KENNEDY AND THE CAMBRIDGE CONSENSUS: CRAFTING "THE NEW LOOK" IN FOREIGN AID

The publication in 1958 of Eugene Burdick and William Lederer's *The Ugly American,* with its powerful indictment of American foreign policy "not only in Asia, but everywhere," made a strong impression on the young senator from Massachusetts. In his zeal, he arranged to send copies to every member of the Senate. The book was written as a fiction, poking fun at exaggerated American stereotypes while calling attention to real problems of waste, mismanagement, and inefficiency in US efforts to help the disadvantaged. The large number of technical advisors and project engineers sent to Asia in the wake of Truman's Point Four program were almost willfully ignorant of local conditions and realities, developing "huge technical complexes" that, according to the authors, were "neither needed nor wanted except by a few local politicians" hoping to enrich themselves.[17]

> We pay for huge highways through jungles in Asian lands where there is no transport except bicycle or foot. We finance dams where the greatest need is a portable pump. We provide millions of dollars' worth of military equipment which wins no wars and raises no standard of living.[18]

No amount of "guns and money alone" would win the hearts and minds of the people of Asia. Neither would sending to the region "a horde of 1,500,000 Americans—mostly amateurs." The goals of American foreign aid policy, including its competition with cadres of better trained and better equipped Communist aid workers, could be realized, wrote Burdick and Lederer, only by a "small force of well-trained, well-chosen, hard-working and dedicated professionals."[19] Such a force would come into official existence in the form of USAID and the Peace Corps three years later. For more immediate purposes, it came to describe the work of a small coterie of leading intellectuals, economists, law professors, and historians at Harvard and the MIT Center for International Studies (CENIS), brought together by Kennedy in 1958 to help forge, in his run-up to the presidency, a new national policy on foreign aid and development.

The group included W. W. Rostow and Max Millikan, economists at CENIS. Rostow would go on to become the president's Deputy Special

Assistant for National Security Affairs and a major architect of the "New Look." From Harvard, law professor Archibald Cox, economist John Kenneth Galbraith, and historian Arthur Schlesinger Jr., together with economist Carl Kaysen and David Bell of the Harvard School of Public Administration, completed the roster. According to one historian, Cox, Galbraith, and Schlesinger formed the "key triumvirate" of Kennedy's pre-presidential Academic Advisory Committee.[20] All would come to take important positions within the new administration: Cox as solicitor general, Galbraith as ambassador to India, Schlesinger as special assistant to the president, Kaysen as deputy for military and strategic affairs under McGeorge Bundy, special assistant for national security affairs, and Bell as director of the budget, deputy special assistant to the president, and later as director of USAID. These and other key Kennedy appointees, including Dean Rusk as secretary of state, Chester Bowles as undersecretary, Adlai Stevenson as US representative to the United Nations, Sargent Shriver as the first director of the Peace Corps, and Teodoro Moscoso as USAID deputy for Latin America, played key roles in crafting and promoting at home and abroad the president's foreign aid program.[21]

The Cambridge consensus emerged in the late 1950s and early 1960s in response to what liberal development economists argued were the deficiencies of foreign aid policy under the Truman and Eisenhower administrations. A task force convened by the president-elect to examine American foreign policy, consisting (among others) of Rostow, Millikan, Galbraith, and Robert R. Bowie, then director of Harvard's Center for International Affairs, voiced some of these criticisms in a final report submitted to the president-elect on the eve of 1961. The current aid program—noted for its nearly exclusive focus on military aid and technical assistance, its rigid commitment to Communist containment, its short-term vision of development assistance (reinforced by an inability to raise adequate funds to meet even the most basic needs), and a preference for private over public investment—was failing "to satisfy the needs and aspirations" of the less developed nations. In the simple organization and administration of aid there was a deplorable "lack of coherence," according to the report. "Today it consists of bits and pieces of policy developed at different times by different people to meet particular situations."

Needed was a "comprehensive Foreign Economic Policy Bill" that would approach foreign economic policy "as a whole," combining in a single program trade regulation, economic aid, commodity policy, and administrative provisions. Such a policy would provide the president with the "tools" necessary to achieve "coordinated action" and a greater sharing of the economic burden between the industrialized nations, strengthening the role, for example, of the newly formed Organisation for Economic Co-operation and Development. The United States would have to take the lead in establishing multilateral agreements aimed at the critical task of "nation building." By the same token, aid recipients would have to demonstrate their ability to "absorb capital and other forms of economic assistance," adducing proof of stable social, political, and economic conditions in their respective countries, and where necessary being willing to carry out institutional changes, such as land reform.[22]

Economic aid would need to be a great deal more generous than in the past, but it would also need to conform to firm criteria set by the donors. This was not the same thing as tied lending, a controversial policy of the Eisenhower administration requiring recipient countries to use their surpluses to purchase American goods and services. Any additional resources resulting from American aid, the report argued, needed to be funneled back into "building democratic nations," not to "subsidizing American exports regardless of price and quality." Tying aid to purchases in the United States was an affront to "competitiveness in world markets."[23] Not incidentally, it also gave support to Communist (and some Third World) claims that American aid proceeded not from humanitarian objectives but from neocolonialist ones of economic self-interest.

The realities of the Cold War and America's very real balance-of-payments problem notwithstanding, Kennedy's advisors were bent on demonstrating that this was manifestly not the case. Indeed, as subsequent events would corroborate, the United States distributed a greater amount of aid on a worldwide procurement basis than any one of its European partners. In the end Kennedy, though sympathetic with the trade liberalism of the Charles River economists, would capitulate to public and congressional pressures for a more protectionist foreign aid policy with "Buy American" strings attached to all procurements.[24]

Faced in 1963 with massive cuts to his foreign aid program, Kennedy and USAID administrator David Bell worried about the connection between development assistance in far-flung lands and American prosperity at home. The president cited Taiwan, Colombia, Israel, Iran, and Pakistan—once "the exclusive market of European countries"— as domestic success stories in the competition here and elsewhere for American markets. But these were only examples of a more general problem, said Kennedy, disarming conservative critics of foreign aid but also confounding an important element of the Cambridge consensus: "Too little attention has been paid to the part which an early exposure to American goods, American skills, and America ways of doing things can play in forming the tastes and desires of newly emerging countries—or to the fact that, even when our aid ends, the desire and need for our products continue, and the trade relations last beyond the termination of our assistance."

To a group of Dallas businessmen in 1964, Bell boasted, "United States foreign aid has probably opened a significant future for American products." He was not far from the truth. Between 1959 and 1963 the percentage of foreign goods purchased with United States aid fell from one-half to one-fifth, a full four-fifths of procurements instead subsidizing domestic manufactures. By linking foreign aid to an international process of demand creation, Kennedy had effectively returned to the mercantilism of an earlier age when the business of the state was commerce and a favorable balance of trade its *raison d'être*.[25]

Flexibility was nevertheless the watchword of the report and of later statements by Kennedy himself: flexibility in the use of loans versus grants; in interest rates and repayment scheduling; in areas of funding (private versus public, local versus national, industrial versus agricultural); and in the level of support for both bilateral and multilateral aid activities. Programming itself, the kind and degree of aid required, would have to be flexible, reflecting the unique needs and historical circumstances of each recipient country. The report recommended five types of resources not only to meet the special circumstances of each country but also "to meet the requirement of different kinds of 'mixes' of aid in each country," an indication of the growing complexity and sophistication of foreign aid thinking among the intellectuals of Kennedy's generation. There would need to be resources for technical assistance and "social development." Not the current type of technical assistance, which often amounted to simply giving "advice," but actual hands-on, operational assistance in running facilities, institutions, and programs.[26]

"Social development" was a new catchall phrase to describe the wide range of public services necessary to achieve greater "growth" and "progress," euphemisms for the social and economic stability, educational levels, and political cohesion required for democracy. Whereas social development was directed at improving government services and husbanding a country's human resources, "capital assistance for development" was needed to strengthen the recipient's infrastructure for greater productivity and a higher gross national product. Whether funds were loaned or granted would depend on the preexisting enabling environment for such growth. Capital assistance could and should consist also of surplus agricultural disposal—the export of American foodstuffs—as a kind of consumption credit and development "cushion" in the event of an emergency or, as many feared, when population growth threatened to wipe out a poor country's economic gains.[27]

Where "normal development assistance is unfeasible" owing to the severity of economic and political conditions, "support and contingency aid" was sometimes necessary not only to bolster a weak government but also to provide emergency relief from the natural and human-made crises that could weaken even a strong one. Multilateral aid and finally private investment were vital supplementary resources in the struggle for human development. It was important, though, to separate them conceptually both from American foreign policy goals, including aid funding, and (in the case of private investment) from the work of development itself. "Political stability" and an "adequate infrastructure" were necessary preconditions for the attraction of foreign investment into underdeveloped areas; more than that, on them hinged the ability of countries to convert private investment into public good. If external capital was to have the promised leveraging effect on a developing country's "take-off point"—the point at which, according to Rostow and Millikan, "sustainable economic growth became possible"—it would have to be relatively free of risk and be managed from above by professional aid workers, not from below by speculators and private entrepreneurs. Investment opportunities, the economists seemed to be saying, were still a field of dreams awaiting an uncertain future.[28]

Memoranda to the president by Rostow, Millikan, Galbraith, George Ball, and others on the eve of his first message to Congress on foreign aid in March 1961 largely reinforced the arguments of the Task Force, focusing instead on "issues in controversy," as Millikan put it. Three important issues, as yet unresolved, were the problem of centralization versus decentralization of aid functions and organization, the question of personnel ("there are differences as to what kind of man [the administrator] should be and what he should do"), and the proper balance between bilateral and multilateral initiatives in the area of economic assistance. Whatever final organizational and administrative arrangements Kennedy and his advisors decided on, Millikan was adamant that "So long as it is easier for a country to get money by waving a Communist threat under our nose or by insisting that we support our friends rather than doing effective programming, designing efficient tax systems, cleaning up government administration, and the like, our development programs will fail of their purposes."[29]

The anti-anti-Communism of the Cambridge liberals was matched only by their commitment to nation building. "We must effectively persuade the underdeveloped world," Millikan continued, "that our main purpose and interest is in nation building rather than in the cold war, an alliance system, or the cultivation of friendship."[30] Somewhat contrary to the views of the Task Force, of which he had been a member, and ultimately to the views of Kennedy himself, Millikan argued against the use of development funds by recipients to solve their political and military needs or to mitigate emergencies. He also doubted the value of multilateralization, arguing that a "revitalized American program" is just as likely to administer development assistance effectively and with "tough" productivity criteria as any international consortium. In any case, "There are many ways in which we can establish multilateral principles in a bilateral setting." Kennedy and his White House staff seized on this idea early in 1961, initiating the call for a Decade of Development; working out, with the help of another task force, the details of such a program; and then handing the concept off more or less intact to the United Nations for implementation.[31]

In his own analysis of current foreign aid policy, Galbraith stressed what the president would repeat time and time again, namely that capital assistance alone could not achieve the desired results and that a negative program of anti-Communism was ultimately self-defeating. Money alone was insufficient to overcome the "decisive barriers to development," barriers of "illiteracy, lack of an educated elite, inimical social institutions, no system of public administration, a lack of any sense of purpose." However, bringing about change in these areas, with or without adequate resources, was no easy task. "To organize a good school system, or reform a bad one, is far harder than to organize an equivalent outlay on dams, turbines, generators and transmission lines. To develop a clear sense of purpose; to get an effective system of public administration when one must build on nothing; and to win social reform when great and perhaps decisive power is held by those to whom reform would be costly are all vastly more difficult." The kind of foreign aid Galbraith had in mind went well beyond the relatively narrow confines of technical and capital assistance. It called for the export to underdeveloped nations not only of money and food stuffs but also of an ideology of national progress and incipient modernization. Kennedy concurred: "If we undertake this effort in the wrong spirit or for the wrong reasons, or in the wrong way, then any and all financial measures will be in vain."[32]

Rostow, whose stages-of-growth theory had captivated Kennedy as early as 1957, became a lead player with the other Cambridge theorists in the evolution of Kennedy's aid program. A memorandum to the president in late February outlined the "crucial issues" in foreign aid, differentiating between "The Old Look" and "The New Look." The differences should be familiar by now. Whereas the old look was defensive and negative in character, its resources directed to propping up weak, often corrupt governments against Communist insurgents alleged to be ubiquitous, the new look was positive and forward-looking, shifting the focus from military to nonmilitary purposes and needs. The old look was long on technical assistance and short on people at home and abroad who "understand the economic development problem"; the new look, by contrast, offered "first-class development planners" and a long-term vision of development needs and aspirations. Finally, the new look would reconceptualize the notion of tied aid, moving it away from the protectionist policies of the past to new criteria related not to the purchase of US products but to the capacity of recipient countries to "absorb capital productively" and to do so "in a reasonably short period." Rostow gave the examples of India, Pakistan, Nigeria, Argentina, Brazil, Colombia, and Venezuela.[33]

The new look would require, however, an entirely new organizational structure, "centralized, simplified, and greatly more efficient" than the old structure. In place of the complex and cumbersome administrative apparatus of the ten-year-old Mutual Security Act (a congeries of a dozen or more separate but related agencies), Rostow proposed a single unifying agency, "The Growth for Freedom Administration," a didacticism renamed the United States Agency for International Development and beginning operation on November 4, 1961. Finally, Rostow counseled "the drafting of a dramatic message which," he told Kennedy, "you may well wish to deliver personally—which would give life to the new look, the turn-around process, and our whole stance towards the underdeveloped areas." The foreign aid message that Kennedy delivered to a joint session of Congress on March 22 was as much the work of Rostow as of the president, who accepted the former's last-minute revisions to the speech almost in their entirety. Behind it was the Cambridge consensus, by now all but indistinguishable from the Kennedy approach to leadership for development.[34]

THE FOREIGN ASSISTANCE ACT OF 1961: LEADERSHIP FOR DEVELOPMENT

Kennedy's first Special Message to the Congress on Foreign Aid was the collective effort of a small but dedicated crew of official and unofficial advisors, including academics such as Rostow, Millikan, and Galbraith, career politicians such as Chester Bowles, and newcomers such as Dean Rusk, Kennedy's secretary of state. As much as he deferred to his advisors on foreign policy and other matters, sometimes with a schoolboy's respect for their intellectual superiority but more often seeking approval for ideas he had already developed on his own, Kennedy always held the reins. "No president," biographer James N. Giglio recounts, "kept a tighter rein on foreign policy, yet few presidents learned to listen to as many divergent viewpoints."

How divergent Kennedy's views were from those of his closest advisors is not clear. By 1959, two years before assuming the presidency, Kennedy had formulated many of the basic elements of his foreign aid policy, looking to learned opinion less for specific recommendations (still less for an introduction to values that would have been unfamiliar to him) than for strategic advice. His aides, wrote Sorensen, "represented his personal ways, means, and purposes." His biggest problem, and the problem on which he turned to them most often, was how most effectively to market his program to a skeptical Congress and an aid-weary public. An analysis of his two major policy speeches of 1961, the

Special Message in March and his address to the United Nations General Assembly in September, both highly collaborative exercises with Kennedy as their prime mover, illustrates the combination of compromise and independence of thought that marked his unique leadership style.[35]

The Special Message on Foreign Aid, like every major presidential address, went through multiple drafts before the final version was delivered before Congress in March. The original draft, according to Schlesinger, was couched in the Cold War rhetoric that the president and others thought was an important selling point at the time. Rostow's rewrite was more muted, emphasizing the more positive aspects of the new program. For himself, Dean Rusk, in a memo to the president on March 10, was sure that "a fresh, positive aid program, scaled to all the requirements and presented with persistence and boldness, has a much better chance of congressional approval and popular acclaim *than another round* of the old Mutual Security bill with the now standard features of 'military assistance,' 'defense support,' 'special assistance,' and all the rest." Rostow's rewrite helped guarantee that the new look would survive intact the demands of public acquiescence. Diplomacy would take care of the rest.[36]

And so whereas in Rostow's rewrite our foreign aid programs were "unsatisfactory in many respects; less productive than they should be; and require radical revision in both concept and administration," in the president's final message they were simply "unsuited for our needs and for the needs of the underdeveloped world." The president's original "two facts" of the foreign aid situation became in Rostow's hands "three facts." The change was accepted. "There is in the 1960s," Rostow wrote into Kennedy's draft, "a major historic opportunity to work together with other nations in the Free World to move more than half the people of the less-developed nations into sustained economic growth."

The president's message replaced "sustained" with "self-sustained" growth to reinforce the theme of self-help and independence, adding parenthetically the clause "while the rest move substantially closer to the day when they, too, will no longer depend on outside assistance." To the phrase "self-help," which appears several times in the president's message, Rostow preferred the phrase "clear mutually-understood criteria," the latter less a euphemism for the former as, in Rostow's mind, a necessary precondition, a "stage" of economic independence. The president, a consummate politician, perhaps better appreciated the impatience of the American people and Congress with aid projects that encouraged dependency, however professionalized. It is telling that in a reference to the current bureaucratic fragmentation of aid, while Rostow struck the original words "haphazard and irrational," Kennedy chose prosaically to keep them.[37]

Some of Rostow's changes were cosmetic, but the text is replete with changes of tone and emphasis and in some cases real substance, whether such changes appear as omissions or emendations in Kennedy's final address. They remind us that the evolution of development policy under Kennedy was a patchwork of competing intellectual and political ideas and objectives and that the liberal Cambridge consensus shared by Kennedy was never adopted wholesale as the basis for his foreign aid policy. In general, "[h]e sought out experts," Rostow later recounted, "but he was systematically suspicious of them. He was conscious that his course of action . . . required him to orchestrate a great many different ideas and considerations that no single advisor or expert could take fully into account."[38]

And so, although Kennedy could agree with Rostow that the United States must continue providing aid to underdeveloped countries "because," in Rostow's draft, "the nation's interest and the cause of political freedom require it," he considered it necessary, when Rostow always did not, to name the alleged enemy of this cause: "world communism." Whether fretting about the growing dependence of developing nations on Russian support or pointing to their vulnerability to "intense subversive activity designed to break down and supersede . . . the new modern institutions they have thus far built," Kennedy, unlike his Cambridge counterparts, was not beneath Cold War mongering to sell his (and their) program. Nor was he quite so willing as Rostow to put the United States at the center of this aid effort—what in his speech became famously the "Decade of Development." He might speak of US goodwill and leadership, but it was to the more important need to "unite the free industrialized nations in a common effort" that he drew particular attention. Thus he omitted the reference recommended by Rostow in this section, "We are the leaders of the Free World and a leader must take the first, firm step"; substituted a reference, struck out in Rostow's rewrite, to the country's "security goals"; and held out instead the promise of an "*end* [emphasis added] of the foreign aid burden."[39]

Nevertheless, Rusk and Bowles had urged a positive approach in the message, and Kennedy followed their advice, hastening to add that the new program "should not be based merely on reaction to communist threats." Restoring a sentence cut by Rostow, the president continues: "We have a positive interest in helping less-developed nations provide decent living standards for their people and achieve sufficient strength, self-respect and independence to become self-reliant members of the community of nations." Kennedy knew enough to appeal to the altruism as much as to the pragmatism of Americans, striking just the right balance between a defensive posture that emphasized national security and military preparedness and a positive one that stressed the global responsibilities of international peace and cooperation.[40]

Kennedy assigned a task force led by Henry R. Labouisse, then director of the International Cooperation Administration (ICA), to translate the proposals of his March 22 message into legislation and programs of action. To ensure continuity with the past, Max Millikan, the director of CENIS, chaired its panel of private consultants. The Task Force on Foreign Economic Assistance publicly released its report, a 189-page "Summary Presentation," to coincide with the president's transmittal of draft legislation on foreign aid at the end of May. Written in vivid yet simple language, and including photographs of "Aid In Action" and colorful charts and tables illustrating a variety of developmental themes and problems, the report was in essence a primer designed to sell to

Congress and to the American public the main tenets and tools of the Kennedy aid program.[41]

Like Kennedy's message itself, the tone of the report was both aggressive and conciliatory. Self-help was essential yet need not preclude "interference with sovereignty to point out defects where they exit." Interference, on the other hand, should not be construed to mean that we "expect countries to remake themselves in our image." Quite to the contrary, the United States considered members of the developing world open societies and, as such, "free to set their own goals and to devise their own institutions to achieve those goals." Nevertheless, aid recipients would need to set firm priorities for their development, although donors would have to use "common sense in applying conditions" for the allocation of funds. From now on, foreign assistance would have to be "a coordinated free world effort" and yet the benefits to the US economy in general, and to its balance-of-payments problem in particular, were unmistakable. Clearly, confining the procurement and shipping of manufactured goods and agricultural commodities to industries based in the United States would have the effect not only of stemming "dollar leakage" but also of stimulating "domestic productive capacities and . . . domestic employment."[42]

With respect to the problem of containing Communism, although it was not the intent of US aid policy to "outbid the communist offers" ("To react this way would involve us in waste, draw us into an undignified posture, and open us to the charge of not being sympathetic to the economic development of other countries except on our own political terms"), aid from the Soviet Union and Communist China had nevertheless reached alarming proportions. A total of twenty-four counties were recipients of bloc aid in 1960. In that year alone, over 6,500 Chinese and Soviet technicians had "penetrated" the developing world, offering assistance as advisors, engineers, construction workers, and farm laborers. Communist advisers had even insinuated themselves into ministerial posts. Generous repayment terms on development loans, including provisions for in-kind credits, and an ideology of long-term commitments made the administration's request for similar lending privileges that much more persuasive. The United States need not emulate the communist model of development, but it still had a responsibility "to provide an alternative to exclusive reliance on Sino-Soviet aid." Revelations of a "bloc offensive" in foreign aid made salient the political machinations of a counteroffensive (not a policy of laissez-faire), in spite of official protestation to the contrary.[43]

American aid policy under Kennedy and as depicted in the Labrouise report was, in this and other important respects, discordant at heart. It counseled self-help but supported an aggrandizement of the helping professions that cut off avenues to independence. It argued for long-term commitments by tying them to short-term economic gains, not in the recipient countries but in the United States itself. It sought a multilateral regime of development aid through bilateral means, through a country evaluation process and country assistance programs supervised largely by the State Department and USAID. As John D. Montgomery has observed, "Foreign aid is more than an extension of the American presence or payments for international favors: it is a strategic reflection of a world outlook."[44] Here too, however, American foreign aid strategy was a compound of opposites, a form of anti-anti-Communism still haunted by 1917 and in the 1960s by the Berlin crisis.

If Kennedy was made uneasy by some of these contradictions, he never showed it, taking every possible occasion to outline and defend his program. Neither did his supporters in Congress, including the chairman of the powerful Senate Foreign Relations Committee, William J. Fulbright, who was Kennedy's bulldog in crucial committee and Senate hearings. Kennedy would get a great deal of what he asked for in the bill for an Act of International Development transmitted to Congress on May 26, including authorization for a five-year program of development lending and funding for the Alliance for Progress, his program targeting the modernization of the American republics. After lengthy committee hearings and debates on the floor of both the House and the Senate as well as within congressional appropriations committees, the

Foreign Assistance Act of 1961 was passed by Congress on August 31. The president signed the act into law on September 4, remarking, "I am hopeful that the Congress will provide funds necessary to fulfill the commitments it undertook in enacting this legislation."[45]

The Foreign Assistance and Related Agencies Appropriations Act of 1961 that was approved on September 30 disappointed but hardly dashed the hopes of Kennedy and his administration. Reflecting the shift from grants to loans, Congress provided $1.1 billion for development lending and $296.5 million for development grants; it gave Kennedy the Presidential Contingency Fund he had requested, appropriating $275 million; and it allotted another $425 million of supporting assistance to nations "whose independence or stability," Kennedy told Congress, "is important to our own security"—countries such as India and Pakistan that, the President and others firmly believed, faced the imminent threat of Communist takeover. Finally, Congress appropriated an additional $600 million for Latin America, for a total of $4.5 billion, including $106 billion for military assistance.[46]

Although Congress provided $860.9 million less than the administration's original request of $4.7 billion, Kennedy and his foreign aid advisors had brought about a sea change in how foreign assistance was viewed in the United States, for the time being moving foreign aid, in Schlesinger's words, "out of the cold war into the context of development." Senator Fulbright, fattened on the modernization theory of Kennedy, Rostow, and the Cambridge economists, put the case before his colleagues in the Senate in words that would once have startled: "The wave of the future is not Communist domination of the world according to Marxian scripture. The wave of the future is social reform and social revolution driving toward the goals of national independence, social justice, and a better way of life for the two-thirds of mankind who live in bitter deprivation." Revolution was in the air. Not a revolution to throw off the yoke of tyranny, real or imagined, but a revolution of rising expectations.[47]

Kennedy understood this—the idea of peaceful, social revolution—yet was able to convey it in terms that people would recognize, as a "struggle" between reactionary and progressive forces of change. In the weeks and months leading up to the passage of his aid program, he stumped the country in support not only of the legislation but also of the deceptively simple, revolutionary concept behind it: development assistance, including the necessary social reforms (not always synonymous with democratization), could serve as America's most effective preemptive strike against left-wing, Communist wars of liberation. On his return from an official visit to Europe in late May, which included a dramatic encounter in Vienna with Soviet Premier Khrushchev ("We have wholly different views of right and wrong . . . of where the world is," asserted Kennedy, "and where it is going"), the president took the occasion to address Americans on radio and television, reaffirming the need for his aid program.[48]

"It was fitting," he pointed out, "that Congress opened its hearings on our new foreign military and economic assistance programs in Washington at the very time that Mr. Khruschev's words in Vienna were demonstrating as nothing else could the need for that very program." And yet, he also pointed out, "I do not justify this aid merely on the grounds of anti-Communism. It is recognition of our opportunity and obligation to help these people be free, and we are not alone."[49] In remarks ten days later to the Eighth National Conference on International Economic and Social Development, he reiterated his policy of social idealism as the only real antidote to Communist insurgency.

> I therefore urge those who want to do something for the United States, for this cause, to channel their energies behind this new foreign aid program to help prevent the social injustice and economic chaos upon which subversion and revolt feed; to encourage reform and development; to stabilize new nations and weak governments; train and equip the local forces upon which the chief burden of resisting local Communist subversion rests.[50]

The latter included strengthening defensive forces in Latin America, through both direct military aid and local police assistance programs, to achieve through violent means what the Alliance for Progress could not by peaceful ones. But it also included a middle-level labor-power approach to skills development, the impetus for which came from the Peace Corps. These two new stars in the constellation, the Alliance for Progress and the Peace Corps, would play essential roles in the internationalization of Kennedy's New Frontier of "unfulfilled hopes and threats."[51]

CONCLUSION: KENNEDY AND THE UNITED NATIONS DECADE OF DEVELOPMENT

Kennedy was one of the last great internationalists of the twentieth century. His foreign aid policy was motivated by the recognition that international cooperation had an essential role to play in development and that development was essential for an acceptable world order. The world of the 1960s was a dangerous place torn apart by growing extremes of wealth and poverty—a widening economic gap against which the two great powers, Kennedy came to believe, were ultimately powerless to act. The United States must play its own strong part in the reduction of poverty and social injustice, but it was not the world's steward. Its solutions were neither the only ones nor always the best ones. "We must face the fact," he told a gathering of students and faculty at the University of Washington in late 1961, "that the United States is neither omnipotent nor omniscient—that we are only 6 percent of the world's population—that we cannot impose our will upon the other 94 percent of mankind—and that therefore there cannot be an American solution to every world problem."[52] In his address at the University of California at Berkeley in March of 1962, he reiterated: "We must reject over-simplified theories of international life—the theory that American power is unlimited, or that the American mission is to remake the world in the American image." Kennedy rejected the idea of an American Century. He rejected the idea, implicit in dependency theory, that to modernize other countries only meant to make them more like ourselves.

The world inherited by Kennedy's generation was made that much more dangerous by the threat of nuclear war. An actual war of this kind would rain down "mutually assured destruction" not only on the United States and the Soviet Union but also on "the great and the small, the rich and the poor, the uncommitted and the committed alike." Modern war was the great leveling force; its undiscriminating effects made the strongest possible case for multilateralism, and for the multilateralism of the United Nations in particular. In his Address before the General Assembly in New York on September 25, 1961, Kennedy made clear the connection between the strength and viability of the United Nations and the world's peace and security, "for in the development of this organization rests the only alternative to war . . . . Were we to let it die, to enfeeble its vigor, to cripple its powers, we would condemn our future." This was more than mere lip service. In the close, intense atmosphere of the Kennedy White House "nearly every significant [foreign policy] decision," according to Schlesinger, the president's liaison to Adlai Stevenson, the US representative, "had a UN angle." Schlesinger further noted: "Considering the fact that JFK is surrounded every day by State Department people, who believe essentially in bilateral diplomacy, and by generals and admirals, who don't believe in diplomacy at all, I think he does exceedingly well to keep the UN as considerably in the forefront of his attention as he does."[53]

The sudden, tragic death of Dag Hammarskjöld gave Kennedy an occasion to recall the UN to first principles (in the words of its charter, "to save succeeding generations from the scourge of war" and "to unite our strength to maintain international peace and security"), renew American and international commitment to nuclear disarmament, and link these and other efforts to the goal of human development. "Free and equal nations," Kennedy was convinced, would not wage war against each other, nuclear or otherwise. For this reason development was necessary for "all nations, however diverse in their systems and beliefs," not simply for the least developed. His call for a United Nations Decade for Development, echoing his call to Congress in March and approved by unanimous vote of the General Assembly, led to two important first steps by the United Nations: (1) the establishment, following a United States initiative, of a $100-million program of multilateral food aid to less developed countries, to be jointly administered by the United Nations and the Food and Agricultural Organization (FAO); and (2) the decision, also based on the US initiative, to hold a world conference on the Application of Science and Technology for the Benefit of Less Developed Areas in Geneva in 1963. The former, taking its inspiration from the Food for Peace program developed by George McGovern and supported by Kennedy, would lead to the World Food Programme (WFP), a lasting achievement of the Decade for Development. By 2000, WFP would account for $1.5 billion of the UN's total expenditures, a fifteenfold increase over its initial 1961 budget.[54]

But perhaps the most important immediate effect of the Decade for Development was to establish a link between development and the social and economic consequences of disarmament. UN officials predicted that reducing worldwide armament expenditures—calculated at approximately $120 billion annually—by half would double national growth rates in underdeveloped countries from an average of 2.5 percent to 5 percent. "The promotion of economic and social development in underdeveloped countries," concluded a high-level conference of economic experts, "is one of the most important ways in which the resources released by disarmament can be put into use."[55]

On the eve of his address, Kennedy's advisors (including Rostow, Stevenson, Schlesinger, Kaysen, and Sorensen) all weighed in on the contents of the speech, outlining what should be the US strategy at the 16th General Assembly. They agreed that "The UN be strengthened in the urgent task of economic and social development"; that however great the UN's interest in disarmament, it was "at least as great in economic development"; and that in any case "the deep political differences which now divide the UN" should not be allowed to slow down efforts to promote "sound and rapid economic and social growth." Only by building "institutions of peace"—Kennedy's system of free and equal nations—could the world hope to "disassemble the institutions of war." The two goals of peace and development, in the view of Kennedy and his advisors, went hand in hand.[56]

Kennedy's foreign aid program, although plagued domestically by congressional cutbacks and in both Latin America and Southeast Asia by suggestions of economic imperialism, nevertheless thrust upon the international stage a new set of ideas about the process of development itself. Through the American example at USAID, national planning for economic development was gaining widespread acceptance as the most rational approach to effective giving. Where once grants-in-aid and technical assistance seemed adequate responses to poverty, Kennedy's "new look" argued forcefully that without structural adjustment—without the underlying economic and social changes associated with modernization and democratization—no amount of money would suffice. To the new lexicon of development, Kennedy contributed concepts of capacity building, skill development, accountability, and performance standards, ideas borrowed less from the world of business than from the social and economic theories of the Cold War intellectuals with whom he shared an affinity.

While Congress debated the domestic consequences of his foreign aid appropriations bill, Kennedy made the decision to take his case before the world's highest tribunal, declaring to the United Nations General Assembly that "development can become a cooperative and not a competitive enterprise."[57] Bilateral aid would not go away, but from Kennedy forward it was necessarily subject to multilateral considerations, not the least of which was international peace and security. In forging this relationship, Kennedy helped give the UN, as an institution greater than the sum of its parts, a new and more meaningful role in economic development.

His finger on the pulse of his times (no less than on the button that in a flash could end them), John F. Kennedy was a transformational leader who nevertheless understood both the limits of transformation and the impossibility of leadership. That he challenged these realities is perhaps the greatest legacy of his presidency, so much of it dedicated to realizing the hopes and needs of the least developed countries. That he kept his sights trained on the larger prize of world peace—left him with a more difficult dilemma than his own leadership: the putative moral superiority of the United States and his dissent from that view. In this one area alone, few American presidents have enjoyed either greater misunderstanding or greater success in the short time given to them.

NOTES

1. Clinton Rossiter, *The Federalist Papers* (New York: NAL Penguin, 1961), 80, 78.

2. Robert Dalek, *An Unfinished Life: John F. Kennedy, 1917–1963* (New York: Little, Brown, 2003), 299.

3. Kennedy's response when asked by Jacqueline Bouvier how he defined himself, reported in Arthur M. Schlesinger, *A Thousand Days: John F. Kennedy in the White House* (Boston: Houghton Mifflin, 1965), 95.

4. Television and radio interview: "After Two Years—A Conversation with the President, December 17, 1962, *Public Papers of the President* (*PPP*), 4, http://www.presidency.ucsb.edu.

5. Ibid., 4–5.

6. John F. Kennedy, *The Strategy of Peace* (New York: Harper, 1960), 53, 46.

7. John F. Kennedy, "Commencement Address at American University in Washington," June 10, 1963, *PPP*, 1–4, http://www.presidency.ucsb.edu.

8. W. W. Rostow, *The Diffusion of Power: An Essay in Recent History* (New York: Macmillan, 1972), 174. As a measure of percentage of GDP, foreign aid was slightly higher at between 0.70 and 1.1. See Curt Tarnoff and Larry Nowels, "Foreign Aid: An Introductory Overview of U.S. Programs and Policies," *CRS Report for Congress*, April 15, 2004, 34, fpc.state.gov/documents/organization/31987.pdf.

9. Kennedy, *Strategy*, 52.

10. Theodore C. Sorensen, *Decision-Making in the White House* (New York: Columbia University Press, 1963), 25–26.

11. Data compiled from the *Public Papers of the Presidents,* American Presidency Project, http://www.presidency.ucsb.edu/.

12. Kennedy, "The President's News Conference of August 20, 1963," *PPP,* 1, and "Statement by the President on Foreign Aid, September 19, 1962," ibid., 1, http://www.presidency.ucsb.edu/. For the comparison between Kennedy's original aid request and the final appropriation for FY 1962, see Office of the Historian, (ed.), *Foreign Relations of the United States* (*FRUS*), 1961–63, Vol. IX: Foreign Economic Policy, section 7, 14, http://dofan.lib.uic.edu/ERC/frus61-63ix.

13. Millikan quoted in Schlesinger, *A Thousand Days,* 588, and James N. Giglio, *The Presidency of John F. Kennedy* (Lawrence: University Press of Kansas, 2006), 31. The "new look" was a phrase coined by W. W. Rostow. See his Memorandum to the President, February 28, 1961, National Security Files (NSF), Staff Memoranda, W. W. Rostow, Foreign Aid 2/24/61–2/28/61, Box 324, John F. Kennedy Library (hereafter JFKL).

14. Sorensen, *Decision-Making,* xxix.

15. "The Presidency in 1960, Address by Senator John F. Kennedy, National Press Club, Washington, DC, January 14, 1960, Historical Resources, JFKL, http://www.jfkl.org.

16. Kennedy quoted in Giglio, *Presidency of John F. Kennedy,* 31; Dean Rusk, Memorandum for the President, March 10, 1961, NSF, Foreign Aid, 3/61–4/61, Box 297, JFKL.

17. William J. Lederer and Eugene Burdick, *The Ugly American* (New York: Norton, 1999 reissue), 283, 281.

18. Ibid., 282.

19. Ibid., 284.

20. Tevi Troy, *Intellectuals and the American Presidency: Philosophers, Jesters, or Technicians?* (New York: Rowan and Littlefield, 2002), 20.

21. See Schlesinger, *A Thousand Days,* 118–145.

22. Report to the Honorable John F. Kennedy by The Task Force on Foreign Economic Policy, December 31, 1960, NSF, Foreign Economic Policy, Box 297, 10–11, 16, 17, 16, 6, 58, JFKL.

23. Ibid., 61.

24. See John D. Montgomery, *Foreign Aid in International Politics* (Englewood Cliffs, NJ: Prentice-Hall, 1967), 19–25.

25. Ibid., 88.

26. Ibid., 66, 68, 70–71.

27. Ibid., 70–72.

28. Ibid., 73–74; W. W. Rostow and Max Millikan, *A Proposal: Key to an Effective Foreign Policy* (New York: Harper, 1957), 56.

29. Max Millikan, "Memorandum on a New Organization for the U.S. Foreign Aid Program," NSF Staff Memoranda Foreign Aid, 1/1/61–1/10/61, 1, 5, Box 324, JFKL.

30. Ibid.

31. Ibid., 9–11.

32. John Kenneth Galbraith, "A Positive Approach to Foreign Aid," NSF, Foreign Aid 12/60–2/61, Summary and 9, Box 297, JFKL.

33. W. W. Rostow, Memorandum to the President, February 28, 1961, op. cit., 1, 4, 3.

34. W. W. Rostow, "Growth for Freedom," NSF, Foreign Aid, 2/13/61–2/20/61, 2–3, Box 324, JFKL. Rostow worked up an organizational chart for his proposed Growth for Freedom Administration in "Plans for the Reorganization of Foreign Assistance," March 4, 1961, NSF, Foreign Aid, Box 324, JFKL. Rostow, Memorandum to the President, ibid., 6.

35. Giglio, *Presidency of John F. Kennedy,* 35. Sorensen quoted in John A. Barnes, *John F. Kennedy on Leadership: The Lessons and Legacy of a President* (New York: American Management Association, 2005), 126.

36. See Schlesinger, *A Thousand Days,* 592, and Rusk, Memorandum for the President, March 10, 1961, op. cit., 2.

37. "Special Message on Foreign Aid," NSF, W. W. Rostow, Foreign Aid, 3/19/61–3/22/61, Pt 1, 1–8, Box 324, JFKL, and John F. Kennedy, "Special Message to the Congress on Foreign Aid, March 22nd, 1961," *PPP,* 1–7, http://www.presidency.ucsb.edu/.

38. Rostow, *The Diffusion of Power,* 67.

39. "Special Message on Foreign Aid," 1–8 and "Special Message to the Congress on Foreign Aid, March 22nd, 1961," 1–7, op. cit.

40. Ibid., 4.

41. Henry R. Labouisse et al., *An Act for International Development, A Program for the Decade of Development: Summary Presentation,* June 1961, Department of State Publication 7224, General Foreign Policy Series 174 (Washington, DC: U.S. Government Printing Office, 1961).

42. Ibid., 13, 12, 167–171.

43. Ibid., 88, 188–189.

44. Montgomery, *Foreign Aid,* 18.

45. John F. Kennedy, "Statement by the President upon Signing the Foreign Assistance Act, September 4th, 1961," *PPP,* http://www.presidency.ucsb.edu/.

46. See *Report to the Congress on the Foreign Assistance Program for Fiscal Year 1962* (Washington, DC: U.S. Government Printing Office, 1962), 5, and John F. Kennedy, "Letter to the President of the Senate and to the Speaker of the House Transmitting Bill Implementing the Message on Foreign Aid May 26th, 1961," *PPP,* 1, http://www.presidency.ucsb.edu/.

47. Schlesinger, *A Thousand Days,* 599, and *Congressional Record—Senate,* vol. 107, August 4, 1961, 14710.

48. John F. Kennedy, "Radio and Television Report to the American People on Returning from Europe, June 6th, 1961," *PPP,* 1–2, http://www.presidency.ucsb.edu/.

49. Ibid., 4.

50. John F. Kennedy, "Remarks at the Eighth National Conference on International Economic and Social Development, June 16th, 1961, *PPP,* 2–3, http://www.presidency.ucsb.edu/.

51. See Edward B. Claflin, *JFK Wants to Know: Memos from the President's Office 1961–1963* (New York: William Morrow, 1991), 119, 149, 189–191, in which the president, in National Security Action Memoranda and in letters to USAID administrator Hamilton Fowler, expresses his concerns and outlines policies for Latin American internal security. In 1962 the Peace Corps sponsored an international conference in Puerto Rico on "Human Skills in the Decade of Development." See John F. Kennedy, "Statement by the President Announcing an International Conference on 'Human Skills in the Decade of Development,' September 3rd, 1962," *PPP,* http://www.presidency.ucsb.edu/. Kennedy quoted in Schlesinger, *A Thousand Days,* 60.

52. Kennedy quoted in ibid., 615 and in John F. Kennedy, "Address in Berkeley at the University of California, March 23rd, 1962," *PPP,* 3, http://www.presidency.ucsb.edu/.

53. John F. Kennedy, "Address in New York City Before the General Assembly of the United Nations, September 25th, 1961," *PPP,* 1, http://www.presidency.ucsb.edu/; Schlesinger, *A Thousand Days,* 467, 466.

54. *Charter of the United Nations,* New York: Department of Public Information, 2005 reprint, 3, and Richard Jolly, Louis Emmerij, Dharam Ghai, and Frederic Lapeyre, *UN Contributions to Development Thinking and Practice* (Bloomington: Indiana University Press, 2004), 4, "The 1960s: The UN Development Decade—Mobilizing for Development," especially 97–99.

55. Ibid., 86, 87, 88.

56. "United States Economic and Social Initiative at the 16th Session of the General Assembly—Organization of United Nations Development Decade," September 19, 1961, NSF, Carl Kaysen, Foreign Aid—General, 1/61–4/62, 1–2, Box 373, JFKL; Harlan Cleveland to Theodore Sorensen, Sorensen Papers, UN Speeches, Memoranda and Speech materials, 7/25/61–9/22/61, 30, Box 64, JFKL.

57. Kennedy, "Address in New York City Before the General Assembly of the United Nations, September 25th, 1961," op. cit., 4.

4

REINVENTING GOVERNMENT IN THE PACIFIC BASIN:

POLITICAL LEADERSHIP AND GOVERNMENTAL CHANGE

G. Shabbir Cheema

The rapid pace of globalization in the world today is resulting in profound and far-reaching changes, manifested in new markets (foreign exchange and capital markets linked globally), new tools (such as Internet links and media networks), new actors (such as the World Trade Organization and networks of global nongovernmental organizations, or NGOs), and new rules (including multilateral agreements on trade, and rules related to intellectual property). With increasing access to information, citizens are demanding greater accountability in the executive branch of the government. To cope effectively with the changes and to take advantage of opportunities provided by globalization, governments are under tremendous pressure not only to be competitive and efficient but also to be accountable and participatory. These demands challenge political leaders and public officials to be highly adaptable and flexible at a time when traditional concepts of training and education have not necessarily prepared them for these tasks.

This chapter examines the role of leadership in reinventing government in the Pacific Basin countries. It identifies some of the critical issues in government reinvention to cope with the demands of the

81

global economy and a more informed citizenry. It reviews leadership characteristics and attributes required to design and implement effective government reinvention programs to promote people-centered development. It also presents case studies on the role of leadership at national and local levels in promoting innovations and good practices to revitalize governance and public administration in Asian and Latin American countries. This chapter identifies areas of competency enhancement to enable top government leaders to function effectively in a globalized world.

CRITICAL ISSUES IN REINVENTING GOVERNMENT FOR DEVELOPMENT

Over the past fifty years, the concepts and practices of good government have evolved through four phases: traditional public administration, public management, new public management, and, most recently, government reinvention to promote partnerships among the public sector, civil society, and the private sector. Each phase has reflected changes in the internal and external environments of government. Globalization has provided new opportunities to both richer and poorer countries through economic liberalization, foreign investment and capital flows, technological change, and information flows. Yet rapid globalization has not led to equitable benefits for millions of people around the world. The United Nations Conferences and Summits held in the 1990s and the historic United Nations Millennium Summit Declaration led to the normative framework, the vision of shared development priorities, and finally the time-bound targets specified in the Millennium Development Goals (MDGs). The MDGs seek to eradicate extreme poverty and hunger, achieve universal primary education, promote gender equality, reduce child mortality, improve maternal health, combat HIV/AIDS and other diseases, ensure environmental sustainability, and promote global partnership for development.

These documents and the theories underlying them assert that reinventing government to meet the challenges of globalization and promote

people-centered development must be built on administrative and political structures and processes that are accountable, transparent, and
decentralized. Governments must be able to manage legitimate elections
and an effective system of justice, and they must operate under the oversight of the parliament. Furthermore, they should combat exclusion,
protect public goods, actively engage civil society and the private sector,
use the power of information and communications technology (ICT)
to promote e-government, and strengthen partnerships among different economic sectors, social groups, and levels of government.[1]

Leadership in reforming public administration is at the core of reinventing government for development. Developing countries face many
challenges in their efforts to reform public administration. They need
to pursue civil service reforms and adapt new personnel policies and
procedures; raise civil service pay scales in order to attract and retain
highly qualified staff; decentralize authority and resources to local governments; and develop further resources to unlock human potential in
the public sector. They also face other challenges in developing communications and information infrastructure; in providing leadership
and vision to cope with the challenges of globalization; in managing
strategically; and in strengthening the relationships among government,
civil society, and leaders in the private sector. Effective structures and
processes for public administration are essential for efficient service delivery. Effectively functioning public-administration systems with motivated and competent staff are needed to design, monitor, and evaluate
programs in education, health, shelter, and other sectors. Competent
local administration with adequate staff and financial resources is necessary to provide.

Establishing and enforcing the rule of law is another pillar of government reinvention. Effective governments create or strengthen institutions, mechanisms, and clear accountability norms for three branches
(executive, legislative, and judicial) in order to establish the rule of law.
An independent judiciary—with adequate infrastructure, well-staffed
courts, accountable bureaucracy, and adequately trained police, lawyers,
and judges—is essential for enforcing laws and ensuring that all citizens

are treated fairly. In the absence of rule of law, services provided by the government are captured by the elite, the poor lack adequate access to justice, and the judiciary cannot independently check abuse of government power or illegal use of public resources. Effective judicial systems are essential to promote foreign investment, allow effective exchanges among commercial enterprises, and enforce property laws.

Promoting accountability and transparency is yet another pillar of good governance. Electoral management bodies with sufficient independence and adequate capacity facilitate the organization of free and fair elections and thereby increase the legitimacy of government. Parliaments with powers to hold the executive accountable through a system of checks and balances enhance the representation of all segments of society in the legislative process. A free press is essential to inform the public, critically analyze government policies, monitor government performance and service delivery, and promote the interests of the excluded and marginalized groups in society. Anticorruption bodies with effective strategies, including codes of conduct and transparent procedures for procurement, are essential to combat corruption and promote integrity in governance. Accountability and transparency facilitate the achievement of development goals. Effective parliaments and systems of checks and balances provide opportunities for representing the interests of different groups and underserved areas in the society and for demanding public review of expenditures. A free press highlights any capture of government facilities and services by the elite and dominant groups in the society and the need to make basic social services such as education, health, and shelter accessible.

Human rights are both an element of good governance and normative standards agreed to by the member States signatory to the UN Millennium Declaration. A rights-based approach to development places people at the center of governance. It states that education, shelter, and physical security are basic rights of the populace, not privileges, because they are essential if people are to fully utilize their capabilities and enjoy life with human dignity. It thus promotes a holistic approach to development. Without economic and social rights, citizens cannot fully exercise their political, civil, and cultural rights. Hence, these rights are complementary.

The promotion of sound economic policy is another pillar of reinventing government for development. The UN Millennium Project has recommended that governments collaborate with the private sector in designing private-sector development strategies that create a favorable business environment: a supportive macroeconomic framework, a favorable legal and regulatory environment, and adequate infrastructure and human capital. A favorable business environment requires government and the private sector to promote business activities in innovative science and technology, to encourage foreign direct investment (FDI), and to help transform the informal economy. Pro-poor policies at the global, regional, and national levels are essential to achieve the Millennium Declaration target of reducing poverty by one-half by 2015.

The final dimension of government reinvention for development is the partnership between government and civil society. The engagement of civil society is essential to government reinvention. Civil-society organizations play an important role in representing different views, monitoring and evaluating government policies and programs, and mobilizing local resources and expertise to meet local and community needs. A vibrant civil society with adequate capacity is central to achieving the MDGs—for example, through facilitating delivery of services such as water and sanitation, primary health care, and education and through its direct support of community-based initiatives to improve environmental education and urban and rural shelter. Civil-society organizations also advocate gender equality and child and maternal health care. More specifically, global civil society has emerged as an influential advocate of debt relief, fair trade practices between developed and developing countries, and increased foreign aid from developed countries.

Effective responses to each of these dimensions of governance reform require national, state, and local leaders with specific attributes who, in consultation with various stakeholders, are able to identify alternative solutions to institutional problems, mobilize support among social groups, forge partnerships among stakeholders, and exhibit the political commitment to designing, monitoring, and implementing government reform.

LEADERSHIP ATTRIBUTES AND GOVERNMENT REINVENTION

A review of the literature on leadership characteristics and their impact on organizational performance shows that strong leaders involved in reform share some personal characteristics but differ significantly in others.[2] Some are transactional leaders, and others are transformational leaders. These differences are due largely to the leaders' personalities, the sociopolitical and cultural context in which they operate, and whether they are working in public- or private-sector organizations. Transactional leadership occurs when the leader receives the support of followers in return for delivering certain things that they value; this is an exchange relationship between leader and follower that may well end once the transaction is completed. Transformational leadership occurs when a bond is created between leaders and followers on the basis of the joint effort of both to achieve higher goals. Based on their characteristics, leaders in government can be divided into several categories: hierarchical, directive, and control-oriented; participative, collaborative, and consultative; delegative and culturally sensitive; meditative; and technical or substantive. Different situations and problems in reinventing government at the national and local levels require different leadership attributes. Globalization has, in many ways, shaped not only the tasks that political leaders must perform but also the attributes they need to influence followers.

First, globalization is a complex process, and its benefits have not been equitably distributed among countries. Political leaders and government officials have to reconcile short-term political necessities with long-term development goals in complex political environments and institutional arrangements. This required leaders with such attributes as technical ability, cultural sensitivity, and ability to forge partnerships.

Second, improved communication and awareness have led to increasing pressures on governments to respond effectively to development problems, sometimes in the context of a stagnant economy. Leaders who are participative, consultative, and collaborative—but decisive at the same time—are more likely than others to build consensus using the expertise and experience of different groups.

Third, growing disparities and gaps between rich and poor countries and within poor countries have created vested interests that limit the policy choices of leaders and the ability of government officials to implement programs. Leaders have to reinvent government processes to achieve both economic growth and social justice. This requires leaders who can forge partnerships among diverse groups, who can mediate differences, who consult with a variety of interest groups, and who are committed to social justice for all.

Other key development issues that leaders face in promoting institutional reform and government reinvention include the rising expectations of citizens from rapid democratization in developing countries that have not seen simultaneous economic gains; marginalization of the poor from growth-oriented policies lacking adequate safety nets; the increasing need to accommodate diverse ethnic and religious groups whose conflicts limit the choices of leaders; and the gradual weakening of government capacity as a consequence of internal conflicts. Responding effectively to these issues requires leaders with such attributes as commitment to the integrity of the mission, genuine interest in the views of all stakeholders, and adeptness at understanding people's individual skills and deploying them in the right places. An effective leader should be able to demonstrate personal integrity to forge partnerships for the common good, commitment to a reform agenda, and consistency in pursuing it even in the face of short-term setbacks.

The case studies of leaders in government reinvention that are presented in this chapter focus on four attributes of leadership.

1. *Ability to communicate a vision to stakeholders.* Political leaders and senior government officials often face many pressures, such as entrenched bureaucracies and highly polarized public interest groups, that business leaders do not. Many leadership scholars argue that one of the key characteristics of good leadership is the ability to formulate and clearly communicate an overall "vision." If leaders can successfully communicate their vision, they can encourage and inspire people to support new policies and institutional reforms by working together for the common good.

2. *Ability to reconcile long-term goals with short-term pressures.* Political leaders and senior government officials often face major obstacles and persistent pressures to focus on short-term gains rather than on long-term goals. Their challenge in achieving development goals, however, is to balance or reconcile these pressures. Doing so requires leaders with such attributes as technical ability, cultural sensitivity, and future orientation.

3. *Ability to forge partnerships.* The rapid pace of democratization in much of Asia and Latin America has increased citizens' expectations of governments. At the same time, growing disparities in income and wealth within poor countries have created vested interests at the national and international levels that limit leaders' policy choices and their ability to implement government programs. Government reinvention requires leaders who can forge partnerships among diverse groups, mediate differences, consult with a variety of interest groups, and stay committed to achieving social justice. Partnerships among governments, the private sector, and civil society have become increasingly important in improving

basic service delivery. Leaders who use participatory and inclusive approaches should have a greater potential to accomplish difficult reforms.

4. *Personal integrity and commitment to reform.* Government reinvention is a long-term process in which conflicts often occur among different groups trying to protect their own interests. An effective leader should be able to demonstrate personal integrity to forge partnerships for the common good. Also required are commitment to a reform agenda and consistency in pursuing it even in the face of short-term setbacks.

In brief, as a recent United Nations report concluded, leadership in the public sector involves vision, mobilization, action, and learning.[3]

CASE STUDIES OF THE IMPACT OF LEADERSHIP ON GOVERNMENT REINVENTION

The five cases of leadership in government reinvention that follow illustrate the crucial role of strong leaders in seizing opportunities and mobilizing human resources to promote government reforms. The cases show that in exercising leadership, there is no one-model-fits-all. Using different styles and attributes of leadership, political and government officials at national and local levels have at different times and places in Asia and Latin America had strong influence on government reform. Some succeeded and others did not. Their success or lack of it was determined in part by their leadership attributes and skills.

President Vicente Fox and Government Reinvention in Mexico

President Vicente Fox's 2000 election victory broke seven decades of continuous one-party rule by the Institutional Revolutionary Party (PRI) in Mexico.[4] His election resulted from a growing public demand for change and raised expectations that he would be able to deliver economic growth, jobs, and public security. Citizens voted for him because they believed that he would be able to bring real democracy, which for most people meant more economic opportunities, more security, and better living standards. President Fox had to tackle the difficult task of managing a collapsed political establishment along with constructing a completely new governance system that would not threaten the many vested interests that were weakened by the collapse of the PRI.

From the start, Fox articulated a clear and specific national strategy to build a government that would be transparent and accountable to citizens. Its primary purpose would be to provide effective and efficient services that met citizens' demands. To carry out these reforms, he created a special unit on government innovation within the Executive Office and established quality networks across all departments and agencies of the federal government to reengineer and align institutions and processes to pursue his national strategy. Fox's vision and leadership of reform were influenced by his previous experience as an executive in the private sector.

His vision was to construct a government for citizens, of citizens, and by citizens. This monumental task meant introducing entirely new institutions and a new culture of governance. He passed a Freedom of Information Act that transformed government from a closed and secretive body to an open and transparent institution where citizens could gain access to information about how government agencies were using public resources and carrying out their public duties. This fundamental transformation in government operations sent a clear signal to all citizens that Mexico was open to a new way of doing business. The overall vision set the tone for the reforms: the citizen was the center of all government action, and the citizen was the government's primary client. To pursue this vision, government had to reinvent itself. It had to establish accountability mechanisms so that citizens could observe progress in an open and transparent way.

With President Fox's declaration that his was "the administration of change," all federal departments and agencies were required to set benchmarks that would lead to visible results for improving and expanding services, based on the needs and priorities of citizens. In order to communicate his message, Fox established the Presidential Office for Government Innovation to launch the "Presidential Good Government Agenda." He personally presided over awards ceremonies to recognize the best practice reforms of his Good Government Agenda.

He promoted partnerships among important interest groups, including public servants who until then had been appointed through a political patronage system. He urged Congress to create a civil service system. But Fox's reform programs encountered serious obstacles, only some of which he was able to overcome. Because public service jobs depended on patronage, bureaucrats were more loyal to their patrons than to the mission of their agencies or the vision of the president. The majority of the approximately 1.5 million bureaucrats simply had no incentives to support the Presidential Good Government Agenda. Also, members of Congress did not fully appreciate and support the need for professionalizing the civil service and for maintaining continuity in the implementation of public policies. The Presidential Good Government Agenda provided a clear road map for a government that was to be at the service of citizens and guided the training that government officials would need to recognize the need for change and to implement the president's reforms. The alignment of vision and strategy from the president to front-line workers provided public servants with the mission of implementing reforms. Under President Fox, the executive branch worked closely with Congress to demonstrate the benefits of a civil service. It sponsored hearings, brought in international experts, and arranged study tours to countries with mature civil services. In the end, Congress became the champion of creating a civil service law but resisted many other elements of Fox's vision.

President Fox's personal integrity and commitment to reform were instrumental in the implementation of government reinvention in Mexico. The Presidential Good Government Agenda meant that the president himself was leading the change to a citizen-based government. All executive departments and agencies were required to report their prog-ress or setbacks in meeting performance benchmarks directly to the Executive Office of the President. Fox took direct responsibility for promoting trust in his administration, even though he was not able to accomplish all of his administration's development objectives during his tenure.

Thaksin Shinawatra, the Former Prime Minister of Thailand

Thaksin Shinawatra's leadership style could be described as decisive and committed to the causes of the rural poor and other underprivileged groups in society. Unlike Vicente Fox in Mexico, however, Thaksin was more likely to use strong-arm tactics to achieve his policy goals. This leadership style helped him to win overwhelming majorities in parlia-mentary elections in 2001 for the first time in the Thailand. But it also led to social and political divisiveness, and his inability to forge part-nerships among different groups and promote bipartisan agendas led eventually to his downfall as prime minister in 2006.[5]

Thaksin elicited strong emotions. His supporters loved his "can do" attitude, and he was quite popular among the poor in rural areas. Others resented what they called his dictatorial management style and his use of political power to channel economic benefits to his family and cronies. In early 2006, Thaksin camped out in a rural area for a week and brought with him an entourage of officials and reporters to record a reality TV show, which he considered a new approach to reach-ing the people and sending a message. His decisive leadership contrib-uted to his popularity and electoral victory. He first took office in 2001 when Thailand was struggling to cope with the Asian financial crisis. Immediately after taking office, he boosted domestic demand through policies promoting cheap loans and government handouts. He declared war on Thailand's drug trade by cracking down on suppliers and small-scale dealers. His war on the drug trade was criticized by human rights advocates, but most citizens supported it. He won high marks for his leadership in response to the tsunami in Southeast Asia in December 2004 and for Thailand's effort to control the spread of avian flu.

His heavy-handed military response to ethnic conflicts and violence in the Muslim majority provinces of the south, however, were severely criticized both within the country and abroad and worsened the situation in the provinces. His appointment of relatives and cronies to high positions in the government, including the appointment of his first cousin, General Chaisit Shinawatra, as first the army chief and then the military's supreme commander, and that of his brother-in-law, Priawpan Damapong, as deputy chief of police, enabled opposition parties to mobilize popular opposition to his government.

In February 2006, many groups in urban areas, ranging from middle-level professionals to Buddhist monks, held public protests calling for Thaksin's resignation. The flames of outrage were fanned by the sale of his family's telecom and media empire, Shin Corp, to the government of Singapore and by the "use of a legal loophole to avoid tax on the nearly $2 billion the deal netted" for his family and clan. Some protested the prime minister's suppression of free speech, including the banning of meetings called by his opponents. In his combative style of leadership, he organized a demonstration of more than 150,000 supporters at the same location where the opposition had organized a smaller demonstration.[6]

In response to the public demonstrations, Thaksin called for new elections and promised a neutral panel to draw up constitutional reforms—one of the opposition's main demands—and to call for further elections once the reforms were adopted. Elections were held in 2006. The opposition parties' boycott gave Thaksin's party another victory, although by a far lower number of votes than it received in 2005. When the demonstrations continued even after his reelection, Thaksin resigned to restore unity in the country. The opposition parties refused offers of reconciliation. Months of street protests and allegations of abuse of power, heavy-handedness, and corruption had created an environment in which the main opposition group, the People's Alliance for Democracy, completely lost trust in his leadership. A military coup ended his regime in 2006.

Jaime Lerner, Mayor, City of Curitiba, Brazil

Curitiba, the capital of Parana state in southeastern Brazil, faced explosive growth from the 1950s onward.[7] It grew in population from a town of 300,000 in 1950 to a metropolis of 2.2 million in 1990, making it Brazil's fastest-growing city. Various trends indicated uncontrolled growth with negative social and environmental consequences. Curitiba's rapid economic surge from a small center of agricultural processing to a regional industrial and commercial nucleus attracted massive waves of migrants from the countryside, who had been displaced by the mechanization of plantations, resulting in widespread poverty and lack of adequate shelter and services.

The city became an international model for integrated and holistic planning and won international awards for the local administration's ability to mobilize local communities to tackle development challenges. From the early 1970s, leaders in Curitiba eschewed top-down policy-making and embarked on a different path, one that followed conscious political decisions backed by popular participation. The driving force for change was Jaime Lerner, the mayor who introduced reforms and pursued their implementation through three terms as the elected mayor of Curitiba.

Mayor Lerner had to balance immediate challenges posed by physical expansion and the growth of slum areas with the tremendous pressure for public transport, water, sanitation, and other basic services. He initiated institutional reforms, including the creation of the Curitiba Research and Urban Planning Institute, an Industrial City, and a plan for the revitalization of the Historic Centre. During his subsequent terms of office, Mayor Lerner focused on environmental preservation, waste management programs, social services (including a network of day care centers), consolidation of the public transport system, and creation of the rapid transit system, among other short-term improvements.

A number of diverse groups were engaged in the approval of a master plan for Curitiba, which addressed the need to define a blueprint for urban development based on consensus among different communities. The plan was shared with the population and widely disseminated. The plan defined medium- and long-term development by outlining a growth structure based on public transport facilities going from the city center to the periphery where the poor live, land use legislation, and the hierarchy of road networks. The plan also addressed the need to promote social services while sustaining economic growth. The transparent dissemination of the plan contributed to controlling land speculation and helped engage various groups representing civil society and the private sector by defining "equations of co-responsibility" through partnerships.

A common "vision" for the future of the city was included in a plan. The mayor was able to promote societal consensus around the main goals of the plan by demonstrating the importance of organized growth for Curitiba. He emphasized the dangers of disorderly growth as exhibited by other Brazilian cities, such as São Paulo. During his first administration the mayor also highlighted the importance of balancing the physical transformation, cultural transformation, and economic transformation of the city. The physical transformation was characterized by the implementation of changes in public transport and land use, the cultural transformation was characterized by the creation of pedestrian malls and the revitalization of the historic center, and the economic transformation was characterized by the Curitiba Industrial City.

Communication and consultation were an ongoing part of the reform process. Reforms had to be properly communicated to stakeholders and to the population in general, through meetings with the City Council, neighborhood associations, and media. Shop owners were engaged in the revitalization of the city center; neighborhood associations in the periphery were widely engaged in the waste management programs; and public transport entrepreneurs had to be engaged in the reform of the public transport system.

Mayor Lerner is widely known in Brazil and worldwide as an example of credibility and competence. Citizens saw results and knew that the mayor was leading by example. He was never accused of any type of malfeasance and did not use his power to make exceptions to the rules defined to guide the development of Curitiba. The population never saw any signs of "unexplained wealth" on the part of the mayor, who lived in the same house and kept the same standard of living throughout his terms of office.

Mayor Lerner also demonstrated a few other qualities that deserve mention. One of them was giving proper credit to the contributions of staff members and external partners. The decision-making process seemed to flow better when the mayor demonstrated willingness to listen to suggestions for further improvement. The process of sharing ideas in a creative environment also contributed to consolidating innovations. Mayor Lerner was able to lead while promoting team spirit and an atmosphere conducive to the free exchange of ideas. He generated trust among financial institutions, thanks to the seriousness of his administration. Banks trusted Lerner enough to finance private-sector operations of pubic transport in Curitiba, and big companies such as Volvo, Bosch, and Siemens and (with some incentives) other companies trusted the municipal administration enough to move to the Curitiba Industrial City.

Mahathir Mohammad:
Former Prime Minister of Malaysia

Mahathir Mohammad's two-decade rule in Malaysia was dominated by his thinking that development policies and institutional responses must change if the country was to move forward.[8] He made no apology for the fact that this change had to come from above, and that it needed strong leadership. Mahathir once said that he did not see why democracy and authoritarianism could go hand in hand in this process, at least during the transition as Malaysia moved toward becoming a developed nation.

He began his premiership with a campaign based on "Clean, Efficient and Trustworthy" government. His privatization and corporatization policies were accompanied by an emphasis on smart partnerships between the public and private sectors and on the new role of the public sector in an economy in which the private sector would be the dynamic engine of growth. He was at times harsh in his criticism of the ethnic Malay for their dependence on the state (through the affirmative action provided by the constitution) and wanted them to get involved in business without the direct aid of the government and to compete in the marketplace. He deemphasized the quota for ethnic Malays, as reflected in the new policy for admission to public universities that replaced the ethnic quota system with one based on merit. He pushed for use of the English language, culminating in a change of policy—partial but significant—regarding the medium of instruction in public schools. He believed in state spending to spur economic activities. He believed that Malaysia must move up in the industrial value chain, toward higher technology to compete in the international marketplace. The Malaysian car and the Multimedia Super Corridor reflected this thinking. His idea of change and reforms was epitomized by his Vision 2020 (to transform Malaysia into a developed, progressive, and democratic nation by that year), which dramatically captured the imagination of Malaysians.

Mahathir was, above all, a pragmatist. He was aware of the competing demands that he had to constantly balance, particularly the demands of competing nationalisms in Malaysia's multi-ethnic society. He needed to balance his trust in the private sector with the entrenched interests of the (Malay-dominated) civil service. Mahathir was fully aware that he led a political party whose fortunes depended much on Malay support, and he had to handle the challenge of the conservative Islamists. But as he repeatedly emphasized, he was the leader of and for all Malaysians. Thus he continuously made short-term adjustments in the face of these realities. The replacement of the ethnic quota in universities was balanced by setting up more colleges and increasing the intake of the all-Malay in the Universiti Technologi Malaysia (UTM). His ambitions for the English language to become the universal medium of instruction were watered down to mathematics and science classes only. In the wake of the 1985–1986 recession, the affirmative action regulations of the New Economic Policy were not enforced; indeed the NEP, which ended in 1990, was replaced by the National Development Policy, with less emphasis on Malay-Bumiputra exclusive concerns. But throughout his premiership, Mahathir never lost sight of his larger 2020 vision.

Mahathir will certainly be remembered for his creative and far-sighted Vision 2020. No official policy or slogan galvanized the nation as that vision did. As a vision, it was clear, focused, and inclusive; all Malaysians—across all ethnicities and party affiliations—could identify with it. Mahathir's rule was dominated by Vision 2020, a mantra repeated everywhere and at all times. Virtually all policy statements and initiatives were benchmarked against the achievement of that vision.

Forging partnerships between diverse groups has been a feature of Malaysian politics, best reflected by the multi-ethnic coalition of the ruling party. Mahathir's rule saw a concerted effort to forge a partnership between the state and the market. The capital controls following the 1997–1998 "financial crisis" notwithstanding, Mahathir was unabashedly pro-market. One characteristic of his premiership was the policy of privatization and the retreat of state economic activism. The forging of state-market partnership must be seen in this context. There were joint committees at the highest level. Although Mahathir's relationship with civil society had been quite antagonistic, there was a flourishing of "non-political" NGOs, especially in community services.

Mahathir was known as much for his authoritarianism as for his creativity and innovativeness. He worked hard; he was a "slave-driver" who drove himself even harder. He was well known for punctuality and thorough preparation. He was confident of his vision; he believed in it and held on to it through thick and thin, and yet he was pragmatic enough to make adjustments in the light of changing conditions and diverse demands. He was articulate and a prolific writer. Mahathir was a strong leader. He was not a consultative leader, however; he pushed his agenda strongly and argued for it passionately.

Chandrababu Naidu, Opposition Leader and Former Chief Minister of the State of Andhra Pradesh (AP), India

In India, former Chief Minister Chandrababu Naidu is seen as a very young leader reflecting an ethos of next-generation political leadership.[9] His tenure as the chief minister of the state set the tone for transformation from the traditional agrarian state to one that is "fast-forwarded" to an information technology (IT) state. Hyderabad, the capital city of Andhra Pradesh, has become the focal point of all the IT industry in the state and attracts large companies from around the world.

Naidu had a clear vision for Andhra Pradesh (AP): to make the state on a par with countries such as Malaysia by following models tested in such places. But the state is predominantly agrarian with a large population. Thus there was always pressure to balance a "fast-forwarded" vision with the practical realities of meeting the immediate short-term needs of different groups, especially those from rural areas. Resistance to Naidu's reform agenda revolved around the need for improved transparency and accountability, the use of IT as a lubricant for economic development, and borrowings from lending agencies to kick-start some of the slowing sectors. The greatest resistance came from the people and groups that benefited from maintaining the status quo rather than reforming it.

Naidu initiated ongoing dialogue with the business community and offered them incentives. He openly expressed the commitment of the government to the business community and made policies that reflected such a commitment. This was especially the case with regard to large IT companies centered in Hyderabad. Concerning administrative reform, he started key action research centers that would advise him in developing effective governance systems. He advocated a clear and direct relationship of his office with the different key units of government and administration at different levels. He tried to develop appropriate institutional and organizational frameworks that would support developing transparent and accountable governance systems. He did follow an aggressive style, sometimes using an iron fist to stop people or groups (within the government, especially bureaucrats) who lobbied for maintaining the status quo.

The Vision 2020 document was a milestone of his tenure. It attracted the attention of the business community, and especially of IT companies. Along with formulating a clear policy framework, he made organizational changes in the departments dealing with investments. This helped in overcoming procedural delays and sent a strong signal to the business community about the commitment of the state government. The combination of all these measures made the state a favorable destination for private companies.

As chief minister, Chandrababu Naidu had a clear agenda and a strategy to pursue that agenda. He mobilized his party fully behind his agenda. He emphasized planning and decision making based on hard evidence. Departments were continuously asked to present the "numbers" that reflected on the performance, and this information was used in planning and policy making.

However, Chief Minister Naidu had to face an unusual situation: losing his position in the electoral battle in which the main opposition of the time, the Congress Party, came back to power in the state. It was a shocking defeat for a person with a reputation for the cleanest image in the next generation of political leadership. But reasons for his defeat were clear. The main reason was his emphasis on the "modern sectors" and his failure to pay enough attention to traditionally strong sectors, such as agriculture, on which the majority of the population depend.

His style of working was a slightly different one from that of earlier state chief ministers. He promoted a culture of "direct reporting"—a path-breaking approach very different from that of his predecessors—in which he maintained direct contacts with district-level functionaries. He focused on establishing a cadre of bureaucrats who would support his vision and mission within the districts. Through his video conferencing and use of some of the latest communication systems, he could establish more direct personal contact with district administrators, especially the collectors and other key district-level officials. This provided him with a clear understanding of the diverse conditions in the state.

Naidu also promoted programs that would make people part of the process. He developed the concept of a mass contact program called Janmabhoomi (motherland). The program aimed at ensuring the participation of the people in all the activities and interventions of the state government. Take, for example, the laying of a road in a remote village. Under this partnership program, the government would bring financial resources and technical expertise, but the people of the village would also be partners in providing labor and other services. Through such interventions, Naidu made it a point to be in touch with the citizens all the time and to bring the administration and the political establishment closer to the people.

During his tenure, then, Chandrababu Naidu maintained a more active involvement in all of the key matters in the state, and his style was more aggressive in reaching out to the key administrative units of state government; in maintaining contact with citizens; in mastering key political, policy, and administrative issues; and in controlling his party and countering the tactics of the opposition.

ENHANCING PUBLIC LEADERSHIP COMPETENCY

As these cases in Mexico, Thailand, Malaysia, and India illustrate, enhancing public leadership capabilities is particularly important in the contemporary world because government leaders, elected and appointed, face complex development issues.[10] They need a better understanding of the consequences of rapid globalization, including the need for collaboration in order to benefit from emerging opportunities. They need to operate in a world of increasing democratization that requires constructive engagement with elected parliaments and with civil society at the local, national, and international levels. Effective leaders need to recognize cultural diversity and citizen demands for greater participation, especially among minorities and marginalized groups. Democratization also requires political devolution and stronger local governments.

A globalizing economy requires government leaders to understand the growing significance of market-based solutions and to engage private and nonprofit organizations in delivering services to citizens. Effective government leaders need to find ways of ensuring the participation of women in decision making and in economic opportunities. One of the greatest challenges facing public leaders is the weakening of state capacity, including the inability of government to recruit and retain high-quality public officials as a consequence of competition with the private sector. They need ways to offset the weakness of political institutions in some countries and periods of stagnation in national economies, while at the same time meeting the increasing pressure of citizen demands for access to services.

In order to deal effectively with these challenges, government leaders need to enhance their competencies in several areas. A recent United Nations report identified the following areas in which government leaders need to enhance their competency in order to reinvent government and promote human development in the rapidly globalizing world.

- Ability to communicate complex ideas to citizens in a clear and understandable way in order to gain their trust
- Ability to adapt to rapid change and complexity and respond in new ways to citizen concerns
- Ability to forge partnerships and build effective collaboration because of the complexity of problems and the need for many agencies to respond
- Commitment of governmental leaders to democratic institutions and processes to promote political legitimacy, protection of human rights, and long-term political stability
- Commitment to ethical behavior and sensitivity in the exercise of power

• Capacity and skills to build and promote an environment of multi-ethnic and multicultural harmony and gender sensitivity in order to fully utilize the contribution of all segments of the society.

Other areas of public leadership that are crucial include strategic planning capacity, entrepreneurship, and the ability to take calculated risks.

NOTES

1. Dennis A. Rondinelli and G. Shabbir Cheema (eds.), *Reinventing Government for the Twenty-First Century: State Capacity in a Globalizing Society* (Bloomfield, CT: Kumarian Press, 2003).

2. There is a large body of literature, most of which is based on experience and practices in the private-sector organization. I am grateful to Meredith Rowen for the literature review. Among others, see L. B. Barnes and M. P. Kriger, "The Hidden Side of Organizational Leadership," *Sloan Management Review* 28, 1 (1986): 15–25; W. Bennis, "Managing the Dream: Leadership in the 21st Century—Training," *The Magazine of Human Resource Development* 27, 5 (1990): 44–46; W. Bennis and B. Nanus, *Leaders: The Strategies for Taking Charge* (New York: Harper & Row, 1985); M. Beer, R. A. Eisentstat, and B. Spector, "Why Change Programs Don't Produce Change," *Harvard Business Review* 68, 6 (1990): 158–166; M. De Pree, *Leadership Is an Art* (New York: Doubleday, 1989); P. C. Duttweiler and S. M. Hord, *Dimensions of Effective Leadership* (Austin, TX: Southwest Educational Development Laboratory, 1987); F. Westley and H. Mintzberg, "Visionary Leadership and Strategic Management," *Strategic Management Journal* 10 (1989): 17–32.

3. United Nations, *Report of the United Nations Expert Group Meeting on New Challenges for Senior Leadership Enhancement for Improved Public Management in a Globalizing World*, Turin, Italy, September 19–20, 2002; United Nations, *Unlocking the Human Factor for Public Sector Performance*," Third United Nations Public Sector Report, United Nations, New York, 2005.

4. I am grateful to Jose Cruz-Osario for his support in preparing this section. The views expressed, however, are entirely mine. Among others, see Ramon Munoz Gutierrez, "Government Innovations: The Good Government

Paradigm in the Administration of President Vicente Fox," *Fondo De Cultura Economica* (Carretera Picacho-Ajusco, Mexico, 2004).

5. *The Economist,* March 11–17 (2006): 39.

6. Ibid., 39.

7. Jonas Rabinovitch with Josef Leitman, "Urban Planning in Curitiba," *Scientific American,* March (1996); *UNEP Magazine—Industry and Environment* 16, 1–2 (January-June 1993); Rabinovitch, Jonas, and John Hoehn. *A Sustainable Urban Transportation System: "The Surface Metro" System in Curitiba, Brazil.* Washington, D.C.: EPAT/MUCIA. May 1995. John Mayer Jr. "Curitiba, the Little *Cidade* That Could," *Time,* October 14, 1991.

8. Khoo Boo Teik, *Paradoxes of Mahathirism: An Intellectual Biography of Mahathir Mohamad* (Kuala Lumpur: Oxford University Press, 1995); Khoo Boo Teik, *Beyond Mahathir: Malaysian Politics and Its Discontents* (London: ZenBooks, 2003); Sivamurugan Pandian, *Legasi Mahathir* (Kuala Lumpur: Utusan Publications, 2005); and S. Syed Ahmad Husein, "Malaysia After Mahathir" at http://www.hawaii.edu/cseas/pubs/papers/syed.html.

9. I am grateful to Srikiran Devara for his assistance in undertaking the background research. The views expressed, however, are entirely mine.

10. For a review of some of the challenges faced by leaders in the process of reinventing government, see, among others, Allan Rosenbaum, "New Challenges for Senior Leadership Enhancement for Improved Public Management," in "Citizens, Businesses, and Governments: Dialogue and Partnerships for Development and Democracy," background papers presented to the Third Global Forum on Reinventing Government, held in Marrakech, Morocco, December 10–13, 2002; United Nations, *Report of the Capacity Development Workshops on Innovation and Quality in the Government of the Twenty-First Century* (New York, United Nations, 2004); United Nations, *Report of the Capacity Development Workshops on Citizens, Businesses and Governments: Dialogue and Partnerships for Development and Democracy* (New York: United Nations, 2003); and Dennis A. Rondinelli and G. Shabbir Cheema, *Reinventing Government for the Twenty-First Century: State Capacity in a Globalizing Society* (Bloomfield, CT: Kumarian Press, 2003).

Part II

Case Studies From the Pacific Basin Experience

5

ECONOMIC SUPERPOWER LEADERSHIP IN ASIA:
LESSONS FROM THE JAPANESE AND US APPROACHES

William Ascher

J apan and the United States have long been global economic superpowers.[1] As such, they have exercised distinctive leadership approaches
vis-à-vis the other countries of the Asia-Pacific region. In reaction,
these other countries have developed their own strategies for trying to
maximize their benefits in interacting with Japan and the United States,
and for coping with the pressures that the economic superpowers have
exerted. Yet other superpowers are fast emerging. China and India are
becoming global economic superpowers, and other emerging economies around the world (Brazil, South Africa, Iran, and, of course, Russia) have growing potential to become *regional* superpowers. Yet China
and India are obviously more important for East and South Asia, and because of their sheer magnitude, they are likely to be more important for
the world economy.

Economic superpower status provides opportunities for nations to
leverage their economic influence through foreign assistance, monetary
policies, dominance in negotiating trade agreements, influence in establishing international economic arrangements, and the power to withhold trade and investment. Yet this status also greatly increases a nation's

capacity to employ *economic* statecraft—the use of economic instruments to pursue geopolitical objectives.[2]

These developments raise the primary questions addressed by this chapter:

> *What lessons will these emerging economic superpowers draw from the leadership behavior of the long-standing global economic superpowers, Japan and the United States?*
>
> *What lessons will the leaders of other nations draw from Japanese and US leadership behavior, in their strategies for interacting with both the existing and the emerging superpowers?*

Despite the huge differences between post-WWII Japan and the United States in terms of political and military power, for several decades Japan and the United States shared the distinction of being the world's two economic superpowers. Since the 1970s, Japan has been second only to the United States in the absolute size of its economy. In the 1990s, Japan was the world's largest donor of "official development assistance" (ODA), and it held this position until its economic stagnation dropped it back to the second position in the new millennium. While maintaining a strong partnership in many respects, the United States and Japan have competed for global leadership in several spheres. They have been rivals in securing natural resources, maintaining favorable trading relations with other countries, securing leadership of multilateral institutions, shaping the global foreign assistance effort, and influencing how developing countries should pursue their economic development.

Japan and the United States have displayed starkly contrasting leadership styles in this rivalry, particularly in how they have interacted with nations that have smaller and weaker economies. This may be obvious in terms of national security dimensions, but much less so in terms of economic statecraft, especially with respect to trade and foreign assistance. If we examine the economic leadership and economic statecraft of Japan and the United States in its several dimensions, we can draw some conclusions about lessons learned and the future behavior of emerging leaders and the nations reacting to them.

DIMENSIONS OF ECONOMIC LEADERSHIP AND ECONOMIC STATECRAFT

Five dimensions define "leader-follower exchange" in the international economic sphere: (1) short-term lending, especially when the borrowing country is in dire financial straits; (2) trade, especially when it is on favorable terms compared to other countries; (3) direct foreign investment, (4) foreign assistance; and (5) leadership in defining broad development strategies.

The fifth dimension requires clarification so that it is not regarded simply as technical assistance. Technical assistance, involving help in designing particular projects or programs, is typically considered an aspect of foreign assistance, because there is a financial cost to the donor country. Yet leadership in defining fundamental development strategies is a different matter, because it often entails adopting strategies, such as free-market capitalism, export-oriented state capitalism, or protected domestic industrialization, that are intended to benefit the country or countries advocating a given strategy. For example, immediately following World War II, the United States had much to gain from revitalizing world trade and advocated trade liberalization out of both practical and "ideological" considerations. This does not mean that countries adopting such orientations would fail to benefit—that depends on the soundness of the strategy for that nation regardless of the impact on the leading country or countries. Nevertheless, leadership on fundamental development strategy typically has a strong ideological basis, and it is sometimes adopted only reluctantly by the government of the recipient country.

All five of these channels of interactions between the more economically powerful and less powerful nations can operate directly through bilateral arrangements (e.g., Japanese grants to Laos) or indirectly through official multilateral institutions, such as the World Bank, the Asian Development Bank, the International Monetary Fund, and the World Trade Organization. Thus the World Bank, the regional development banks, and the International Monetary Fund make loans to low-income or financially challenged countries. Multination trade organizations, such as the World Trade Organization, the European Union, and the North American Free Trade Association, can decide whether to take in new members and whether to give favorable treatment to nonmembers. Multilateral institutions, such as the World Bank Group's International Finance Corporation, invest directly in developing countries. All of the development banks provide foreign assistance, as do other multilateral organizations such as the European Union. Many of these organizations, but especially the development banks and the International Monetary Fund, attempt to provide orientation in defining development strategies. We shall see that many of these multilateral organizations have been arenas of Japanese-US rivalry in economic superpower leadership.

For the purpose of brevity, this chapter looks at economic superpower leadership largely through the prism of foreign assistance and efforts to define development strategies. This narrowing of focus is also justified by the fact that economic superpower behavior with respect to developing countries generally ties together foreign assistance, trade concessions, investment opportunities, and lending. Foreign assistance often involves "tied aid" that requires that foreign assistance funds be used for purchases from the donor country, which often increases the likelihood that further purchases will be made. Favored nations are likely to be provided a package of foreign aid, trade concessions, and concessional loans. In addition, short-term loans, trade, and investment, though indisputably important, are conducted largely by private actors. Finally, foreign assistance is a vehicle for much more than money and technical assistance: it conveys development strategies; provides leverage for political, military, and economic influence; and conveys lessons about leadership. The matrix of interactions between developed and developing countries over foreign assistance sends many signals, intentional or not, about what forms of leadership, and what leadership strategies, are likely to be effective. Using Harold Lasswell's broad definition of the leader-follower relationship as the "giving and taking of orientation,"[3] we can explore how the current economic superpowers have tried to provide orientation for development through foreign assistance; how recipient countries have learned, from the leadership of the economic super-powers, how to behave toward those superpowers; and what lessons are likely to endure even when new economic superpowers take leadership roles. The easier part of the analysis is to assess the nature of leadership exercised by Japan and the United States; the more difficult part is to assess the *possible* impacts of the Japanese and US foreign assistance ap-proaches on leadership within Pacific Basin developing countries. In-sofar as we can do these assessments, we can also address the question of how providing orientation on appropriate leadership (that is, lead-ership in shaping leadership) can be effective. This last question is cru-cially relevant to leading developing nations to adopt more democratic leadership.

The comparison of foreign assistance efforts also demonstrates the importance of the multiplicity of *strategic* dimensions. One is the choice of countries to receive foreign assistance. Despite the widespread im-pression that Japanese foreign assistance has been simply an extension of Japan's economic policy, Japan has often followed US leadership in selecting the recipients of foreign assistance when security and geo-political concerns were at stake. A second dimension is the degree to which foreign assistance is used as a lever to influence the recipient na-tion's use of the funds, or even broader policies. Japan and the United States have taken very different stances in this respect. Finally, there is the *content* of the advice and pressures regarding how foreign assistance should be used, and there was a prolonged rivalry between Japan and the United States over development strategies for recipient countries, espe-cially in East Asia. This rivalry persisted until the reputation of the Japan-ese development approach suffered blows from the East Asian economic collapse in the late 1990s and Japan's continued economic stagnation.

Yet another facet of foreign assistance is the choice of how much of the total foreign assistance commitment will be channeled through multilateral institutions. In one sense the diversion of foreign assistance from bilateral to multilateral channels reduces the direct impact of the donor country, but it offers the potential for a leading nation to shape the agenda and approaches of the multilateral institutions, thereby magnifying the impact of that nation's initiatives.

FOREIGN ASSISTANCE STRUCTURES AND APPROACHES

This chapter does not attempt to detail the structures of Japanese and US foreign assistance machinery, enumerate all of the differences between aid approaches, or assess all the implications of these differences. This tall task is done very ably in David Arase's recent essay on "Japan's and the United States' Bilateral ODA Programs," in the book Arase has edited on comparisons of Japanese approaches with those of many other donor countries, and several other country-specific and comparative analyses.[4] Nevertheless, it is useful here to sketch out the structures and orientations in broad outline, because the structures both reflect and implement the different strategic rationales of foreign assistance adopted by the two nations.

Japanese Structures and Approaches

Japanese foreign assistance has been delivered by several agencies[5] with direction coming essentially jointly from four executive entities: the Ministry of International Trade and Industry, the Ministry of Finance, the Ministry of Foreign Affairs, and the Economic Planning Agency. It is significant that three of these four entities focus not only on economic issues but largely on the management of the Japanese domestic economy. Parliamentary and public discourse was minimal for decades, and civil-society participation in the discourse over foreign aid was, and still is, modest compared to that in other donor nations.

Japanese foreign assistance was, from the very beginning, distinctive for the so-called "request-based system," by which a recipient government's requests for assistance would be honored as long as the projects were judged technically sound and any tied-aid requirements could be fulfilled. Much of Japanese foreign assistance has supported very large physical infrastructure projects involving Japanese construction companies, using Japanese contractors and Japanese-manufactured heavy equipment.[6] Many projects have targeted the production of raw materials needed by the Japanese economy. This is not to say that the infrastructure and industrial projects financed by Japanese foreign assistance loans were ill-advised; many projects have been technically proficient, showing off Japanese technical competence. Yet the image that recipient-country governments have been free to request projects of any sort has to be highly qualified; in fact, Japanese corporations have typically led the process of identifying and proposing foreign assistance initiatives, reinforced by the fact that recipient-country officials generally have assumed that projects identified and prepared by Japanese firms would find favor.

Even though Japanese aid officials could not be overtly directive following the discredited paternalism of the pre-WWII "Co-Prosperity Sphere," in practice the decision making over the generation and selection of foreign assistance proposals has been predominantly among Japanese ministries, Japanese firms, foreign assistance technical personnel, and counterpart ministries within the recipient governments, with relatively little (but recently growing) interaction with nongovernmental groups. These recipient-country ministries generally have been content with the emphasis on infrastructure projects and raw-material development. Infrastructure projects are often politically advantageous in their visibility and in the benefits they bestow on the areas receiving new roads, expanded ports, and so on. Raw-material projects (such as oil, mining, and forestry) bring in export earnings that are more easily captured by the government than those earned by domestically oriented projects. Yet this confluence of interests between recipient governments and Japanese aid objectives does not negate the fact that recipient-country officials have generally played a rather minor role in the design and selection of the projects. In short, Japanese foreign assistance has not accorded a leadership role to recipient-country officials.

Japanese foreign assistance has also been strongly loan-based rather than grant-based, with the formal rationale that loans instill more discipline and accountability than do grants. Although below-market interest does constitute concessionary assistance, the emphasis on loans is claimed to make recipient governments more cognizant of cost recovery and the economic returns of projects. Notwithstanding the possible ulterior motives for such a policy (Japanese foreign assistance obligations were initially imposed by the terms of the 1951 San Francisco Peace Treaty requiring foreign aid as a form of war reparations[7]), this form of assistance conveys a message of discipline and caution.

Japanese overseas foreign assistance staffing is very thin, compared to the United States and other donor countries. For various reasons, ranging from language barriers to the relatively late start of Japanese foreign assistance, far fewer recipient-country nationals have been educated in Japanese universities, and in-country training has been largely confined to technical subjects.

US Structures and Approaches

US foreign assistance has largely been delivered by a single agency, the US Agency for International Development (USAID). USAID has long had a large Washington-based policy analysis staff, as well as a very large field presence (with both US personnel and recipient-country citizens working in USAID country offices). USAID has taken a highly interventionist approach to foreign assistance. Whereas Japanese aid agencies have largely responded to requests (albeit often instigated by Japanese firms), USAID officials have been much more assertive in trying to steer recipient governments into particular sectors, projects, and programs, and they have been much more willing to impose policy conditionalities. Thus USAID has played a very assertive role in trying to mold the development strategies of recipient countries, a posture that is perhaps not surprising in light of the dominant political, military, and economic position of the United States vis-à-vis the recipient countries.

Domestically, USAID and the smaller US foreign assistance efforts have been subject to intense and often hostile congressional scrutiny, and there have been numerous attempts to gut the foreign assistance budget. The independence of USAID has long been contested in terms of how much orientation the agency is required to take from the State Department, and there is virtually universal consensus that geopolitical considerations have indeed dominated in the allocation of foreign assistance across recipient nations, whether USAID formally reports to the State Department or not. It is important to note, however, that geopolitical considerations have less to do with the choice of projects within the recipient countries.

US foreign assistance has long been spread across a broad range of sectors, from health and education to large-scale infrastructure.[8] As the agenda of development objectives broadened to include conservation and environment, the role of women in development, micro-enterprise finance, appropriate technology, the development of nongovernmental organizations (NGOs), combating corruption, and the like, US foreign assistance embraced all of these objectives. Of particular relevance for this assessment is the growing emphasis on explicit leadership training, although the training of leaders and future leaders has always been a mainstay of US foreign assistance, both in-country and in US academic and professional institutions.[9] It is difficult to overestimate the importance of the fact that US foreign assistance has supported a huge number of scholarships for university-level and mid-career people from developing countries to attend US universities.

US foreign assistance—and especially the policy conditionalities—have long emphasized the importance of the private sector and free markets. Yet this has always been complicated by both the practical and the geo-political realities that have led US foreign assistance to be channeled through governments, many of them presiding over highly state-centered economies (for example, with Israel and Egypt receiving the largest shares of US foreign assistance until the occupation of Iraq, much of US foreign aid has gone to quite statist governments). Yet US foreign assistance has also specifically targeted the development of nongovernmental institutions ("civil society") as part of the democratization theme of foreign assistance. The other obvious constraint has been that first the Cold War, and later regional security concerns in the Middle East (Israeli-Arab conflicts, oil, and terrorism) and Latin America (drug trafficking and leftist regimes), have resulted in US foreign assistance being targeted to many decidedly nondemocratic governments.

SUPERPOWER LEADERSHIP INTERACTIONS BETWEEN THE UNITED STATES AND JAPAN

The United States has had very strong influence in setting the direction of Japanese foreign assistance, and this dominance persists to some degree in the current era, despite the rivalries that have arisen at various times.[10] One reason was Japan's constraint against participating militarily in security arrangements, which left the United States with the financial and personnel burden of ensuring Asian security for Japan and other Western allies.[11] If Japan's foreign assistance was at least indirectly part of, or reciprocity for, the security effort, its choices of how much aid should go to which recipient nations would be shaped by security priorities largely set by the United States. Akitoshi Miyashita documents five important cases from the late 1980s through the mid-1990s in which the Japanese government followed US direction in crucial foreign assistance decisions related to China, Iran, North Korea, Russia, and Vietnam. Miyashita convincingly argues that the decisions to reduce foreign assistance to China (at the time of the Tiananmen Square massacre), to Iran, and to Vietnam were not in Japan's commercial interest, nor were the increases in foreign assistance outlays to post-Soviet Russia and North Korea (following the 1994 Framework Agreement).[12] It is significant that this compliance occurred precisely when Japan was the world's largest provider of foreign assistance. In fact, the huge expansion of Japanese foreign assistance in the 1990s had a strong element of the same reciprocity to the "aid-fatigued" United States.

Another factor, which adds an ironic twist to our understanding of power and leadership, is that Japan has long been dependent on the United States economically because of the importance of the US market for Japanese exports (as reflected by the US trade deficit). US protectionism, which had strident advocates during Japan's economic boom, could have severely damaged the Japanese economy.[13] Yet another factor is that the increasingly common practice of cofinancing development projects and programs placed a portion of Japanese foreign assistance within the framework of development approaches led by the World Bank and other multilateral institutions, which in turn are strongly oriented toward the so-called "Washington consensus" espousing "the neoliberal belief that the combination of democratic government, free markets, a dominant private sector and openness to trade [a]s the recipe for prosperity and growth."[14]

In fact, even while Japan was expanding its bilateral foreign assistance in the 1990s, it was also tying its foreign assistance efforts closer to the multilateral effort.[15] In 1992 the new Japanese Official Development Assistance Guidelines were in conformity with the OECD Development Strategy, emphasizing participation, human rights, and "people-centered development." For the first time, the Japanese foreign assistance doctrine permitted political conditionalities, as well as the use of foreign aid in support of UN peacekeeping efforts.[16] That said, however, Japan's effort has lagged behind meeting OECD Development Assistance Committee standards calling for a shift from loans to grants, targeting the poorest countries, and shifting away from large-scale physical infrastructure and industrial projects to small-scale "people-centered" projects.[17] On the other hand, Japan has been a leader in untying aid involved in cofinanced projects.

The challenge that the Japanese government had faced since its emergence as a major provider of foreign assistance was to balance five distinct goals: (1) its aspirations to development leadership, (2) the pressures from Japanese business interests, (3) the growing demands by the Japanese public and NGOs that foreign aid focus on poverty alleviation and human rights, (4) the geopolitically driven pressures from the US government, and (5) the multilateral commitments required to cooperate with other bilateral donor agencies and the multilateral institutions. The Japanese government's response to this enormously complex challenge had three elements. The first was the "two-track" approach of financing some poverty alleviation and democratization programs as well as the more traditional infrastructure and industrial projects catering to Japanese corporations.[18] The second element was complying with US leadership on the amounts of foreign assistance targeted to particular countries, but taking an essentially autonomous position on the targeting of such aid within each country, except when cofinancing required coordination. Finally, but perhaps more surprisingly, the Japanese response involved competing for the "hearts and minds" of recipient-country officials regarding development strategies, through the demonstration effects of Japanese-funded projects; as well as the efforts during the early and mid-1990s to lead the multilateral institutions into a more state-centered orientation toward development strategy.

The effort to exert leadership in the multilateral forums has receded dramatically since the year 2000, along with the sharp drop in the volume of Japanese foreign assistance. Japan's relinquishing of foreign assistance leadership apparently stems from a host of factors. Fiscal weakness and aid fatigue (exacerbated by the huge effort to shore up East Asian economies following the 1997 financial crisis) were immediate concerns. But there was also a shift in the Japanese government's overall assessment: the realization that Japan's economic dominance in Asia had eroded, the reassertion of the traditional Japanese perception of Japan as highly vulnerable and resource poor, and the free-market availability of raw materials and opportunities for infrastructure contracting as a result of the general liberalization of the world economy. More than a decade and a half of Japanese economic stagnation, along with the South East Asian economic meltdown beginning in 1997, may have also eroded the Japanese confidence that the state-led model is as successful and replicable as once was thought. It may be that Japanese foreign assistance decisions and technical assistance still provide an alternative model whenever state-led approaches are compared to more free-market approaches within particular recipient nations, but the high-profile efforts by the Japanese government have certainly declined.

Leadership in Multilateral Aid Efforts

However, before Japan made at least a partial retreat from the competition over development leadership, two confrontations between Japan and the United States over the World Bank's operations revealed a great deal about the nature of the rivalry and the complexities of where development leadership can be found. With Japan's greater overall ODA effort in the 1980s and 1990s, the financial resources were available to increase Japan's standing and influence over the multilateral assistance provided by the World Bank, other regional development banks, and other official international organizations. At that time, the US government, facing tight budgets and domestic opposition to foreign assistance, was not averse to having Japan increase its contributions to multilateral agencies such as the World Bank and to have greater voting shares in the World Bank affiliates. Yet the question was whether the Japanese government would have a stronger voice in shaping multilateral foreign assistance and determining the orientation of development strategies.

Despite Japan's bilateral-aid focus on East Asia and, consequently, its relative neglect of the poorest nations, Japan strongly supported the World Bank Group's "International Development Association" (IDA), the soft-loan facility that provides virtually interest-free loans to the poorest countries. Because of IDA's highly concessional terms, the IDA fund needs periodic replenishments from donor countries, which requires complex and often contentious negotiation among the donor governments. When the US government balked at providing its share of the replenishment in 1986, the Japanese government led the effort to tie

Japanese and other governments' contributions to the US contribution.[19] These efforts succeeded in preventing the United States from free-riding in this costly aspect of the World Bank's efforts. Several other IDA replenishments pitted the reluctant US government against Japan and other, more enthusiastic supporters of IDA.

Rivalry over Development Doctrines

In 1991 Yasushi Mieno, governor of the Bank of Japan and alternate Japanese governor of the World Bank, requested an in-depth study of the successful role of governments in promoting economic growth in East Asia. He stated that

> Experience[s] in Asia have shown that although development strategies require a healthy respect for market mechanisms, the role of the government cannot be forgotten. I would like to see the World Bank and the IMF take the lead in a wide-ranging study that would define the theoretical underpinnings of this approach and clarify the areas in which it can be successfully applied to other parts of the globe.[20]

Behind the request was Japanese dissatisfaction with the World Bank's strategies, advice, and myriad publications that emphasized the importance of macroeconomic stability and the reduction of government intervention in the economy.[21] Many in the Japanese government believed that the World Bank's doctrine slighted the lessons behind the remarkable economic growth of the East Asian countries, which, according to Japanese development thinking, was attributable to wise interventions of governments in coordinating industrial strategy so that the most promising industries, especially those with strong export potential, could emerge. Moreover, they believed that the World Bank's development doctrines, so influential because of the prominence of the bank, were driven by the outlooks of the US government and the so-called "Washington consensus." Under this prod by the Japanese government, the World Bank undertook a major study that culminated in the book *The East Asian Miracle:*

Economic Growth and Public Policy.[22] But this book and its aftermath provided little support for the Japanese strategy. As the authorized "First Half Century" World Bank history concludes, the World Bank

> had so little regard for governmental initiatives to "pick winners" and alter comparative advantage in the manner that had been practiced with alleged success by South Korea and Taiwan that Japanese representatives began to lobby insistently for more attention to the more interventionist "Japanese" mode of industrial development. The result—the study, *The East Asian Miracle,* which appeared in 1993— gave only grudging support to interventionist doctrine and did not signal any substantive shift in adjustment lending—at least none that was evident by the mid-1990s.[23]

There is little evidence that the US government intervened to counter the Japanese influence on the World Bank team writing *The East Asian Miracle,* and it is noteworthy that the World Bank economists who conducted the study were largely Asians trained at US universities.[24] One important leadership lesson is that the orientation of the World Bank staff, which made it resistant to the orientation pressed by the Japanese government, came not from the US government but rather from the American educational establishment. The true leaders were the economics faculties at Chicago, Yale, Harvard, Berkeley, and other US institutions, joined by their counterparts at select European universities who had also been trained in the United States or were otherwise influenced by US economic thinking.[25]

The Japanese experiences with foreign assistance multilateralism offer important insights into the nature of international leadership. Multilateralism, as with any other collective action, in general entails a reduction of discretion of the nations involved, and the possibility of a de-politicization of aid in comparison with bilateral foreign assistance relationships. However, those who can lead within a multilateral assistance arrangement have additional power insofar as they can shape the orientation of the aid effort. For the nations vying for leadership roles, the discretion of independent action is sacrificed for the potential influence over others.

LESSONS OF US–JAPANESE INTERACTIONS OVER FOREIGN ASSISTANCE

The US–Japanese interactions, whether they involved compliance or rivalry, highlight an important complexity of international leadership. One could say that the Japanese government was following the lead of the US government regarding the targeting of foreign assistance country by country and was increasing its commitments to multilateral organizations largely influenced by US intellectual orientations. Yet to a large degree this compliance was part of an effort, at least partially successful, to achieve a position of equal partnership as a leader. At stake was not just reputation but also a permanent seat on the UN Security Council (an objective of Japanese foreign policy still very much at issue, with strong opposition from China and other East Asian nations). Leadership of other international organizations is at issue as well. In 1988 a Japanese was chosen as director general of the World Health Organization, but personal and political issues led to his replacement in 1998 following a bitter dispute. In 1999 a Japanese director general of UNESCO was appointed and still holds that position. Japan continues to be the major contributor to the Asian Development Bank (ADB), with a Japanese president. The ADB has long had a more state-centered orientation than the World Bank. Contributing more to multilateral cooperative efforts also reduces Japan's client-state status vis-à-vis the United States insofar as it offsets US military spending. In short, some aspects of following have strengthened other aspects of Japan's capacity to lead—accepting orientation has been the price to pay in order to provide orientation.

To assess the impacts of Japanese and US foreign assistance approaches on leadership in the emerging economic superpowers and other countries, it is useful first to outline relevant dimensions of leadership styles and then to enumerate the *potential* channels through which foreign assistance may shape the nature and distribution of leadership roles. The following lists will provide the framework for characterizing Japanese and US foreign assistance approaches and their possible impacts on leadership in other countries.

Relevant Dimensions of Leadership

Signals regarding appropriate and effective forms of leadership are relevant only if important distinctions in leadership styles can be found. The following distinctions are among the most salient to foreign assistance and to the issues that developing countries face.

1. *Democratic leadership* is based on the willingness to share power, the acceptance of rules of competition, responsiveness to public preferences, respect for minority rights and views, and willingness to relinquish power when the public chooses other leaders through legitimate mechanisms such as elections. Of course, some circumstances would counter the most democratic of predispositions, such as the risk that relinquishing power would result in enormous losses, or even death, for those with whom the leader identifies, or the circumstance in which public preferences are morally repugnant to the leaders.

2. *Authoritarian leadership* is based on limiting the access of others to power, whether out of selfish considerations or to accomplish objectives seen as jeopardized by broader sharing of power.

3. *Transactional leadership* is based on exchange between leaders and followers, regarded in an instrumental vein rather than entailing common cause or loyalty. The term describes one pole of the continuum running from purely instrumental to purely emotional, ideological, or spiritual. Obviously, we would not expect a real case of leader-follower interaction to be purely transactional, inasmuch as emotional attachments, loyalties, and commitment to a common cause is likely to emerge to a certain degree in virtually any group or formal organization.

4. *Transformative leadership* is marked by leaders' efforts to elevate the goals and actions of members and other leaders such that they pursue the common good beyond the rewards received by the individuals involved.[26]

5. *Charismatic leadership* is characterized by the acceptance of the leadership of individuals who are regarded by followers as having "special gifts" that legitimize their leadership, apart from the benefits that are expected to flow from that leadership.[27] Often charismatic leaders are perceived as strong, aggressive, physically attractive, and mysterious; the appeal may be the followers' vicarious enjoyment of the behaviors of the charismatic leader—whether or not these behaviors would be acceptable if the follower were to engage in them. Yet charismatic leadership cannot be defined in terms of a common set of leader characteristics; different characteristics resonate with different types of followers and different types of circumstances. Although charismatic leadership has recently attracted great interest in the leadership literature, largely reflecting the hope that charismatic leaders can inspire followers to break out of stodgy inertia, the lack of accountability of charismatic leaders to their followers raises serious concerns about charismatic leadership. Although charismatic leadership is in fact defined by the reactions of followers, leaders often have some control over how strong their charismatic appeals will be, inasmuch as the leaders can shape their public images.

6. *Apprenticeship paternalism* is a leadership orientation marked by initial directiveness and strong paternalistic guidance, but with the expectation that this guidance or tutelage will eventually bring the subjects of this guidance to equal or nearly equal standing. The apprentices are viewed as initially lacking an educational, administrative, or political background, but with appropriate training and collaboration, they can be brought into the circle of the proficient. This is in sharp contrast with the permanent paternalism of "looking after our little brown brothers."

Potential Channels of Influence

Orientation can be provided through numerous aspects and dynamics of the interactions between aid donors and recipients. The following list is distinctive in that some of these aspects are intentional on the part of the donor, whereas others may be unintended or even unwelcome consequences. It is obvious that in many respects, Japanese and US foreign assistance interactions with recipient governments have the potential to convey very different messages.

1. *Selection of foreign assistance recipients.* The choice of recipients through which foreign assistance will be channeled influences the power relationships within the recipient country, putting certain leaders in positions of greater power. For example, donor governments can try to channel their aid through national governments, subnational governments, NGOs, and so on. They can try to channel assistance through government agencies that have a more technical orientation or through those with strong political coloration. Technical assistance, one important aspect of foreign aid, can be used to strengthen both the analytic capabilities and the standing of particular entities within and outside of government.

   The strengthening of "civil society" by working through recipient-country NGOs has long been a formal objective of US foreign assistance. In sharp contrast, the Japanese aid establishment has been leery of NGOs[28] and has relied instead on the government-to-government emphasis emerging from the Japanese request-based system.

   The US foreign assistance approach has also placed more emphasis on sectoral programs and policy reforms that involve the recipient-country policy-setting ministries and subministerial agencies, especially those that participate in economic policy making. In many instances, officials from these ministries and other agencies have gone through short- and long-term training in their home countries or in the United States. In many countries, high-level officials of finance ministries and planning agencies have become allies with US officials (as well as those of multilateral financial institutions such as the International Monetary Fund and the World Bank) in pressing for such economic policy reforms as reduction of budget deficits, tax reform, and elimination of subsidies. These interactions have strengthened the standing of the technical economic-policy cadres in the political battles that pit one agency against another in the competition for jurisdiction and influence. In contrast, in adhering to the request-based system, Japanese foreign assistance has largely confined the interactions to the sectoral ministries, such as transportation, industry, and mining.

This US-led development of a technical cadre has ambiguous implications for strengthening democratic leadership. Technical cadres, such as Indonesia's "Berkeley Boys," sometimes stand up to the rent seeking, corruption, and unwise populist policies of authoritarian leaders. Yet strong concerns have been raised, particularly in Latin America, about the tendency of some technical cadres to ally themselves with authoritarian regimes because these governments face less opposition in imposing the economic reforms formulated by the technical cadres. This was a highly publicized issue with respect to the "Chicago Boys" within the economic policymaking apparatus in Chile during the Pinochet military dictatorship.[29] These concerns may by based on an exaggerated assessment of the power of the technical cadres, who typically are, in Lasswell's terminology, "mid-level elites" without enough political power to change the nature of regimes in which they work.[30] Insofar as these technical cadres do not view their participation in governmental policymaking as determining whether the government is democratic or authoritarian, their primary focus of attention is typically on how best to pursue the technically preferred reform agenda, regardless of whether the government is democratic or authoritarian.

2. *Conveying a sense of donor-country motives.* The "spirit" of leadership, which is often framed in terms of whether leader-follower interactions are transactional or transformative, can be influenced by the manifest motives conveyed by donor officials. If foreign assistance is conveyed as mere horse-trading of aid transfers in exchange for commercial access or foreign-policy support, the message is that unity, partnership, and "common cause" are merely rhetorical cover for self-serving exchange on both sides. When, in contrast, foreign assistance is part of broader, more transcendent efforts, it may be viewed as responding to a higher calling, thereby legitimizing more "heroic" leadership styles. However, it must be noted that even where higher, transformative motives are truly prominent, as in genuine efforts to foster democracy for its own sake, there may well be great skepticism on the part of recipient-country observers.

The US government has long articulated its formal motives for foreign assistance, which throughout the post-WWII period have invoked democratization along with economic development. This began with the Marshall Plan to aid in Europe's reconstruction and to insulate Western Europe and then Southern Europe from the threat of Communism, and it was extended to developing countries thereafter. However, governments around the world could hardly be unaware that the allocation of US foreign assistance would favor governments, whether democratic or authoritarian, that faced a perceived Communist threat or could claim a "strategic location" with respect to potential US–Soviet confrontations. Thus for those who saw the "fight against Communism" as superpower rivalry rather than a principled struggle for democracy, the US support for nondemocratic governments certainly undermined the credibility of the transformative standing of US leadership in foreign assistance.

Japanese foreign assistance, generally of much lower visibility than US efforts, has been widely perceived as driven by commercial considerations. Insofar as recipient governments in the early years were aware that Japanese aid was a required aspect of war reparations, and given that Japanese companies have clearly been a driving force in the development of foreign assistance proposals, it would be difficult to imagine that Japanese aid would be seen as anything but an economic exchange. This perception was reinforced by the emphases on loans and on infrastructure projects involving large Japanese contractors and manufacturers of heavy machinery. The dramatic increase in total Japanese foreign assistance beginning in the late 1980s[31] may have changed this perception, but skeptics were aware that the increase in foreign assistance coincided with the increasing challenges in securing natural-resource supplies.

3. *Conditionalities.* The conditions imposed along with foreign assistance can have several impacts. They can strengthen the power of particular government agencies within the sphere of bureaucratic politics. For example, if macroeconomic conditionalities require major reforms in economic policy, the government entities that oversee these reforms may well have more power, and their top personnel may have greater influence in the long run.

The greater aggressiveness of US foreign assistance in imposing conditionalities reinforces the centrality and standing of the recipient-country policy-setting ministries and subministerial agencies, especially those involved in economic policy making. The assertiveness of the United States in imposing conditionalities reinforces the message that power will be used to exert influence. In a number of respects, US foreign assistance has been engaged in a rather paternalistic relationship with recipient-country officials.

On the one hand, US foreign assistance officials have been far more assertive in selecting development priorities and rejecting projects that were judged to be either technically inadequate or inconsistent with these development priorities. For this reason it is fair to characterize the US approach as apprenticeship paternalism.

In contrast, in adhering to the request-based system for projects outside of the social sectors, and still largely confining its interactions to the sectoral ministries, Japanese foreign assistance has placed much less emphasis on policy conditionalities, even at the height of the Japanese aid effort.

4. *Direct pedagogy.* Foreign assistance can support training, from short courses to long-term education in donor-country universities, to try to instill leadership lessons pedagogically. Long-term educational stays in donor-country universities provide not only the lessons embedded in the formal education but also a cultural immersion that is far deeper than the interactions with foreign assistance officials could ever provide.

The US foreign assistance effort has long emphasized explicit training and education. Arase concludes that

> Japan cannot match America's strengths, which derive from a strong emphasis on field presence and from intense, far-reaching efforts to reform and improve aid effectiveness . . . U.S. technical assistance is often managed through field offices and has developed a focus on building recipient capacity at various levels, in dialog with a variety of local and international donor actors. In comparison, Japan's aid philosophy envisions technical assistance being extended from a base in Japan . . . Japan's technical cooperation has played a more limited and subordinate role in an aid philosophy that emphasizes costly capital- and skill-intensive projects. Promoting technical assistance to a more independent, field-oriented and central role, as required by the new client-centered and poverty alleviation development agenda, will require a basic rethinking of its aid philosophy.[32]

With the rising concern over sound leadership, short-term training has increasingly focused explicitly on "leadership development." USAID has mounted myriad leadership training programs, combining "leadership techniques" with admonishments about the importance of broad stakeholder participation.

Formal education within the donor country is an under-appreciated factor in shaping the perspectives of recipient-country leaders who have the opportunity to study abroad. The huge US investment in educating potential leaders over the entire post-WWII period has produced an enormous number of foreign attendees and graduates of US universities. Of course, not all of the roughly 11 million foreign enrollees[33] at US universities were funded directly by the US government, yet the federal government deeply subsidizes both private and public universities in various ways. Japanese universities have remained far behind in providing university training to foreigners: they had just over 50,000 foreign students on average each year in the 1990s,[34] compared to roughly 450,000 studying in the United States, and since the year 2000 roughly 100,000 foreign students have been studying in Japan each year, compared to 550,000 in US universities. Roughly two-thirds of the foreign students in Japan are from China, Taiwan, and South Korea; the foreign students in the United States come from all over the world.

Leadership through education implies the student's subordinate role relative to the donor-country professor, reinforcing the apprenticeship paternalism expressed even more directly by the heavy US pressure to execute policy reform. Yet the leaders who have received US degrees, especially advanced degrees in economics and other policy-related fields, can hold their own technically and in reputation with their developed-country counterparts, as witnessed by their influence in the multilateral organizations and (increasingly) in international business. The apprenticeship does have a graduation to peer status.

5. *Modeling.* The behavior that donor-country foreign aid officials present to their recipient-country counterparts and others within recipient countries is a potential model for those within the recipient countries. Whether the behavior of foreign assistance officials will be seen as a model of how recipient-country officials ought to behave depends, of course, on the perceived effectiveness of foreign assistance efforts and the level of respect that donor-country officials earn in their interactions with recipient-country counterparts. The presumption that positive lessons will "rub off" has been prevalent for both Japanese and US foreign assistance. Japanese pronouncements often emphasize the role model of the careful, technically expert Japanese aid official. With respect to US foreign assistance, José Abueva, the prominent Philippine public administration expert, noted that early on, US foreign assistance operated on the "basic thesis . . . that 'modern' and 'sound' administrative technology developed in the United States is transferable or adaptable to the administrative systems of developing countries and that this diffusion will improve their efficiency and effectiveness."[35] Exposure of recipient-country officials to sound leadership practices, especially through collaboration with donor-country counterparts, may encourage the adoption of these practices.

6. *Advocacy of development models.* The debates over foreign assistance—and by extension the debates over general development strategy—have significant implications for the norms of leadership. The strategies that win out in the marketplace of ideas will shape attitudes toward effective leadership on such dimensions as the degree of leadership sharing with nongovernmental entities, the degree of directiveness in shaping the economy, and the degree of politicization of policy leadership.

We have already seen the rivalry on development strategies, and the marked differences between Japan and the United States in their advocacy of or opposition to state intervention. The controversy surrounding this issue has been widely interpreted as just as ideological as pragmatic. It is likely that the decisions of governments on the role of the state in the economy have hinged more on the lessons drawn directly from the apparent success or failure of state-led economies and the domestic politics of each country.

7. *Lessons from interaction.* Leadership styles may emerge not from direct teaching or modeling but, rather, from the strategies found to be effective in influencing the behavior of foreign assistance officials. If the coping strategies appear to be successful in obtaining more foreign assistance, or in ensuring that the foreign assistance goes in desired directions, these strategies are more likely to be adopted as part of the repertoire of the developing-country leaders. Recipient-country officials may thus learn to be straightforward or devious, aggressive or submissive, more transactional or more transformative, more technically analytical or more political, and so on. Obviously, this sort of learning is less intentional on the part of the donor-country officials, yet it may have quite a significant impact.

In one sense, both Japanese and US foreign assistance have been transactional: Japanese aid has been very clearly linked to expanding Japanese commercial ties, US aid to foreign-policy cooperation. Yet the latter has aspired, at least to some degree, to take a transformative leadership role, in pursuing the anti-Communist and democratization agenda. Moreover, whatever motives people in recipient countries attribute to US government motives, US foreign assistance is clearly more than just an economic exchange.

THE NET IMPACTS OF "LEADERSHIP LESSONS"

Reasonable speculation on the impact of leadership messages conveyed through the channels enumerated above would yield the following possibilities. Although it is virtually certain that leaders in recipient countries have taken in some lessons about leadership through their interactions with donor-country officials, *demonstrating* the nature and magnitude of this influence with any degree of certainty is simply impossible. Even if we can hypothesize about the perceptions that developing-country leaders have of Japanese and US foreign assistance, we do not have access to the inner workings of the minds of recipient-country leaders that would link these perceptions to attitudes toward leadership. Yet this difficulty is not unique to tracing the impact of foreign assistance; it is a pervasive limitation in establishing patterns of the "socialization" (that is, inculcating attitudes and norms) of leadership. Nevertheless, it is important to emphasize that the speculations here focus on *possible* influences on leadership patterns in the recipient countries, rather than on empirically demonstrated effects.

Japanese Lessons

An official or activist of an aid-recipient country could well draw the following lessons from interactions with Japanese foreign assistance efforts.

1. Governmental leadership is and should be dominant over leadership efforts of other sectors.
2. Government leadership requires openness to new priorities (such as environmental protection), but these are more effectively assessed within the governmental structure than through dialogue that gives high standing to nongovernmental groups.
3. Managerial expertise is a very important credential for leadership, as distinct from charismatic leadership.
4. The skills of bureaucratic maneuvering are also important for effective leadership.
5. Leader-follower and leader-to-leader relationships are essentially transactional rather than transformative.
6. Leadership entails working within the existing decision-making structure, rather than trying to mobilize new entrants into the structure.

7. Leadership, even if transactional, is collaborative rather than directive or overtly paternalistic.
8. "International leadership" by national governments is essentially the pursuit of national interest.
9. Leadership on development strategy is clearly a reflection of the economic and military power of the rivals. Following a remarkable increase in Japan's foreign assistance and influence over development strategy in the 1990s, both have declined in the new century. Yet Japanese foreign assistance efforts have put Japan into a stronger position of leadership in various other aspects of international affairs, by reducing Japan's client-state status as a recipient of US security spending without reciprocation.

US Lessons

A recipient-country official or activist might derive the following leadership lessons or principles from participating in or observing interactions over US foreign assistance, or from involvement in US aid-assisted training.

1. All interactions are, to a certain extent, politicized, even if the matters at hand are ostensibly technical or economic.
2. Transactional leadership is the usual mode; however, the political aspects mentioned in the point above are sometimes part of the patterns exhibited by transformative leadership, in its emphasis on anti-Communist efforts and democracy.
3. Strong leadership entails the willingness to engage in confrontation and strong directiveness.
4. Technical expertise can put a leader into a very strong position to influence policy, particularly economic policy.
5. Technical expertise and managerial skills (but especially technical expertise) are appropriate criteria for leadership, as opposed to characteristics that can serve as a base for charismatic leadership.

6. Promoting participation is an important responsibility of leadership.

General Lessons

Two general lessons can be derived from the contrasts and commonalities of Japanese and US behavior regarding foreign assistance. First, the likely impacts have probably been compromised by the self-serving nature of foreign aid and the fact that leadership lessons are derived from the nature of the interactions as well as from the lessons that the donors intend to convey. It is not clear that Japanese foreign assistance has been significantly motivated by the objective to cultivate leadership in recipient countries, but this objective has been quite explicit for US foreign assistance. For various—perhaps obvious—reasons, it is likely that interactions with US foreign assistance efforts have had more influence than Japanese efforts. Many more leaders of Pacific Basin countries have been educated in the United States than in Japan, often supported by US foreign assistance programs. In-country training has also received much greater emphasis in US foreign assistance. The US efforts have been much more explicitly directed to conveying leadership models than the Japanese efforts. Even so, the direct impact of US efforts to provide orientation on development strategies, emphasizing the close connections among free markets, the autonomy of civil society, and democratization, is difficult to assess. This is in part because of the intrinsic difficulty of tracing such impacts. Yet it is also likely that conveying the intended orientation has been undercut by the variety of messages sent by different foreign assistance agencies of the various donor nations, the multiple channels through which lessons may be drawn, and the skepticism that transactional leadership engenders. Moreover, any given donor government's leadership in conveying development strategies is offset by the increasingly multilateral nature of foreign assistance and the increasing role of nongovernmental actors—ranging from university-based experts to environmental and human rights activists.

Second, if the "messages" likely to be conveyed through foreign aid interactions seem ambiguous, this is not necessarily a failing of foreign assistance officials. Foreign assistance is always fraught with ambivalence and ambiguity, for a host of reasons. Decisions related to foreign aid are complex outgrowths of both donor-country domestic politics and the relations between the donor and recipient countries.[36] The impulse to contribute to the development of the recipient country and to help alleviate poverty within it is tempered by geopolitical and economic considerations of the donor country. The salience of different motives often varies across the levels of personnel within the aid agency, in-country staff being more likely to identify with recipient-country interests. Finally, motives that are highly salient in one period may give way to priorities that emerge later.

The messages related to the motives for giving foreign assistance, the articulation of development strategy, and other signals regarding foreign aid are often muddled by the need to defend foreign assistance in the donor country as well as to present a helpful stance in the recipient country. One would imagine that recipient-country leaders groping for effective leadership models may well be perplexed by these mixed messages. When no single set of norms is supported by experience or common international understanding, it is likely that leaders will choose the norms most congruent with their own individual or institutional interests.

It is also important to take into account the remarkable diversity of sources of orientation on development issues that have emerged over the past several decades. Multiple governments, myriad NGOs, multilateral foreign assistance institutions, and the universities and think tanks that shape development thinking are all providing leadership in enormously complicated ways. Peter Dauvergne points out that even as Japan's foreign assistance converged with the international foreign assistance effort, Japan adopted "a more assertive, confident, and coherent aid philosophy."[37] Providing orientation is often a two-way street.

WHAT MIGHT CHINA AND OTHER EMERGING ECONOMIC SUPERPOWERS DO?

China and other potentially emergent economic superpowers have certainly witnessed and participated in foreign assistance exchanges with the United States, and some (including China, India, and Brazil) have done the same with Japan. Of course, every nation has its own distinctive situation and objectives, but the backdrop of the impacts of the existing superpowers' efforts provides an important element of the context.

China and India are distinct from past economic superpowers in several respects. Barring an unforeseen economic collapse, they will be the first economic superpowers that are, in many respects, still poor countries. A huge foreign assistance effort on the part of China or India would be politically as well as economically foolhardy. Their economic power lies not in a surplus to be dispensed to poorer countries but, rather, in the sheer magnitude of their economies, in terms of both domestic market and export potential. Nevertheless, both China and India have foreign assistance programs.

China

China, even while accepting more than US$1.5 billion of official development assistance annually in the mid-2000 decade,[38] funds Asian and African countries through a conventional foreign assistance grant and loan program, debt forgiveness, and financing of mega-projects connected to Chinese overseas investments and pursuit of raw materials. Although the amount of such foreign assistance reported is highly ambiguous, the total in the middle of the 2000 decade was probably roughly on the order of US$10 billion, with commitments to increase dramatically in the near future.[39] Other estimates have put China's conventional official development assistance at roughly US$4 billion (44 percent of which goes to sub-Saharan Africa),[40] but these estimates do not incorporate the likely value of China's subsidies to North Korea in supplying energy and food, the occasional writing off of official debt of heavily indebted countries, and loans at particularly favorable interest rates for oil-exporting African countries such as Angola.[41] Chinese foreign assistance has gone not only to most of the countries of Southeast Asia and numerous sub-Saharan African nations, but also to Central Asia and South Asia.

Chinese foreign assistance imposes far less conditionality in terms of meeting environmental standards, resettlement programs for displaced people, or good governance than do the bilateral donors or the multilateral aid institutions such as the World Bank and the Asian Development Bank.[42] In particular, Chinese foreign aid has been roundly criticized for supporting the "rogue states" in Africa, such as Sudan and Zimbabwe, that have been condemned by the Western nations and by the United Nations for repression and corruption.[43] This reveals an important contrast between the image that the Chinese government is trying to convey through its international interactions, and its true priorities. Wang's analysis of the 1958–2002 issues of the *Peking Review* and the *Government Works Report*, both written for international audiences, reflects the international image that the Chinese government has tried to convey. He finds that the desired image entails portraying China as

> a peace-loving country, [a] victim of foreign aggression, [a] socialist country, [a] bastion of revolution, [an] anti-hegemonic force, [a] developing country, [a] major power, [an] international cooperator, and [an] autonomous actor. These data also indicate that over time, there have been both changes and continuities in the images projected of China by the Chinese government. On the side of continuity, the government has consistently—though with different levels of vigor—pursued the images of China as a peace-loving nation, a victim of foreign aggression, an opponent of hegemony and a developing country. On the side of discontinuity, the Maoist era saw the government emphasizing the images of China as a socialist country and supporter of revolution. During the reform period, the government has de-emphasized those images. Instead it has highlighted the images of China as an international cooperator and a major power.[44]

Clearly, the role of "international cooperator" clashes with the dominance of commercial considerations that motivate China's dealings with these African countries. China also has close relations with Myanmar,[45] despite the Western nations' economic sanctions in force since 1988, and in fact vies with India for primary influence in Myanmar, competing primarily for access to Myanmar's gas fields.[46]

In fact, the dominant motivation of Chinese foreign assistance, judging by both these departures from cooperation in economic statecraft with the West and the very generous concessional terms of loans extended to recipient countries, has been to secure access to raw materials. And the motif of competing with India for such access is widespread. As Evans and Downs note,

> The most prominent example [of infrastructure investment] is the $2 billion soft loan agreement China Eximbank signed with Angola in 2004 to finance infrastructure projects presented by Chinese companies. The terms of this line of credit were extraordinarily generous—1.5% interest over 17 years. Chinese and international observers agree that this offer persuaded Luanda to reject Royal Dutch/Shell's plan to sell its stake in Block 18 to the Indian firm ONGC Videsh and award it to the Chinese firm Sinopec. China Eximbank's largesse probably also contributed to Luanda's decision to award Block 3/80 to Sinopec.[47]

In short, Chinese foreign assistance in the new millennium is quite similar in motive and policy to Japanese foreign assistance in the past three decades, though somewhat more assertive in terms of departing from the geopolitical and humanitarian positions of Japan and the Western nations.

India

In the middle of the 2000 decade, India has been providing roughly US$400 million in grants and loans to other countries. Yet during this period, India has been receiving more than US$4 billion annually in official development assistance in the form of grants and loans, with two-thirds coming from two multilateral sources: the World Bank Group and the Asian Development Bank.[48] As part of the British Commonwealth, India also receives substantial foreign assistance from the United Kingdom. But India receives very little foreign assistance directly from the United States, in part reflecting the closer ties that the United States has had with Pakistan, in contrast with India's "nonaligned" status.

Some of India's foreign assistance comes in the form of concessional lending, particularly for projects requiring Indian inputs. In 2003, India wrote off roughly US$20 million in official loans to heavily indebted poor countries in sub-Saharan Africa and Latin America. A significant portion of India's foreign assistance outlays has gone through the Special Commonwealth African Assistance Programme in collaboration with the United Kingdom and other Commonwealth members.[49]

India has tried to reduce public dissatisfaction with providing foreign assistance to other countries despite India's own poverty by portraying the foreign assistance program explicitly as part of the "Indian Development Initiative," emphasizing how assistance, particularly to Africa, promotes Indian exports and secures raw-material supplies.[50] Foreign assistance is largely channeled through the Economic Division of the Ministry of External Affairs. Like those in Japan, Indian engineers and project managers are heavily involved in the development and selection of large-scale infrastructure projects; Indian teachers and health workers are heavily involved in social projects. Like China, the main thrust has been commercial, with a similar concentration on securing raw materials. One indication of the dominance of economic considerations is that although the Indian government has taken strong public stands against the tied aid practiced by Japan and the Western nations, India continues to tie its own foreign assistance in the same way.[51] Yet a considerable portion of India's foreign assistance has been devoted to neighboring countries, such as Bhutan and Myanmar, and has involved geopolitical considerations as well.

Since the collapse of the Soviet Union and the consequently di-minishing rationale of adopting a nonaligned foreign policy, India has pursued its foreign assistance as a fairly faithful partner with the West-ern powers. Following the invasion of Afghanistan by the United States and US allies, Afghanistan became by far the largest recipient of offi-cial Indian assistance. Although India has also pursued closer relations with Myanmar, in general India's foreign assistance has been more aligned to the goals of the Westerns' power.

In some respects, the emerging economic superpowers face the same *economic* constraints that Japan has faced. China, like Japan before it, is dependent on the US appetite for imports. India is somewhat less de-pendent on trade with the United States, partly because of India's closer ties with the Commonwealth and partly because China has simply been more efficient in producing goods that are attractive to the US market. Nevertheless, India depends more on the Commonwealth and Euro-pean Union market and would also be vulnerable to economic sanctions, consumer boycotts, or other trade-damaging measures. The question may boil down to how desperate the scramble for natural resources will be-come if affordable substitutes do not replace the apparently diminishing world supplies of hydrocarbons and other raw materials.

The countries that are eligible to receive foreign aid from the newly emerging economic superpowers have also learned from their experi-ences with the geopolitically oriented US foreign assistance approach. Drew Thompson notes that "several African countries have played China and Taiwan against one another, seeking massive aid packages and switching recognition. In order to compete with China's dominating presence on the continent and support in international forums, Taiwan must offer substantial aid packages to its African allies."[52]

China and India's Pursuit of International Leadership Roles

Like Japan before them, China and India display aspirations to increase their roles in shaping the international economic regime, largely through greater influence in the multilateral financial institutions. There has long been an effort to increase the voting weight of economically emerging countries in the International Monetary Fund.[53] The argument is that the weighting should take much more account of the size of the economy than of such other factors as original voting weights, market openness, hard-currency reserves, and initial contributions. Thus far, these efforts have met with only limited success—in 2006 China's share has increased modestly, along with those of several other emerging nations, whereas India's has actually declined slightly.[54] Undoubtedly there will be continued challenges to the voting dominance of the wealthy countries.

Neither China nor India—as of yet—has attempted to reorient the development doctrines of these multilateral institutions the way the Japanese government did in the 1990s. Of course, to many leaders of authoritarian governments, the Chinese model is attractive in its own right. On the broad question of whether market-oriented economic reform should precede or occur simultaneously with democratic reform, China's remarkable growth contrasts sharply with the calamity of Russia. Will China become ideologically assertive through its foreign assistance and other instruments of economic statecraft? For the short- to medium-term future (that is, within the next decade), China is likely to exert transactional rather than transformational leadership, if only because economic prosperity will still be regarded as the *sine qua non* of future progress.

Yet in the long run, insofar as Chinese national and cultural pride as the "Middle Kingdom" is restored, Chinese leaders may be motivated to be far more ideologically assertive in advocating state-led development, just as Japan did in its halcyon days. How much emphasis would be placed on authoritarian rule to pursue this form of development would depend, of course, on whether the fledgling democratic reforms, now emerging at the local level in China, will lead China to evolve in a manner similar to South Korea and Taiwan. Certainly the model of "apprentice paternalism" vis-à-vis less developed neighbors is consistent with the reemerging Chinese cultural chauvinism. The answer will depend on how thoroughly the goal of economic prosperity remains dominant over the older ideological commitment, or over the emerging commitment to state-directed capitalism.

If its rapid growth can be sustained, India is likely to assume a stronger partnership role among the Western-oriented nations. India's inexorable movement to a market economy undercuts any distinctive development message, and assuming that India remains democratic, coordination of foreign aid and other economic instruments with the democratic nations is also highly likely. Like China, India will continue to exercise apprenticeship leadership vis-à-vis poorer neighbors.

Will China and India become even more assertive in using economic statecraft geopolitically? In contrast with Japan, neither China nor India has been subject to the constraint of having to reciprocate for operating within the US security umbrella. India is not beholden to the United States regarding India's most relevant conflict with Pakistan; China is even less entangled in Western alliances. Therefore, there is less reason to believe that Chinese economic statecraft will be coordinated with that of the United States or, for that matter, with that of any other nation, whereas Indian economic statecraft is more likely to develop in concert with that of the United Kingdom and the European Union. Both China and India have learned from the US example that economic power can be translated into geopolitical power, and it is no exaggeration to say that both nations have serious geopolitical issues within their regions. Economic statecraft is likely to be exerted increasingly in the context of these issues as China and India gather more capacity to provide assistance and to promote or withhold investment or trade. And both China and India are likely to be even more aggressive in securing raw materials, especially if resource scarcity continues to grow as a problem for these nations and the rest of the world. Yet it is also true that nations that will long depend on economic expansion for their own standing and stability are therefore highly dependent on global stability as well.

CONCLUSIONS

The idealistic expectation that economic superpowers would use bilateral foreign assistance and other economic instruments primarily to bring poorer nations out of poverty has not materialized in the Asia-Pacific region; that policy has been pursued by neither the established nor the emerging economic superpowers. The lessons of leadership to be drawn from the long-standing behavior of Japan and the United States, replicated currently by China and India, emphasize self-interest and therefore transactional interchange with recipient nations, occasionally with aspects of apprenticeship paternalism. The farsighted view that making alleviation of global poverty the first priority would ultimately reduce international conflict and promote prosperity for all has been dominated by considerations of trade, access to raw materials, and geopolitics. This is certainly understandable, in light of the political constraints arising from domestic opposition to giving assistance to other countries, especially when poverty is still widespread within the donor country.

These constraints on bilateral actions highlight the importance of multilateral assistance as the primary vehicle for relatively disinterested support of economic growth and alleviation of poverty. The activities of the World Bank, the International Monetary Fund, and other multilateral institutions that channel resources to developing countries are inevitably controversial, but even so, these institutions have had considerable success in de-politicizing their decisions. Although clouded by a petty personnel scandal that was the ostensible reason for the forced resignation of World Bank President Paul Wolfowitz in 2007, the fundamental opposition to Wolfowitz came from the World Bank staff and executive directors over the favoritism shown to US allies.[55] This episode also eroded the legitimacy of the practice, never formalized but in effect at the World Bank since its birth, that the World Bank president would be chosen by the president of the United States.[56] Some might take this episode as reflecting the problems of the World Bank;

it is fairer to see it as reflecting the limits to the pursuit of geopolitical objectives by the United States through this multilateral institution. In addition, multilateral institutions remove the specific trade and investment advantages of donor countries. For example, the World Bank has long had a procurement policy that enables donor countries to secure goods and services from the most affordable, quality sources. Japan, the United States, China, and India are all heavily involved in multilateral economic collaborations. China, the latest to engage with the "Bretton Woods institutions" (the International Monetary Fund and the World Bank) still has more than twenty-five years of experience with these multilateral entities[57] and has been pressing for a greater role. Thus the multilateral institutions, for all their difficulties, represent the best vehicles for global economic leadership. It is no wonder that a significant part of the rivalry over global economic leadership has been—and probably will continue to be—centered on the governance and development doctrines of the multilateral financial institutions.

NOTES

1. For discussions of Japan as an economic superpower and its role in economic statecraft, see Samuel Huntington, "Why International Primacy Matters," *International Security* 17, 4 (1995): 68–83; and Michael May, "Correspondence: Japan as a Superpower?" *International Security* 18, 3 (1993): 182–186.

2. David Baldwin, *Economic Statecraft* (Princeton, NJ: Princeton University Press, 1985), 1–5.

3. Harold D. Lasswell, "Conflict and Leadership: The Process of Decision and the Nature of Authority," in A. de Rueck and J. Knight (eds.), *Conflict in Society* (Boston: Little, Brown, 1966), 210 –228, quotation at 211.

4. David Arase, "Introduction," in David Arase (ed.), *Japan's Foreign Aid: Old Continuities and New Directions* (London: Routledge, 2005), i–xx; David Arase, *Buying Power: The Political Economy of Japan's Foreign Aid* (Boulder, CO: Lynne Rienner, 1995); Richard Grant and Jan Nijman, "Historical Changes in US and Japanese Foreign Aid to the Asia-Pacific Region," *Annals of the*

Association of American Geographers 87, 1 (1997): 32–51; Bruce Koppel and Robert Orr Jr. (eds.), *Japan's Foreign Aid: Power and Policy in a New Era* (Boulder, CO: Westview Press, 1993); Alan Rix, *Japan's Foreign Aid Challenge: Policy Reform and Aid Leadership* (New York: Routledge, 1994); Alan Rix, "Japan's Emergence as a Foreign-Aid Superpower," in Steven Hook (ed.), *Foreign Aid Toward the Millennium* (Boulder, CO: Lynne Rienner, 1996): 75–90; Alan Rix, "Japanese and Australian ODA," in David Arase (ed.), *Japan's Foreign Aid: Old Continuities and New Directions* (London: Routledge, 2005): 104–116; Peter Schraeder, Steven Hook, and Bruce Taylor, "Clarifying the Foreign Aid Puzzle: A Comparison of American, Japanese, French, and Swedish Aid Flows," *World Politics* 50 (1998): 294–323; David Seddon, "Japanese and British Overseas Aid Compared," in Arase, *Japan's Foreign Aid,* 117–132.

5. The Japanese International Cooperation Agency (JICA), the Overseas Economic Cooperation Fund (OECF), the Export-Import Bank of Japan (JEXIM), and the Japan Bank for International Cooperation (JBIC; a merger of OECF and JEXIM).

6. See Richard Grant, "Reshaping Japanese Aid for the Post-Cold-War Era," *Tijdschrift voor Economische en Sociale Geografie* 86 (1995): 235–248; and Saori Katada, "Japan's Two-track Aid Approach," *Asian Survey* 42, 2 (2002): 320–342.

7. David Arase, "Japan's and the United States' Bilateral ODA Programs," in Arase, *Japan's Foreign Aid,* 117–132; quotation at 118.

8. For a recent overview of US foreign assistance, see Kurt Tarnoff and Larry Nowels, *Foreign Aid: An Introductory Overview of US Programs and Policy, Report to Congress* (Washington, DC: Congressional Research Service, January 19, 2005).

9. José Abueva, "Administrative Doctrines Diffused in Emerging States: The Filipino Response," in Ralph Braibant (ed.), *Political and Adminstrative Development* (Durham, NC: Duke University Press, 1969): 536–587.

10. Mikio Oishi and Fumitaka Furuoka, "Can Japanese Aid Be an Effective Tool of Influence? Case Studies of Cambodia and Burma," *Asian Survey* 43, 6 (2003): 890–907; pages 904–905 recount how, because of current US opposition to the government of Myanmar, "Japan's freedom to act independently in applying positive sanctions has been severely limited."

11. Arase, "Introduction," in *Japan's Foreign Aid,* 12.

12. Akitoshi Miyashita, *Limits to Power: Asymmetric Dependence and Japanese Foreign Aid Policy* (New York: Lexington Books, 2003).

13. This instance of economic weakness providing leverage brings to mind the famous adage attributed to the Brazilian finance minister Roberto Campos in the 1980s: "If I owe you a million dollars, I have a problem; if I owe you a billion dollars, you have a problem."

14. Christopher Gilbert and David Vines, "The World Bank: An Overview of Some Major Issues," in Christopher Gilbert and David Vines (eds.), *The World Bank: Structure and Policies* (Cambridge: Cambridge University Press, 2004), 10–36; quotation at 16. However, Gilbert and Vines (17) also point out that the Washington consensus did not mean the same thing to all people and that the originator of the term, John Williamson, intended it to convey a commitment to a certain degree of governmental activism in health, education, and poverty reduction.

15. Edith Terry, "The World Bank and Japan," Japan Policy Research Institute Working Paper 70, Tokyo, August 2000.

16. Japan devoted $13 billion for the 1990 Desert Storm effort and to help the economies of countries affected by the Gulf War, and became the largest foreign assistance donor to Cambodia and Vietnam following the 1989 Cambodian disengagement and the withdrawal of Vietnamese troops. See Keiko Hirata, *Civil Society in Japan: The Growing Role of NGOs in Tokyo's Aid and Development Policy* (New York: Palgrave Macmillan, 2002), 173–174.

17. Arase, "Introduction," 7.

18. Katada, "Japan's Two-Track Aid Approach," 322–323; Stine Nielsen, "Improving Japanese Official Development Assistance Quality: Discussing Theories of Bureaucratic Rivalry," *Kontur* 7 (2003): 32–40.

19. Devesh Kapur, John P. Lewis, and Richard Webb (eds.), *The World Bank: Its First Half Century,* Vol. 1: *History* (Washington, DC: The Brookings Institution, 1997), 1146.

20. Cited in Toyoo Gyohten, "Japan and the World Bank," in Devesh Kapur, John P. Lewis, and Richard Webb (eds.), *The World Bank: Its First Half Century,* Vol. 2: *Perspectives* (Washington, DC: The Brookings Institution, 1997), 275–316; quotation at 301–302.

21. See Robert Wade, "East Asia's Economic Success, Conflicting Perspectives, Partial Insights, Shaky Evidence," *World Politics* 44, 2 (1991): 270–320;

and Niels Hermes, "New Explanations of the Economic Success of East Asia: Lessons for Developing and East European Countries," Centre for Development Studies Working Paper No. 3, University of Groningen, June 1997. http://72.14.207.104/search?q=cache:Dg20u0GtFwAJ:www.ub.rug.nl/eldoc cds/199703/199703.pdf+%22east+asian+economic+miracle%22+debate+%22 world+Bank%22&hl=en&gl=us&ct=clnk&cd=10. Accessed February 19, 2006.

22. World Bank, *The East Asian Miracle: Economic Growth and Public Policy* (New York: Oxford University Press, 1993).

23. Kapur, Lewis, and Webb, *The World Bank,* 526.

24. Gyoten, "Japan and the World Bank," ibid., 302.

25. The dominance of this thinking in Western economics faculties is documented and analyzed in A. W. Coates (ed.), *The Post-1945 Internationalization of Economics* (Durham, NC: Duke University Press, 1997). The dominance of US economics training among the most influential South Asian economists is documented in George Rosen, *Western Economists and Eastern Societies* (Baltimore, MD: The Johns Hopkins University Press, 1985).

26. The terms *transformational* and *transformative* have both been prominent, without any consistent difference in their usage. James MacGregor Burns, in *Leadership* (New York: Harper & Row, 1978), popularized the term *transformative* with the strong implication that the objective is to inspire higher-level aspirations among followers.

27. The term was introduced by Max Weber, *Economy and Society,* trans. and ed. Guenther Roth and Claus Wittich (New York: Bedminster Press, 1921/ 1968), 215–216. An insightful book on the virtues and pitfalls of charismatic leadership is Jay Conger and Rabindra Kanungo, *Charismatic Leadership in Organizations* (Thousand Oaks, CA: Sage Publications, 1997).

28. Michelle Beaudry-Someynsky, "Japanese ODA Compared to Canadian ODA," in Arase, *Japan's Foreign Aid,* 133–151; quotation at 139.

29. Patricio Silva, "Intelectuales, tecnócratas y cambio social en Chile: pasado, presente y perspectivas futuras," *Revista Mexicana de Sociología* 54, 1 (1992): 139–166.

30. Harold D. Lasswell, "The World Revolution of Our Time," in Harold D. Lasswell and Daniel Lerner (eds.), *World Revolutionary Elites: Studies in Coercive Ideological Movements* (Cambridge, MA.: The MIT Press, 1965), 29–96.

31. By 1989, Japan was the world's largest provider of official development assistance, exceeding US "ODA." In the present decade, however, Japan

has cut back on its foreign assistance while US foreign assistance has increased, such that by mid-decade, the $20 billion US foreign-assistance total was more than twice the Japanese total.

32. Arase, "Japan's and the United States' Bilateral ODA Programs," in *Japan's Foreign Aid,* 123.

33. Institute of International Education, *Open Doors 2005* (Washington, DC: Institute of International Education, 2005).

34. The Japanese data come from the Japanese Ministry of Education, Culture, Sports, Science and Technology. "Ryugakusei Ukeire no Gaikyo" (General state of accepting foreign students in Japan) Student Exchange Division, Tokyo, December 9, 2005. http://web-japan.org/stat/stats/16EDU61 .html.

35. Abueva, "Administrative Doctrines," in *Political and Administrative Development,* 557–558.

36. Grant and Nijman, "Historical Changes," in *Annals.*

37. Peter Dauvergne, "The Rise of an Environmental Superpower? Evaluating Japanese Environmental Aid to Southeast Asia," Working Paper 1998/3 (Canberra: Australian National University, 1998), 4.

38. Organisation for Economic Co-operation and Development, "Statistical Annex of the 2007 Development Co-operation Report," "China." http:// www.oecd.org/dataoecd/1/21/1880034.gif.

39. Phillip Saunders characterizes the uncertainty of official development-assistance estimates for China, but he does venture a rough estimate:

The limited official data available are insufficient to accurately determine the total volume of Chinese grant and loan aid or the precise breakout in terms of recipients. Open source data describe many projects that receive Chinese assistance and sometimes report aggregate totals for Chinese bilateral assistance. However, press reports typically lack details on the nature and form of Chinese assistance, report total project costs without specifying the percentage of Chinese support, and confuse commercial investments with foreign assistance. Reports often incorporate previous and prospective assistance to arrive at exaggerated totals. Despite these caveats, some important details emerge from an analysis of open source reports on Chinese development assistance:

- China provided more than $5 billion in assistance to Indonesia and Thailand in 1998 during the Asian financial crisis.
- Chinese assistance to Pakistan increased dramatically in 2003–2004, with press reports citing more than $6.8 billion in assistance for projects such as a nuclear reactor, power plants, railroad improvements, and general development assistance. This assistance follows a major Chinese project to expand the Pakistani port of Gwadar and is likely intended to help stabilize Pakistan politically (or to build a presence that will ensure good ties with any successor regime).
- Chinese development assistance in Africa includes numerous large grants and loans to oil-producing states such as Angola, Sudan, and Nigeria. Some grants fund infrastructure projects such as railroads, power plants, and power lines. Others involve debt relief or provide financing for the purchase of Chinese goods.
- Open source analysis suggests a crude estimate of total Chinese grant and loan development assistance in 2004 is approximately $10 billion. Iran, Pakistan, and North Korea appear to be the largest beneficiaries. The total amount of development assistance announced appears to have increased significantly in the last 2 years.

Phillip C. Saunders, "China's Global Activism: Strategy, Drivers, and Tools," Washington, DC: Institute for National Strategic Studies, National Defense University, Occasional Paper 4, October 2006, 21. http://www.ndu.edu/inss/Occasional_Papers/OCP4.pdf.

40. Alden and Sidiropoulos estimate China's development assistance [US$4.09 is the base from which 44 percent would equal $1.8 billion] in Chris Alden and Elizabeth Sidiropoulos, "China and Africa: Friendship and Revival in the New Century," *Beijing Review,* December 15, 2006. http://www.bjreview.com.cn/expert/txt/2006-12/15/content_50879.htm.

41. Peter C. Evans and Erica S. Downs, "Untangling China's Quest for Oil Through State-Backed Financial Deals," Brookings Institution Policy Brief 154, Washington, DC, May 2006, 3–4. http://www.brookings.edu/~/media/files/rc/papers/2006/05china_evans/pb154.pdf. Estimating conservatively that this rate is 2 percent lower than commercial rates, this is equivalent to more than US$1 billion in aid.

42. Jane Perlez, "China Competes with West in Aid to Its Neighbors," *New York Times Online,* September 18, 2006. http://www.nytimes.com/2006/09/18/world/asia/18china.html?n=Top/Reference/Times%20Topics/People/P/Perlez,%20Jane.

43. Robert Rotberg, "China's Mixed Role in Africa," *Boston Globe,* June 23, 2007. http://www.boston.com/news/globe/editorial_opinion/oped/articles/2007/06/23/chinas_mixed_role_in_africa/.

44. Hongying Wang, "National Image Building and Chinese Foreign Policy," *China: An International Journal* 1 (2003), 46–72; quotation at 52.

For a brief history of China's foreign assistance and the shift from ideological/geopolitical considerations to economic considerations, see also George Yu, "Africa in Chinese Foreign Policy," *Asian Survey* 28, 8 (August 1988): 849–862.

45. Embassy of the People's Republic of China in the United States of America, "Foreign Ministry Spokesperson Liu Jianchao's Regular Press Conference on 9 October 2007." http://www.china-embassy.org/eng/fyrth/t370983.htm.

46. Power and Interest News Report, "Pipeline Politics: India and Myanmar," September 10, 2007. http://www.pinr.com/report.php?ac=view_report&report_id=679&language_id=1.

47. Evans and Downs, "Untangling China's Quest," 3–4.

48. Gareth Price, "India's Aid Dynamics: From Recipient to Donor?" Asia Programme Working Paper. London: Chatham House, September 2004, 6. http://www.britac.ac.uk/institutes/SSAS/projects/Price.pdf.

49. "Foreign Relations," in James Heitzman and Robert L. Worden (eds.), *India: A Country Study* (Washington, DC: US Government Printing Office for the Library of Congress, 1995). http://countrystudies.us/india/122.htm.

50. Price, "India's Aid Dynamics," 10.

51. Sonia Chaturbedi, "India's Double Standard on International Aid as Donor and Receiver," September 27, 2004. http://www.indiadaily.com/editorial/09-27b-04.asp.

52. Drew Thompson, "Economic Growth and Soft Power: China's Africa Strategy, Jamestown Foundation China Policy Brief 4, 24 (December 7, 2004). http://www.jamestown.org/print_friendly.php?volume_id=395&issue_id=3170&article_id=2368982.

53. Dennis Leech and Robert Leech, "Voting Power in the Bretton Woods Institutions," in Alberto Paloni and Maurizio Zanardi (eds)., *The IMF, World*

Bank, and Policy Reform (New York: Routledge, 2006), 29–48; Edwin Truman, "Rearranging IMF Chairs and Shares," in Edwin Truman (ed.), *Reforming the IMF for the 21st Century, Special Report 19* (Washington, DC: Institute for International Economics), 201–232.

54. BBC Business News, "India Attacks 'Flawed' IMF Reform," September 19, 2006. http://news.bbc.co.uk/1/hi/business/5358774.stm.

55. Steven R. Weisman, "World Bank's New Chief Will Also Focus on Corruption, *International Herald Tribune,* June 25, 2007. http://www.iht.com/articles/2007/06/25/business/wbank.php.

56. Amid all the diatribes launched in the wake of this episode, few objective assessments are available. One of them is Sofia Biller, "The Wolfowitz World Bank Presidency," University of Iowa Center for International Finance and Development, October 5, 2007. http://www.uiowa.edu/ifdebook/briefings/docs/wolfowitz.shtml. http://www.uiowa.edu/ifdebook/briefings/docs/wolfowitz.shtml.

57. World Bank, *China and the World Bank: A Partnership for Innovation* (Washington, DC: World Bank, 2007). http://siteresources.worldbank.org/INTCHINA/Resources/318862-1121421293578/cn_bank_partnershp_innovation.pdf.

6

CHINESE AND JAPANESE LEADERSHIP:
A STUDY IN CONTRASTS

William H. Overholt

For the last quarter century, Chinese leadership has provided the world with a model of decisiveness and rapid change, while Japan's leadership has provided a model of stasis and inability to adapt to changing conditions. In both countries, the structure of leadership has changed over time, in very important ways, so it is important to avoid reliance on models that are too simplistic, but the basic contrast remains. A comparison of the two countries' response to parallel financial crises will illuminate the differences in leadership.

From 1955 to 1975, Japan was one of the world's most dynamic economies, raising fears in the West that its superior manufacturing prowess would overshadow US and Western European accomplishments. Japan's fearsome image remained through the 1980s, even though its growth rate gradually decelerated. In the 1980s, gigantic financial bubbles made Japan seem even more formidable. The Japanese stock market came to have a capitalization equal to 49 percent of all world stock markets combined, and land in Tokyo was said to be roughly equal in value to all the land in the United States. Japanese banks towered over all the world's other banks, with larger market capitalization and superior competitiveness. In competitions for international deals, particularly in

Asia, US banks generally had to content themselves with the deals that were left over after the Japanese banks had taken what they wanted.[1] Western fears contrasted with the confidence of Japanese leaders, who expected that Asia would lead the twenty-first century and Japan would lead Asia, overshadowing its impoverished neighbors and an economically incompetent America.

In 1990 the financial bubble burst. Japan's economy stagnated for a dozen years. Its banking system nearly collapsed and, at its worst, threatened to drag Japan and possibly much of the rest of the world economy into a severe recession or depression. China in the 1990s faced a problem parallel to that of Japan. The banks in both countries were endangered by nonperforming loans on a vast scale.[2]

The contrasting experiences of Japan and China over the last generation have multiple roots. The current relative performance of the two economies is deeply rooted in demographics, because China has a relatively young and increasingly educated population, with a favorable ratio of workers to nonworkers (children and retired people). Japan's population is declining, with a bad and worsening ratio of workers to nonworkers and escalating costs for pensions and medical care. China's advantage in this respect is not permanent; by 2020, because of its one-child policy, China itself will have quite unfavorable demographics. At that point both Japan and China will be gray, but Japan will remain rich, whereas China, however impressive the absolute size of its GDP, will remain relatively poor in terms of per capita incomes and numerous aspects of technological development.

China's 10 percent growth rates, compared with Japan's 1–2 percent growth rates, also reflect the fact that China is engaged in catching up from a very low economic and technological base, whereas Japan is already one of the world's richest countries. When a country's technology, education, and productivity are abysmally low, as China's were at the start of the reform period, it is easier to grow very rapidly than a country that is already at the leading edge of technology, education, and productivity, such as Japan.

That having been said, different qualities of leadership have been crucial in these two countries for the recent past and may remain crucial for the indefinite future. Both Chinese and Japanese banks suffered catastrophically from, respectively, the collapse of China's state enterprise system and the collapse of Japan's property and stock market bubbles. Their different responses reflect differences in leadership structure.

THE MOBILIZATION SYSTEMS AND THEIR DIFFICULTIES

Both Japan and China had economies structured by what I call financial mobilization systems. These are financial and economic management systems structured by the government to serve an overriding national purpose, usually war. They have characteristic strengths and weaknesses.

Japan

The Japanese financial mobilization system was created, with lessons learned from Hitler's Germany and Stalin's Russia, in order to prepare for coming war. Much of what many Americans believe to be ancient Japanese culture is actually a system that was created between 1937 and 1945 to mobilize resources for World War II.[3] Most of the characteristic qualities of Japanese management, including lifetime employment and banks being more important than capital markets, were created in order to mobilize resources for World War II. They had nothing to do with ancient Japanese culture. The system was designed to squeeze resources out of families and channel them through the government into the big companies that were the key to fighting the war. When a country is fighting a war, it doesn't want its ammunition company to go out of business. Thus Japan created the *Convoy System* and the *Main Bank System* whereby groups of companies would support each other, banks were responsible for groups of companies, and the government propped up banks as necessary.

Before the war preparations began, if a bank was insolvent, it went bankrupt. If a company was insolvent, it went bankrupt. But that couldn't be allowed in the middle of a war. Moreover, the government supported the war-critical big companies through cartels at home and protectionism abroad. National planners curtailed shareholder rights because they wanted the government to be able to guide some corporate strategies, and in doing so be able to reduce the role of capital markets. Before 1937, if a company wanted to raise money, it would usually go to the stock market or the bond market. But it's hard for the government to manipulate the stock markets and bond markets. It's easier for them to tell a bank, "Give that company a loan." Therefore, the government created a system very *bank-centered* and a system of very strong bureaucratic management of the economy. They created a lifetime employment system for the big companies and set of new social values that deemphasized the family in favor of loyalty to the company.[4] Foreign traders and investors were kept at arm's length, because foreign involvement was inconsistent with preparing for and prosecuting a war.

This system worked beautifully for two phases of modern Japanese history. In mobilizing resources for the war, it was effective. And in rejuvenating the economy after the war it was spectacularly effective—Japan was the first major country to achieve nearly 10 percent annual growth for two decades.[5] (A version of the same system also proved effective for kick-starting the primitive economy of South Korea in the 1960s and 1970s.) To understand the success of the postwar system, imagine a hypothetical steel mill that has excellent management, excellent workers, and excellent technology but was physically destroyed by wartime bombing. If the government funnels a lot of money to such a steel company, it just might stimulate the fastest growth of a steel company in world history. That in microcosm was the story of Japan for thirty years after the war. In addition, the social-bonding techniques made it possible to get industry organized and disciplined more thoroughly than elsewhere in the world. Fear—of hunger, of domestic subversion, of Soviet invasion—kept government leaders focused on efficient management. They built needed roads and other infrastructure, helped important companies, and phased out sunset industries (such as aluminum smelting after the 1973 rise in oil prices). Rarely, perhaps never, had the world seen such efficient economic management.

Then, long before the rest of the world noticed, a gradual deterioration of the system set in.[6] From 1975 onward, Japan's economic growth rate gradually decelerated. The focus of the country's leaders shifted from moving the economy vigorously into the future (for instance, by shedding old industries) to defending existing industries and companies at vast expense. Industries such as construction that had been supported by the government to reconstruct essential infrastructure after the war were now supported by the government in spending more on highway construction than all of the United States, in lining virtually every river and stream with concrete, in building hugely expensive bridges used mainly by rabbits and deer, and so forth.[7] With government protection and encouragement, key industries—most notably property, construction, banking, agriculture, and retail distribution—metastasized into vast cancers depleting the resources that would have otherwise been available to other, more innovative, more modern industries.

Strong government protection from overseas competition and overseas investment enabled these industries to keep prices very high, depleting the real incomes of Japanese citizens. For many years the Japanese staple food, rice, was priced at eight times the world price. A pound of high-quality beef or one high-quality melon often sold for more than US$100. The Japanese phrase for the system that produced these absurdities is "the high-cost economy." As a consequence, although the Japanese people enjoyed incomes among the world's very highest, they typically lived in tiny apartments, with lifestyles typical of consumers in far poorer countries.[8] Because consumer demand was limited, economic growth depended on rising net exports, but foreign countries made it clear that there were limits to their willingness to accept the huge trade deficits with Japan that such a growth path entailed. The economic model had inherent limits.

By the late 1980s this system was malfunctioning spectacularly. Low interest rates encouraged reckless spending. Special ties with the banks, a rising stock market, and support from the government glutted the big companies with cash and enabled them to spend wildly on overseas acquisitions, to support "zombie" companies that elsewhere would have died, and to maintain a variety of other inefficient practices. A rapid increase in the stock market made investors willing to finance companies at negligible cost. The shift of corporate financing from banks to the stock market left banks bereft of important customers and led them to pour money into mortgages. Stock market and property prices soared, creating the biggest financial bubbles in the history of the world. Many families could buy an apartment only through a "three-generation mortgage" that bound parents, children, and grandchildren to service the debt for a small apartment.

In 1990 the bubbles burst. Property prices collapsed by more than half. The stock market declined from an index of 38,915 to 7,607. So many companies foundered, and so many families had difficulty paying for homes, that most banks landed in severe trouble. Families lost much of their assets.

China

Revolutionary and postrevolutionary China also developed initially on the basis of a mobilization system. As in Japan, the mobilization system was a manifestation of wartime needs. Both the Chinese Communist Party and its old foe, the Guomindang, relied on bank financing rather than capital markets, insisted upon government ownership and control of major companies, provided government direction for corporate strategies rather than relying on autonomous corporate governance, and propped up companies in difficulty. They rationalized their economic structures with different ideologies, but the fundamental structures were quite similar to each other and were natural consequences of decades of warfare and competitive struggle for political control. Socialism facilitated political control and assurance of steady military supply.

As in Japan, the early post-1949 mobilization system served the Chinese economy relatively well. Excluding periods of upheaval from

Maoist political campaigns (the Great Leap Forward of 1958–1961 and the Cultural Revolution of 1966–1976), infrastructure improved dramatically, domestic peace was maintained, health and nutrition improved, and longevity rose dramatically. The results were very far from the Japanese economic miracle of 1955–1975, but they were remarkably positive compared with the previous two centuries of Chinese history.

After the reform era began, economic growth ascended to the level of the Japanese economic miracle: about 10 percent GDP growth per year, based on increasingly market-oriented domestic policies and increasing openness to foreign trade and investment. However, by the 1990s the fundamental institutions of the mobilization system—the banks and the giant state enterprises—were in even deeper trouble than their Japanese counterparts. Like many favored Japanese corporations, the big state enterprises had become accustomed to easy money and limited competition, and many could not survive in an economy where there was real competition and where bank loans actually had to be repaid. In consequence, the banks nearly foundered under bad loans that proved proportionately even worse than the Japanese counterparts.[9]

REFORM AND RECOVERY

In this situation, as in the aftermath of the 1997–1998 financial crises in Thailand, South Korea, and Indonesia, and the US savings and loan debacle of the early 1980s, the customary remedies include insuring the banks' depositors, shutting down insolvent companies, cleaning out the banks' management, forcing bank shareholders to take their losses, imposing far greater accounting transparency, radically improving standards of corporate governance, increasing competition, welcoming strategic shareholders (usually foreign, in the Asian cases), and putting both banks and companies on a more market-oriented basis.

Faced with national crisis, the Japanese and Chinese governments responded in drastically different ways. The Chinese government initiated probably the most sweeping, socially strenuous reform program in all of modern world history. In contrast, the Japanese government, despite having far greater national wealth, administrative resources, and access to international experience, dragged its feet in all the areas where reform was needed. China emerged from the crisis dynamic, confident, and growing rapidly, with the government in a sound financial position and with a stirring vision of the future. Japan emerged from the crisis dispirited, listless, politically crippled, hampered by government debt exceeding 170 percent of GDP, and utterly devoid of a positive vision of the future.

Japan

Japan managed individual bank failures relatively smoothly, but it mostly consolidated big banks into huge banks, thereby limiting competition and saddling the country with banks that were hard to reform and politically divided. Managements were heavily protected rather than thoroughly purged. Stockholders who elsewhere would have been completely wiped out were heavily protected. Big companies, including ones like giant retailer Daiei (proportionately about as big as its US counterpart K-mart, which went under uneventfully) were rescued by government fiat rather than being allowed to fail. The true scale of the banks' nonperforming loans was covered up until late in the process; government officials sometimes intervened to limit what bank examiners were allowed to research and insisted on publishing numbers more positive than the banks' own numbers. Likewise, the government assigned high credit ratings to companies such as Mycal that independent agencies uniformly rated as poor credit risks. The recovery agency RCC certified that all loans it was buying were from financially sound institutions, whereas in reality none of the institutions was sound. To enable Japan's major banks to continue doing overseas business, which requires a capital adequacy ratio of 8 percent, the government helped the banks fix their numbers so that the big ones came out above 8 percent rather than the 1.07 percent calculated properly by respected Japanese authorities. The RCC warehoused loans and had them valued by its own experts, rather than selling them off quickly at market value in line with the practice in the United States and other more market-oriented economies. All these practices distorted perceptions and delayed reforms.

Large numbers of loans were forgiven or sold to the RCC for 1 yen rather than incur the wrath of established customers, influential politicians, or the yakuza gangsters who were often behind the transactions. Unlike other Asian countries with financial crises, Japan sharply limited foreigners' ability to buy strategic stakes and influence the management of Japan's banks. (One bank was sold to foreigners, and a major political controversy arose when the foreigners actually imposed tough reforms and made a large profit.) More broadly, the authorities relied overwhelmingly on setting interest rates barely above zero for many years in order to save most banks and big companies, rather than allowing the market to winnow out incompetent institutions and thereby reallocate the nation's capital and labor into more productive uses.[10] The result of all this was a banking system that, eighteen years after the onset of the crisis in 1990, had a drastically curtailed international presence compared to 1989 and has no foreseeable prospect of becoming internationally competitive in the manner of the US and European banks that Japan once overshadowed.[11]

As soon as the crisis-era prime minister, Junichiro Koizumi, retired in 2006, politics as usual resumed, and economic reform essentially ended.

China

China started from a much lower base in all respects, and was in a much worse financial situation, but under Premier Zhu Rongji, with backing from President Jiang Zemin, imposed the most sweeping reforms in modern history. Thousands of state enterprises—the vast majority, in fact—were absorbed, devolved to local governments, privatized, or sold to foreigners. Risking his job, Prime Minister Zhu insisted on bankruptcy for the second most prestigious foreign borrower in China, Guangdong International Trust and Investment Company (GITIC) after mismanagement rendered it insolvent—despite universal expectations that, in the mode of other third world countries, China would bail out prestigious and politically influential, albeit corrupt, institutions. The whole system of ownership and management of state enterprises was revolutionized in order to reduce (though not eliminate) political influence over such management. State-enterprise employment declined by 50 million in a single decade after 1994. The government went on a campaign to increase competition in major sectors.[12] The banks were completely restructured. Accounting transparency was steadily and dramatically improved. Bank managements were completely overhauled. Foreign financial institutions were invited to take major strategic ownership positions and encouraged to influence management. The bank and securities regulatory systems were transformed, with ruthless idealistic reformers in charge of banking regulation and a large number of foreign experts appointed at high and medium levels in the China Securities Regulatory Commission (CSRC). Many new banks emerged, and the roles of foreigners and foreign financial institutions in China's financial system drastically increased.

Given the low base from which these reforms began, China in 2008 still had a long journey to fully modern standards of accounting, corporate governance, freedom from political control, and many other dimensions of modernity. But the rate of progress was remarkable, and implementation of reforms has strongly continued.

Moreover, China's response to crisis occurred in the context of sweeping, politically painful reforms designed to address related problems. Employment in the central and provincial levels of government was cut nearly in half. Pay was then doubled, and later doubled again, to reduce incentives for corruption. At the turn of the century, forty ministries had become twenty-nine. Ten vice ministerial industrial bureaus in charge of running various industries were consolidated into one. The military was ordered to give up most of its businesses—a step that governments such as those of Thailand and Indonesia could not even imagine implementing. The government subjected the military to additional civilian controls, and generals were eliminated from the Politburo

Standing Committee. The year 2008 saw another major reorganization of the government around five superministries. Although China's economy was far more vulnerable than Japan's, the Chinese economy was opened far more than Japan's to foreign trade and investment. Trade as a share of GDP became about three times Japan's level, and the proportionate difference in foreign direct investment was even more pronounced.

A more thorough review of the detailed reform and recovery process would divert us from our main focus on leadership qualities and structures. Very detailed reviews are available elsewhere. The central point is that China, starting from a much more difficult situation, implemented far more sweeping and politically difficult reforms that left the country far more competitive and feeling dynamic and confident about the future, whereas Japan, starting from a comfortable point, allowed a similar but somewhat less severe problem to stagnate the economy, demoralize the citizenry, and leave the country without a vision of the future.

CONTRASTING LEADERSHIP STRUCTURES

Different contexts affected the leadership responses. A high level of prosperity enabled Japan to be more complacent, whereas poverty discouraged complacency in China; the role of fear as a motivator of reform should never be underestimated. As noted, different demographics meant that success in China would inevitably produce faster economic growth than similar success in Japan. Conversely, China was digging out from a deeper hole than was Japan, so success in reform was more difficult. After controlling for these contextual factors, the difference between Chinese and Japanese leadership performance remains remarkable.

Japan

The genius of Japan's 1955 political system was that in the face of domestic political instability and foreign subversion, the country's leaders stabilized the country by merging the two major conservative parties into a single Liberal Democratic Party that controlled so much of the country's organizational talent and financial/economic resources that it could hold free elections without significant risk of being defeated. The resulting predominance depended heavily on the evolved version of the 1940 economic system, which enabled the government to manage the economy in far more detailed and politically advantageous ways than are possible in North America or Western Europe. For instance, the postwar system was designed to keep about half of government expenditures out of the official budget and therefore not subject to public or legislative scrutiny. Part of this gigantic slush fund came from the Postal Savings Bank, the world's largest deposit-taking bank, which collected trillions of dollars of savings at low interest rates and made those funds available for spending on public-works projects. It also had roots in a legal system where judges were heavily influenced by LDP political priorities and over 98 percent (currently over 99 percent) of people arrested are convicted. This far-reaching control has made it possible for the LDP to run the country continuously, except for one brief, anomalous Socialist prime ministership (Tomiichi Murayama, June 30, 1994, to January 11, 1996), from 1955 until the present.

The other side of the resulting stability is that the system is very stable even in the face of drastically needed change. Even though LDP candidates have overwhelming financial resources to defeat their opponents, they are also heavily dependent on the sectors that make up the key LDP constituencies, notably property, construction, retail, banking, and agriculture. The result is a legislature divided into "tribes" (*zoku*) that are effectively owned by these interest groups. Of course, in any democracy, key interest groups are influential constituents of any legislator, but the price Japanese legislators pay for their overwhelming financial resources is that, to a greater extent than in any Western democracy, the legislature is the almost wholly owned subsidiary of a small number of powerful interest groups. This exceptional power of key constituencies leads to a phenomenon that the Japanese call "structural corruption," the inability of the government to act in the national interest because of the exceptional political influence that key interest groups have over the decision-making process. Again, the general phenomenon is common to all democracies, and probably to all polities, but in Japan it is greatly magnified.

In the United States or the United Kingdom, although legislators represent local constituencies, the president or prime minister is acknowledged to represent the country as a whole and as such is endowed with great power. In Japan, the prime minister has in recent times been very weak. (Yasuhiro Nakasone, prime minister from 1982 to 1987, was a notable exception.) Rather than winning by primary elections followed by a direct popular vote like a US president or running as clear leaders of their party in the manner of a UK prime minister, they have in recent times typically been men of bureaucratic demeanor and no detectable charisma, chosen by their colleagues with little popular input. (We shall discuss the recent exception, Koizumi, below.) Most Japanese prime ministers serve for very short periods of time and then give another loyal party stalwart his turn. Moreover, the power that most Western democracies associate with their top leader is dispersed to other institutions.

In recent times the prime minister has usually not been the leading power in the LDP. Instead, on the model of ancient times, when the emperor was actually overshadowed by a shogun, the real power has been held behind the scenes. After his fall from office as a consequence of the Lockheed scandal in 1972, former Prime Minister Kakuei Tanaka held the real power behind the scenes to the extent that he selected the six prime ministers who succeeded him. For years Hiromu Nonaka, who served as chief cabinet secretary from 1998 to 1999, exercised power vastly exceeding that attached to his official government and party posts. These shoguns have controlled such great resources that they can overshadow prime ministers; in so doing, they connect the interest groups that provide the resources directly to critical decisions.

The Japanese Diet has far more power relative to the executive than in other democracies, so local interests have proportionately more sway than in countries where the national leader has great power.

The bureaucracy of the executive branch has typically chosen the prime minister's key advisors, who remain primarily loyal to, for instance, the ministry of finance, rather than to the prime minister. The major bureaucracies have had far more power than their counterparts in other countries, and the prime minister has been proportionately weaker.

The political vetting of policy initiatives and legislative bills has usually been far more intrusive in Japan than elsewhere. Typically the Policy Research Committee of the LDP has vetted a bill before it goes to the legislature. This decisive, politically focused vetting process greatly diverts and dilutes the kind of influence that in the United States would be exercised by the National Security Council, the Council of Economic Advisors, and other bodies that feel loyalty primarily to the president and to the national interest. Of course, in the United States, key political advisors—for instance, Karl Rove for President George W. Bush—exercise very important influence. But the Japanese situation is quite different, with a powerful, institutionalized group of political advisors taking the first and dominant cut at legislation and policy initiatives, secondary bureaucrats dominating the prime minister's office, and a weak prime minister trying to manage without a powerful staff of his own choosing.

Finally, Japanese voters have typically been apathetic. In a polity dominated by one party, at the height of the financial crisis, half of voters were unaffiliated with any political party. That is a huge anomaly. Those who do vote have usually had negligible influence over policy. They do not vote for a candidate with a clear platform. They vote for a local figure who will have marginal influence over the eventual negotiated choice of a prime minister and cabinet.

The inability of the standard candidates and canonical system to cope with the financial crisis led to an anomalous development, the emergence of Prime Minister Junichiro Koizumi during Japan's financial crisis. Unlike his immediate predecessors, Koizumi was flamboyant, sporting an unusual haircut and an unusual personality. He understood that the patronage structure of the LDP inhibited the drastic steps needed to cope with the crisis, so he campaigned on a promise to "destroy the LDP" if necessary. He understood that the system was sustained by vast flows of funds, of which the postal savings system provided the largest stream, so he bet his job on (gradual) privatization of the Postal Savings Bank and held an election in which he took the unprecedented step of running reformist candidates against LDP stalwarts. He understood that reform was impossible without transparency, so he empowered a determined economics professor, Heizo Takenaka, as minister of state for economic and fiscal policy and as minister of state for privatization of the Postal Savings System, among other appointments, to impose more transparency and lead financial reform. He understood that the prime minister's weakness was creating national weakness, so he began centralizing power; for instance, he chose his own advisors, relied heavily on informal advisors, ignored the LDP Policy Research Council, and called for an eventual constitutional amendment to allow direct election of the prime minister.

Koizumi's reforms were painfully slow and were barely enough to save the system from collapse. Their overreliance on monetary policy and their inability to deal with the protected, politicized, and cartel-heavy industrial structure left Japan burdened with an extraordinary national debt, but they saved the country—or at least the system.

Japan's emergence from its financial crisis was the perfect time for the emergence of new leadership that would articulate a fresh and inspiring version of Japan's future. It seemed that Japan could be the first mature society, showing the rest of the world (which was mostly graying too, only more slowly) how a mature civilization could create a model of dignity, of efficiency, of peace, of equity, and even of growth through a more open and competitive economy and more modern roles for women, small companies, and others hitherto pushed aside by the old mobilization system.

But that did not happen. Instead, the next prime minister, Shinzo Abe, restored the positions of the anti-reformist politicians ejected from the party by Koizumi, while the leader of the opposition Democratic Party of Japan, Ozawa, mounted a successful Upper House campaign based on the old LDP model of mobilizing the agricultural and other reactionary lobbies.

The only new vision articulated by leading political figures was confined to the hawkish nationalists (such as Shinzo Abe and Taro Aso), and it focused on the past: rearming Japan, advocating restoration of some of the discipline and pride of prewar Japanese society, and reinterpreting the country's history in a nationalistic fashion that ensured conflict with Japan's neighbors. Abe fell from power quickly, but his successor, Prime Minister Yasuo Fukuda, a decent and balanced figure with great skill at international politics, was seen as a man of the old, obsolete LDP and quickly became quite unpopular. Fukuda completely foreswore any economic reform agenda.

The lack of leadership imperiled Japan's international position as well as its domestic economic strength. With a larger and more modern economy than China's, Japan continued to aspire to regional Asian leadership and seemed reasonably positioned to succeed in that ambition. But Japan's refusal to open its economy meant that China's smaller economy had far more trade with each of its neighbors, and more dynamic investment relationships with them, than Japan did.[13] Japan insisted on being relatively closed to immigration, so its economy could not surmount demographic decline. Therefore, Japan's leaders locked themselves into a position of fearing China's rise but refusing to take the necessary steps to compete, as well as trying to leverage an alliance with the United States to limit China's influence but resenting subordination to the United States. This failure to make choices is a core aspect of leadership failure.

Both major Japanese political parties now are seen as waves of the past, gradually decaying, but it is not clear what might replace them or revive them. Japan, although saved by a new kind of leader, Koizumi, is again drifting for lack of leadership. The 1955 political system saved Japan from the risk of anti-Western instability, but it evolved into a form of stability that resisted the emergence of vitally needed leadership for new times.

China

In the reform period since 1979, Beijing has consistently delivered superior economic management and superior political inspiration to a people arising from two centuries of impoverishment and humiliation. It has not provided democracy or human rights, but, as occurred earlier in places such as Taiwan and South Korea, it has delivered what the country's people felt they needed most at the time, and it has made substantial progress in improving personal liberties—from an extremely low base.

The superiority of Chinese leadership flies in the face of many expectations. Chinese and Indians often say that China's leaders can deliver the goods because China is a dictatorship. But dictatorship elsewhere does not consistently, or even in a substantial proportion of cases, deliver superior results. Latin America, Africa, and Asia have historically been full of dictators who focused on lining their own pockets or served as the face of one or another greedy interest group. China's success results not from dictatorship per se but from a particular form of leadership typical of the Asian Miracle economies, most notably South Korea, Taiwan, Hong Kong, and Singapore.

Most US commentators would assume that democracy would draw on such a diversity of constituencies that it would readily adapt to social changes, whereas Chinese Communist Party dependence on the revenues of the state enterprises and communes should make Communist leadership in China, rather than democratic leadership in Japan, the captive of the obsolescing economic establishment. They would likewise assume that, with virtually every hand in China held out for a bit of graft, China would be crippled by corruption, whereas Japan, endowed with the transparency and competition of democracy, would be relatively free of corrupt influence. Instead, China, despite having a billion hands potentially reaching for graft, has been able to move forward with policies and performance clearly designed in the national interest, while Japan has been hobbled by "structural corruption."

China benefits from the relative absence of legacy institutions that drag the country back to the past. Ideological Maoism destroyed many of the old Confucian institutions, and Maoist excesses destroyed many of the key institutions of Mao's era, while discrediting the rest. Reformist Chinese after 1979 did have the legacy of financial and political dependence on the communes and the state enterprises, but the communes disintegrated in a wave of popular takeovers that canny Deng Xiaoping and his colleagues subsequently decided to bless.[14] They realized quickly that the spectacular increase in popular living standards created a political base—and potentially a fiscal base—greatly superior to the one that was being destroyed.

In the era of Jiang Zemin and Zhu Rongji, the Communist Party made a similar calculation about the state enterprises. Yes, the state enterprises had, from the time of the revolution, provided the financing and the political power base of the regime; the foundation of socialist economic power is control of production, and the foundation of socialist political power is control over jobs. But China's leaders were wise enough to learn the lesson of their neighbor economies South Korea, Taiwan, and Singapore: you could abandon your old power base and develop a new one. Create an economic dynamo, and taxes would broaden your fiscal base while rising standards of living broadened your political base. Anyway, the communes had failed and the state enterprises were running losses rather than making profits. The decision was obvious in retrospect, but it required foresight, a clear understanding of what had happened in the smaller Asian economic takeoffs, and considerable political courage.

In this evolution lies the most important secret of the difference between Chinese and Japanese leadership. The Japanese leadership is heavily controlled by a few key interest groups, but the Chinese leadership cut itself loose from its old owners and provides professional management as though the country were a business conglomerate.

As in South Korea under Park Chung Hee and Taiwan under Chiang Ching-Kuo, China's leadership is quite conscious that its continuation in office depends on business performance, not on ideological or religious belief or on democratic or interest group legitimacy.

Notwithstanding omnipresent graft, the Chinese top leadership takes great pains to maintain its integrity. Whereas the purpose of becoming a leader in the Philippines or Paraguay or the Congo is typically to make more money, the purpose of becoming a leader in South Korea or Taiwan or Singapore or China during the era of the Asian Miracle economic growth is to secure an admired place in the history books. Aside from personal values, there are perennial efforts in China to prevent the capture of the leadership, or of large segments of the economy, by particular interest groups. The Politburo Standing Committee has been gradually purged of soldiers, policemen, ideologues, and the immediate offspring of former top leaders. Whereas a Marcos or a Suharto strives to consolidate as many monopolies as possible, China has implemented a relentless drive to increase competition. Unlike Japan and South Korea, China has been relatively inclusive of foreign as well as domestic competition.

Under Zhu Rongji, as noted, the government was cut down rather than, as is more typical elsewhere, continually expanded to provide increased patronage. Zhu out-Reaganed Reagan.

Unlike India and the Philippines, where infrastructure and education are allocated on a patronage basis, China's leaders allocate infrastructure and education on a business performance basis. China's roads, telecommunications, and ports form a carefully planned network that gradually knits the country together. China builds more first-class freeways in a few months than India has built since independence in 1947. The standard for political and governmental advancement is performance. Mayors and governors and party secretaries must meet quotas of growth, local investment, foreign investment, and employment if they want promotion. Zhu Rongji's annual Work Reports read like a Western corporate CEO's annual reports: facts, figures, accomplishments, weaknesses, not ideological harangues in the manner of Mao or rationalization of patronage decisions as in India.

One of the most impressive aspects of China's business model is its selection process for middle- and upper-level leaders. As noted, rigorous performance-based criteria are employed. Prior to promotion there are 360-degree interviews; all of the person's bosses and immediate subordinates are interviewed, and the findings are carefully recorded. Although political consideration is never excluded anywhere in the world, China's system emphasizes concrete performance to an extent rare outside the Asian Miracle economies. The result has been outstanding national and provincial leadership.

That having been said, the system breaks down almost completely at the lower levels—for instance, in the towns and villages. The government has resorted to elections in the villages, not because of any love for elections but because elections have provided the only theory of how to avoid complete descent into village corruption and chaos. There are limits to the applicability of the business model.

Because the leaders are intensely conscious of other limitations of the business model, they have continually altered the details of governance until the polity of today bears little resemblance to the polity of two decades ago. They make ever more use of elections, and increasingly competitive elections, within the Communist Party. They have changed their image of society from a Marxist one of widening class polarization to a post-Marxist one of shaping an increasingly middle-class society. That has enabled them to change their view of political process as continual class struggle to one of rule in the general interest. They have learned that scientific progress and innovation of all kinds depend on allowing open debate. They have learned that as economic progress continues, people become assertive about not being arbitrarily moved from their homes to accommodate a new business venture and about not having their environment sullied by pollution from a new chemical plant.

For a time, such learning encourages incremental modifications within the business model, and then at some point, these alterations accumulate into a transformation of the nature of the model. China's leaders are all conscious that Chinese politics today bears little resemblance to Chinese politics of two decades ago, and all of them understand that Chinese politics a generation hence will have to change at least as much. There are no Brezhnevs, Chernenkos, or Andropovs (leaders who blithely assume that the old political structures will suffice eternally) at the top of Chinese politics. That is why the leaders allow debates on national television about which of several models of democracy China should aspire to. This does not mean that China will inevitably end up as a Western-style democracy, but it does mean that it can only continue to succeed if it becomes increasingly sensitive to demands for representation.

Internationally, unlike their Japanese counterparts, Chinese leaders have made necessary strategic choices. In order to focus on economic development, they have settled twelve of fourteen land border disputes to the satisfaction of their neighbors. (Such compromises are a sharp contrast with Indian and Japanese behavior.) They have abandoned all efforts to impose their ideological preconceptions on other countries. They have done whatever was necessary to develop friendly diplomatic relations with most of their neighbors. By joining the ASEAN Free Trade Area without detailed negotiations and then opening their economy to ASEAN neighbors more rapidly than promised, they have consolidated an image of cooperative, multilateral economic behavior that is the opposite of Japan's. The result of all these differences is that Japan finds itself relatively isolated on key issues such as energy security, whereas China enjoys broad support. Decisive leadership and a willingness to override domestic interest groups in pursuit of the national interest is a key reason for China's success.

The leadership model under Hu Jintao and Wen Jiabao has evolved in important ways from the model under their predecessors, Jiang Zemin and Zhu Rongji. At the turn of the century, China's leadership decided that it was time for the era of great men to end. Mao, Deng, and Jiang had wide latitude for their rule, with increasing but limited encumbrance by rules. Jiang was called the "Core of the Third Generation." There is no core of the fourth generation. China has decided that collective leadership, with each leader constrained by a rule-based system, is an important step forward in the rule of law and in political development. The new leaders are right about that, of course, but they have also paid a price. The system is not as dynamically reformist or as nimble as it was when Zhu Rongji was axing government jobs and laying waste to the state enterprise system. Under the new leaders, who emphasize social harmony in sharp contrast to Zhu's ruthless efficiency drive, inflation has gone from zero to just under 9 percent—and that is an underestimate because rice and energy prices have been suppressed. Weak financial management has allowed the emergence of financial bubbles, particularly in the stock and property markets. Interest groups have become far more assertive. Premier Wen's reputation for indecisiveness is the opposite of Zhu Rongji's. It remains to be seen whether the new form of maturity can be made consistent with the ongoing need for decisiveness.

Western commentators often underestimate the power of the business model in the medium term. One never sees mention in the Western press that Chinese longevity has increased from forty-one to seventy-three years. Every literate Chinese knows that and appreciates it. In an equal but opposite fallacy, other Western commentators lack a sense of history and think that business model leadership has shown that it can persist indefinitely. Ironically, Chinese leaders, who feel the social pressures and have studied the historical experience of neighboring polities such as South Korea and Taiwan, have a much more realistic appreciation that change is inevitable. The precise nature of the change that will occur remains obscure, but there is no doubting the inexorability of change.

NOTES

1. The author of this chapter ran investment bank research teams in New York (1980–1984) and in Hong Kong and Singapore (1985–2001) for Bankers Trust, BankBoston, and Nomura. This comment and much of the paper rely on that experience.

2. The authoritative work on Chinese banks' crisis and reform measures is Kumiko Okazaki, "Banking System Reform in China: The Challenges of Moving Toward a Market-Oriented Economy," Occasional Paper, National Security Research Division (Santa Monica, CA: RAND, 2007).

3. For a detailed account of the construction of the financial mobilization and its motivations, see Tetsuji Okazaki and Masahiro Okuno-Fujiwara, (eds.), *The Japanese Economic System and Its Historical Origins*, trans. Susan Herbert (New York: Oxford University Press, 1993). Much of this system was dismantled and reassembled after the war. In its broadest outlines, Japanese refer to the mobilization system as the 1940 System. See also William H. Overholt, "Japan's Economy: At War with Itself," *Foreign Affairs* 81, 1 (2002).

4. I spent three years as chief strategist of Nomura for Asia Ex-Japan, the biggest Japanese investment bank, and our salespeople in Tokyo were out until the wee hours of the morning, nearly every morning, with customers. The really good ones were out until 4 o'clock in the morning and then were back in the office at 7. They slept through many important meetings, but they had that camaraderie that created bonds within the company and bonds with customers. That's like wartime when you work hard with a lot of discipline during the day and during the week, and then you let go on the weekend— but often with colleagues and customers rather than family. The whole culture was essentially organized on a quasi-wartime footing. To give one more example, my area covered eight countries, and virtually all the Americans, Brits, Chinese, Koreans, and Filipinos brought their families with them when they were assigned overseas. We didn't have one Japanese executive who brought his family with him. Some were overseas for ten or fifteen years, during which time they would visit home a few times each year; the whole focus was on the company. This is now changing for the younger generation.

5. To understand the reconstruction and reshaping of the 1940 system after the war, see John W. Dower, *Embracing Defeat: Japan in the Wake of World War I* (New York: W.W. Norton, 2000).

6. The most thorough account of the process of deterioration is Richard Katz, *Japan: The System That Soured* (New York: M.E. Sharpe, 1998). The shifting politics that accompanied these changes is chronicled in T. J. Pempel, *Regime Shift: Comparative Dynamics of the Japanese Political Economy* (Ithaca, NY: Cornell University Press, 1998).

7. For a lively account of some of the extremes created by this metastasis, see Alex Kerr, *Dogs and Demons: Tales from the Dark Side of Japan* (New York: Hill & Wang, 2001).

8. Typical middle-class Japanese families live in housing that would seem cramped to middle-class Filipinos. On a 2001 trip to visit Chinese companies, my Nomura colleagues concurred that typical farmers in a large area around Shanghai, with their two-story homes and high-quality $30 DVD players, live much better than mid-career Tokyo stockbrokers, with tiny apartments, long commutes, and $600 DVD players. (Despite low nominal incomes, Shanghai farmers are of course far better off than farmers in much of the rest of China. Farmers in Guizhou are often impoverished by any standard.)

9. For the details, see Kumiko Okazaki, op. cit.

10. In May 2008, eighteen years after the onset of the crisis, Bank of Japan had just reaffirmed its benchmark interest rate at 0.50 percent—up from the 0.25 percent that prevailed for years of crisis.

11. The details in this paragraph are drawn from William H. Overholt, "Financial Reform in Japan: The Social Context," presented at a Harvard University conference on Asian financial reform, December 10–11, 2002.

12. For instance, the government broke up the telecommunications monopoly in order to increase competition. The intense competition that resulted is the reason why China hit 200 million cell phone subscribers when India, which still supported a traditional dominant provider, was just hitting 10 million. So great was China's success that India subsequently copied China's example, with similarly spectacular results.

13. China's trade with every country in the region exceeds Japan's. Japan's cumulative investment around the region remained much larger than China's, but regional investment in China was much more substantial and dynamic than in Japan, because of China's more open economy. And economic relations with China were much more welcome in the region, because Japanese firms nearly always sought dominant managerial, technological, and financial

positions, whereas investment relations with China involved every imaginable permutation of different relationships.

14. The dismantling of China's communes began with peasant takeovers in Anhui Province, against the policies of the central government and contrary to the core ideology of the Chinese Communist Party. But Deng and his colleagues saw the spectacular economic consequences and, instead of suppressing the movement, spread it throughout the country.

7

ECONOMIC REFORM POLICY AND DEVELOPMENT LEADERSHIP IN LATIN AMERICA:
CHILE AND MEXICO

Judith Teichman

In general, the era of globalization has not produced sustained growth and generalized prosperity for Latin America. Although a variety of external factors, such as declines in the terms of trade and the debt crisis, have certainly been important ingredients in this general malaise, domestic politics has undoubtedly been of paramount importance. In particular, political leadership plays a crucial role in mitigating or exacerbating political conflict and in building a consensus toward equitable and well-formulated policy decisions. An examination of leadership, therefore, sheds considerable light on past practices and future possibilities.

This chapter focuses on two Latin American countries: Mexico and Chile. While Mexico has confronted recurrent economic crises since the early 1980s and has continued to be mired in high levels of poverty (41 percent in the year 2000), Chile has been characterized by steady economic growth rates and substantial poverty reduction: between 1990 and 2000, poverty was reduced from 38.6 percent of households in 1990 to 20.67 percent by 2000.[1] Both countries, however, continue to face a common development challenge: that of high levels of inequality with gini coefficients in 2000 of 57.1 (Chile) and 54.1 (Mexico).[2]

This chapter explores economic (market) reform policies and continuing development challenges as they relate to the evolution of leadership styles, strategies, and decisions. The heyday of market reform policies (Mexico, 1985–1995, and Chile, 1975–1988) witnessed remarkable similarities in leadership and decision-making styles, in both cases, but subsequent years have been characterized by growing criticisms on the social policy front and by reluctance to open up the policy process to wider civil society participation

HISTORICAL LEGACIES: PERSONAL POWER AND EXCLUSIONARY DECISION MAKING

Latin American leadership styles have been markedly hierarchical in nature; exclusionary processes of decision making have frequently characterized a variety of regime types in the region from military to electoral democracies. Even in electoral democracies, willingness on the part of both government leaders and opposition groups to negotiate, to compromise, and to make concessions has often been only weakly in evidence. As this chapter shows, hierarchical leadership styles have been shaped by both institutional and informal power arrangements constructed in the face of very difficult historical political challenges. Overcoming current political challenges over the long term, however, will probably require a more open policymaking approach. As the latter part of this chapter demonstrates, more open and conciliatory leadership styles are slow to emerge.

By the time economic reform projects were introduced in Chile and Mexico (Chile under military rule, 1973–1989, and Mexico under the Institutionalized Revolutionary Party, or PRI, 1985–1994), both countries were characterized by highly authoritarian political arrangements. But even though Mexico and Chile have since established themselves as electoral democracies, providing contexts that have challenged authoritarian leadership styles, exclusionary decision making has demonstrated considerable resiliency, even in the face of mounting pressure to open up the decision-making process to wider civil society participation. In Mexico, this pressure for the opening up of the policy process is coming from opposition parties in the legislature and from civil society; in Chile, it is coming largely from labor and from civil society.

Latin American political systems stand out for the high concentration of political power in the hands of the president. Generally absent has been an effective system of checks and balances by which the various branches of government could mitigate presidential power. Constitutionally sanctioned presidential decree powers, for example, have often served to substantially strengthen the ability of presidents to take policy initiatives and keep policies from being altered by the congress. But informal power arrangements have also been a predominant feature of Latin American politics, just as they have of other polities of the global south.[3] Perhaps the most important informal power arrangement is Latin America's variant of neopatrimonialism, known in the literature on Latin America as *caudillismo*.[4] This is a form of personal authority, not sanctioned by laws or institutions, of enormous importance in concentrating political power in the hands of political leaders. It has allowed presidents wide discretionary power, enabling them to flout laws, the congress, and other institutions such as the judiciary. Caudillismo (personal discretionary power lodged in the hands of the president), as we will see, became an important ingredient in the market reform process in both countries.

In Chile, market-liberalizing reform, put into place following the 1973 military coup, coincided with both a resurgent caudillismo *and* the institutionalization of heavily concentrated presidential power. The essential backdrop to this development was a political history that enormously reduced the space for political negotiation and compromise. Between 1965 and 1970, the ability and willingness of the presidents of the day to negotiate with their opposition declined as power contenders became increasingly mobilized. Highly contentious issues such as land reform and nationalization of privately owned copper companies came to sharply divide the left- and right-wing parties and the population, a context that eventually made negotiation and compromise impossible. At the same time, institutional developments such as the 1970 amendment to the constitution, giving constitutional status to the practice of presidential decree legislation, helped to bolster presidential power.[5] Seeing his socialist reform program blocked by congress and unable to negotiate a solution, socialist President Salvador Allende (1970–1973) further alienated political opponents by pushing through property expropriation laws via the questionable use of presidential decree power.[6] The military government, which overthrew Allende in 1973, immediately embarked on a mission of dismantling the state; it removed price controls, reduced tariffs, and privatized state companies. The "shock treatment" of 1975, involving steep trade liberalization, drastic cuts in government expenditure, deregulation of financial markets, and a stepped-up privatization program, was followed by privatization of the social security system and health care.

The extreme hierarchical nature of decision making under military rule took a few years to fully establish itself. The military regime began as a four-man military junta and, during the first year, consulted a variety of center-right civilian leaders on matters of policy. But Pinochet, aided by renewed economic crisis and increased inflation at the end of 1974, maneuvered himself into a position of predominance by first granting himself the title of President of the Republic and then, in 1978, securing the ouster from the junta of his strongest opponent, General Leigh, head of the air force and a proponent of an early return to civilian rule. The stage was set for economic decision making to fall into the hands of a cohesive cluster of decision makers that included Pinochet, a small group of technocrats known as the Chicago Boys,[7] and the executives of the country's three biggest conglomerates (the Edwards group, BHC [Mortgage Bank of Chile], and Cruzat-Larraín). These conglomerate executives were virtually the only members of civil society with access to the policy process prior to 1985, and they were also the major beneficiaries of the new economic program, buying up public companies at bargain basement prices and reaping the benefits of trade liberalization.[8] Meanwhile, the repressive apparatus of the state (and the fear and insecurity that repression created) denied opposition critics the opportunity to question or alter the market reform program. It was only as a consequence of the severe economic crisis of the early 1980s that the economic policymaking process opened up to a wider cross section of business interests.[9] But labor and civil society remained firmly excluded.

A crucially important aspect of the consolidation of power under Pinochet was his use of personal power. Although Chile's caudillo strain had receded in importance, it resurfaced with President Pinochet, for whom personal trust and loyalty were paramount prerequisites for government appointments.[10] Of crucial importance was Pinochet's use of personal power to ensure that the army, the branch of the military that was the most nationalistic and the most resistant to the Chicago Boys' market-liberalizing reforms, did not block the favored economic program. Pinochet moved quickly to clear out the old guard such that within three years of the coup, Pinochet loyalists monopolized all of the command positions. Then, particularly within the army, loyalty was rewarded with appointments to boards of public enterprises and public commissions, and defense spending soared by 30 percent in 1974 and by 44 percent in the second half of 1975 alone.[11] Ties of personal loyalty also bound the Chicago technocrats to the Pinochet leadership, helping to insulate economic policy makers from opposition critics[12]

But the highly closed policymaking process of the early period of military rule, dominated as it was by Pinochet's highly personalistic and closed decision-making style, had a number of long-lasting consequences. The failure to devalue the currency quickly enough in 1982 and the wholesale liberalization of financial markets—policies developed by Pinochet and the closed group of decision makers described above—made the economic crisis, when it hit, far deeper than it would otherwise have been.[13] With the collapse of the banking system in the early 1980s and the bailout of a number of the county's major banks, the public debt skyrocketed and was passed on to the Chilean taxpayer in the form of the "subordinated debt."[14]

The legacy of the period of military rule would be long-lasting and would help to shape leadership styles and decision making long after the return to civilian rule in 1990. The 1980 constitution, constructed to keep the new economic model in place, established institutional mechanisms that bolstered hierarchical decision making and helped to ensure that policy making would exclude civil society and rank-and-file party militants of the ruling alliance, both inside and outside of the congress. One of the most important provisions in this regard was the requirement for nine appointed senators, all of whom were appointed by Pinochet.[15] This arrangement made it possible for the political right in the congress, after the return to civilian rule, to block executive initiatives they did not like. Another important legacy of the military years, which constrained the power and policy impact of cabinet ministers, was the 1975 law giving the finance minister ultimate authority over all decisions with financial implications. Finally, the military years bequeathed a marked inequality of political power, one in which the private sector received privileged access to the state while other societal groups were excluded.

Mexico's exclusionary policymaking process and hierarchical leadership style arose from a combination of formal and informal political arrangements. Between 1940 and 2000, Mexico was ruled by the Institutionalized Revolutionary Party (PRI), which maintained what has been described as "the perfect dictatorship" through a combination of clientelist and corporatist political controls.[16] The key decision-making figure during most of that period was the president of the republic. Whereas the Chilean tendency toward hierarchical leadership styles and decision making was shaped by a history of political polarization, Mexico's stemmed from a struggle for political stability. Mexican presidents from 1917 to 1940 faced a host of challenges to their rule, particularly from the congress. The arrangements that arose out of those challenges set the stage for a highly exclusionary form of leadership and decision making over the next fifty years

A combination of legally sanctioned and meta-constitutional powers resulted in enormous power in the hands of the president. The 1917 constitution gives the president a variety of powers, including the power to initiate legislation; to veto legislation in its entirety or in part; definitive agenda-setting powers in the budget, including exclusive powers over expenditures; and extraordinary decree power in the case of emergencies, a power that has been used by presidents in situations that were not periods of emergency. Despite such powers, periodic wars emerged at the end of each succession struggle as incoming presidents were presented with fierce challenges from caudillo party leaders.[17] It was only when Lázaro Cárdenas (1934–1940) was able to defeat the caudillo leader of the party (Plutarco Elías Calles) and unite the positions of president of the republic and president of the party that political stability was firmly established. In this way, the Mexican presidency acquired a variety of powers not bestowed constitutionally, such as the power to appoint and remove state governors and to control the naming of all party candidates. This latter worked in concert with the prohibition on candidate reelection (instituted in 1940) to ensure presidential control of congress. Under these arrangements, legislators became tied to the president not only for their initial entry into the legislature but also for continued career advancement, either in the party or in the state bureaucracy, after their term in office ended. Indeed, the exchange of loyalty for material rewards was an arrangement that ensured loyalty and political control from the top to the bottom of the political system.[18]

The state bureaucracy also had marked authoritarian features. In addition, at the end of each term, state employees were cleared out in large numbers and replaced by loyal supporters of the new president and his team.[19] The most important source of recruitment of political leaders has been the *camarilla*, a network of public officials bound by

ties of strong personal loyalty to a camarilla leader. Although historically, the president headed up the "primary" camarilla, secondary camarillas were led by his closest associates. The dominant value of loyalty to
the camarilla leader ensured that bureaucratic teams usually did not
question (or debate) the policy preferences of their camarilla leader;
they saw their role not in terms of offering policy advice but, rather, in
terms of working toward and achieving the leaders' goals.[20]

The implementation of market reform in Mexico (1989–1994) coincided with a notable increase in what was already a hierarchical decision-making process, and as in the Chilean case, closed technocratic
decision making became the order of the day on matters of economic
policy reform. This situation was in contrast with the process prior to
1980, in which, although negotiation and concession were not generally present, Mexican presidents had become accustomed to making
themselves aware of the spectrum of viewpoints both within their cabinet and within the party.[21] In addition, more and more of the top political leadership was drawn from the government bureaucracy, especially
the finance ministry (rather than from the party), and most of these
new recruits sported graduate degrees, particularly in economics, from
US universities.[22] These Mexican technocrats were thrust into predominance by the 1982 debt crisis because of their purported economic know-how and their contacts with the multilateral lending
institutions. A clique of closely knit economists linked to Carlos Salinas de Gortari took over the key cabinet appointments once their leader
become president in 1989.[23] Very much like Chile's Chicago Boys, these
technocrats formed a tight, ideologically homogeneous group, bound
by personal friendship and with a sense of their own mission.

Although it was not dealt with as harshly as in the Chilean case,
labor was most certainly excluded from the policy process. Opposition
from within the state bureaucracy (which was considerable) was addressed through the removal of reform resisters. The prospect of intra-
state opposition was minimized through measures such as excluding all
but a select few cabinet ministers from economic policy making and by

handing over the responsibilities of the ministry of budget and planning to the finance ministry [24] As in the Chilean case, however, there was one group—the executives of the country's most important conglomerates—that was able to heavily influence the policy process. The already inordinate influence of this group on policy increased further during the Salinas years. It exercised enormous influence on policy, partly through formal channels and most notably through the Mexican Council of Businessmen (the MCHN), which had direct access to the cabinet. But ongoing personal contacts remained even more important.[25] As in the Chilean case, the owners of powerful conglomerates benefited from export promotion programs and were the purchasers of the privatized companies. By 1992, the country's most important financial, industrial, and service activities were in the hands of four conglomerates.[26] It was this closed and insulated decision-making process that drove market reform; indeed, the process was explicitly constructed that way to remove political obstacles that might slow down the reform process. A large number of companies were privatized, subsidies were eliminated, and a variety of trade agreements (including the North American Free Trade Agreement) were signed.[27]

Personalistic and concentrated decision making corrupted the privatization process; cronies of the president agreed to pay higher than market prices for public companies in exchange for monopoly market control. Here, just as in Chile, the combination of liberalization of the capital market and the inordinate personalized access of big conglomerate executives to the highest reaches of political power deepened the country's economic crisis. Once unregulated, the newly privatized Mexican banks borrowed heavily in dollars to take advantage of lower interest rates, lending out to their circle of industrial enterprises in pesos at higher rates, thereby producing, even prior to the collapse of the peso, a rise in nonperforming loans. Like Chilean technocrats, Mexican ones, under pressure from conglomerate interests holding debt in US dollars, resisted devaluation,[28] thus exacerbating the economic crisis when devaluation eventually occurred.

CHILE UNDER CONCERTACIÓN:
THE RESILIENCY OF HIERARCHICAL LEADERSHIP

The three civilian Concertación governments,[29] led by Presidents Patricio Alywin, Eduardo Frei, and Ricardo Lagos, which held power between 1990 and 2006, have all had to grapple with the social and political legacies of military rule. These administrations approached this task first by taking measures to deepen the neoliberal economic model. The country's civilian rulers liberalized trade; privatized the airlines, mining, electricity, and ports; sought new export markets; and kept a careful watch over government expenditures. The Concertación sought to address the legacy of poverty and inequality bequeathed by military rule[30] through increased social spending, reform of the labor code, and measures to equalize access to and quality of health care. As the following discussion will show, successive political leaders have found it very difficult to bring opposing sides together to find policy solutions to such challenges. Political leadership style and decision making have remained stubbornly exclusionary, a product of Chile's historical and policy contexts.

For the most part, decision making has remained firmly lodged in the hands of a small policy elite, one bound together by both policy commitment and loyalty. Congress, on the other hand, is generally weak; for example, it can only approve or reduce expenditures; it cannot increase or redistribute them. Because it has been dominated by the political right (for reasons explained in the previous section), negotiations with the congress, when they occurred, have been with the right-wing parties, while discussions with Concertación's own rank-and-file members of congress have often been minimal.[31]

The commitment of the country's political elite to the neoliberal economic model and their fear of its being undermined by "populist" pressures on expenditures are important factors in the resiliency of a closed policy process. The experience of the Popular Unity years (1970–1973) shaped the belief that high levels of political mobilization were harmful to both economic growth and poverty reduction, a notion that was reinforced by the more recent experiences of Peru and Argentina, where popular pressure and expectations had contributed to fiscal disequilibrium and inflation.[32] The fact that a commitment to this viewpoint and personal loyalty to the president were the criteria for cabinet appointments guaranteed a cohesive policy elite and reluctance to allow broader policy participation.

In addition to this, the top political leadership has shared a common set of characteristics (being highly trained in the social sciences) and a common source of recruitment (being largely drawn from the think tank CIEPLAN, the Corporation for Economic Research on Latin America).[33] Whereas a small group of ministers (the president, the secretary of the presidency, the minister of finance, the head of the Central Bank, the minister of public works, and the minister of labor) controlled macroeconomic policy under President Alywin, under the presidency of Eduardo Frei, macroeconomic policy came to rest almost exclusively in the hands of the finance minister and his technocratic team. Neither macroeconomic policy nor the nation's budget was discussed at the full cabinet level—a conscious decision designed to insulate economic policy makers from pressure within the cabinet to increase public spending. The 1975 law granting control over all financial matters to the minister of finance remained firmly in place. Thus it ensured the overwhelming predominance of the finance ministry and has been an important institutional support for this insulated policy process. As a consequence, finance ministry officials play a leading role in virtually all policy areas. The ministry became heavily involved in the development of social policy, linking up directly with officials of sectoral areas (such as health and education) in which it wished to see policy developed. Indeed, the role of the Social Planning Ministry (MIDEPLAN) declined through the 1990s, and at one point it was threatened with extinction.

At the same time, the private sector has continued to have privileged access to the policy elite through both institutionalized and personalized channels. Working commissions on economic policy, a yearly conference during which ideas on economic policy are exchanged, and monthly meetings with the head of the Central Bank have all given the private sector regular opportunities to press its point of view. Direct personal access to the president and cabinet ministers continued to be important; indeed, in 1996, business leaders claimed that business involvement in economic policy was greater under Concertación than it had ever been under military rule. Although tensions with the business community increased under President Lagos, business, generally, had high praise for economic policy under Concertación.[34]

However, this closed policy process was, by the mid-1990s, generating increasing tensions. Labor was particularly restive, given its exclusion from policy access and the failure of government reform of the labor code. Labor argued that the restrictive labor code contributed to labor's organizational weakness, undermining its ability to improve the living standards of workers, especially in the rural sector. Reform of the labor code in 1991 was deemed insufficient because collective bargaining above the firm level was possible only if management agreed. Another reform attempt was proposed in 1995 but was blocked by opposition from both the business community and the political right in the Senate, including opposition from the appointed senators. Strikes and demonstrations through the 1990s and growing criticisms from rank-and-file members of the Concertación, particularly members of the Socialist Party, reflected unhappiness with failure to reform the labor code, as well as opposition to the government's commitment to further privatizations.

Unrest among socialist rank-and-file militants within Concertación was reflected in the growing demand that the next Concertación presidential candidate be a socialist. The strength of society's demands was, however, mitigated by two factors. First, although labor protest among urban workers and miners was on the upswing, the once highly mobilized rural masses remained politically quiescent. Second, civil society organizations, though very active in the struggle for political transition, have had a lower profile on the political scene following the return to civilian rule. The subordination of civil society organizations to the political parties, which began in 1986 when the political parties took leadership of the democratic transition, is no doubt an important part of the explanation.[35] The "culture of fear" arising from the prolonged period of military rule is also cited as discouraging political involvement.[36] Finally, the fact that many grassroots organizations have become dependent on the government for funding to carry out training programs and establish micro-enterprises is viewed as another important reason for their withdrawal from activist politics.[37] The Concertación leadership takes the position that it is the elected representatives who should make policy, not civil society organizations or NGOs, because these, particularly the latter, can have very particular interests that are not necessarily related to broader societal needs.

The tensions arising from the closed leadership style described above gave rise, by 2000, to an initial commitment on the part of incoming Concertación president Ricardo Lagos (2000–2006) to a more inclusionary policy process and to leadership-mediated policy outcomes. Upon assuming power, Lagos also announced a reform of the labor code, equality-enhancing reforms to the health system, and a new program to end extreme poverty, known as *Chile Solidario.* He immediately set up a Social Dialogue Council (a tripartite bargaining council involving government, business, and labor) to reach a consensus on a new labor bill. He also established a new civil society consultative mechanism, the Citizens' Council, as part of his "Program for Strengthening the Alliances Between Civil Society and the State." Despite these efforts, however, his initial more inclusive leadership style came up against the deeply polarized positions that continue to characterize many policy areas in Chile. Two attempts to arrive at a consensus on labor reform through the Council of Social Dialogue failed. It was only in 2004, as economic growth returned and business profits shot up, that the government introduced a new labor bill that, it claimed, would distribute the benefits of economic growth more equitably by reducing the working day and regulating over-time pay.[38] This initiative, negotiated only with labor representatives, angered business.

Attempts to reform the health-care system have similarly fallen victim to polarized positions. The establishment of a two-tier system in health care under military rule, involving a private system for the well-off and a public system for the remaining 85 percent of the population, had produced a sharp deterioration of health services as middle- and upper-class financial contributions to public health were eliminated and government contributions dropped. In an attempt to equalize the quality of health care, the government proposal called for the establishment of a Solidarity Fund, to be funded by contributions from both the public and the private health-care systems. However, because this proposal entailed a reduction in the flow of funds to private health-care providers, it incurred the wrath not just of the private health-care companies but also of the private sector more generally.[39] Business and the political right eventually succeeded in having the Solidarity Fund removed from the legislation, while the socialist parties continued to campaign for its reinsertion.[40]

At the same time, little progress has been made in the area of civil society involvement in social policy. This administration, in the end, appears to have preferred an acquiescent civil society excluded from the policy-making process. One of the most telling cases of the state's rejection of civil society involvement in policy is that of its program to alleviate extreme poverty, Chile Solidario. In this case, senior officials in the Ministries of Finance and Social Planning developed the new policy. Senior officials flatly rejected the policy participation of societal organizations, even when World Bank funding for such consultations appeared to be forthcoming.[41] Furthermore, by 2003, the work of the Citizens Council, established by President Lagos at the beginning of his presidency, had ground to a halt when its recommendations for measures to strengthen civil society went unheeded and it failed to receive most of the funds it had been promised. Unsurprisingly, by 2003, civil society leaders were claiming to be virtually excluded from social policy.[42]

MEXICO UNDER VICENTE FOX:
THE FAILURE OF EFFECTIVE LEADERSHIP

In 1997 the PRI lost its control of congress. For the first time, the executive (President Ernesto Zedillo, 1995–2000) was forced to think about serious negotiations with opposition parties in the House.[43] But macroeconomic policy making remained in the executive (as did social policy) during the twilight years of PRI rule, while the private sector retained its privileged access to the highest reaches of political power. The national election of 2000 marked the country's transition to electoral democracy. For the first time ever, a non-PRI candidate, Vicente Fox, the candidate for the opposition "Alliance for Change" was elected president of Mexico and took office.

President Vicente Fox's lack of leadership success as illustrated by his failure to accomplish most of the original aims of his presidency— has been widely recognized. Certainly, assessments of ineffectiveness are heavily influenced by the very high expectations raised at the beginning of Fox's presidential term when the new president made too many difficult-to-keep promises: the eradication of corruption, an economic growth rate of 7 percent, and the creation of more than a million jobs per year. Without a majority in the congress,[44] bringing all those presidential policies to fruition would have required an outstanding willingness and ability to negotiate and compromise. Although the emergence of electoral democracy in Mexico was the key institutional ingredient shaping a less hierarchical policy process and forcing the president to discuss important legislation with the congress, the legacy of authoritarian leadership shows considerable resiliency, and strong executive resistance to a more inclusive policy-making process has remained in place.

Discussion of Fox's leadership is complicated by the fact that it was full of contradictions; for example, it combined personalism in government appointments with what appeared to be an attempt to make appointments based on expertise. Initially, at least, there seemed to be a genuine effort to incorporate a wide spectrum of opinions, including those of non-civil society organizations. Much of Fox's initial openness stemmed from the fact that many civil society organizations, including those on the political left, had played an important role in his election campaign. In the period leading up to the 2000 election, civil society organizations clamored for a hearing with the presidential candidates. In response, the Fox election campaign's social transition team established twenty working groups that in total came to involve the representatives of more than 3,000 organizations.[45] These groups would ultimately present policy proposals to the new government.

Once Fox was in power, well-known figures on the political left received top political appointments. Leftists Jorge Castañeda and Adolfo Zinzar were appointed minister of external relations and head of the super-ministry in charge of law and order, respectively,[46] while activists among the NGO community were appointed to important bureaucratic positions in the state.[47] However, Fox left the macroeconomic policy team largely intact: Francisco Gil Díaz, architect of Mexico's trade liberalization drive under the PRI, was appointed finance minister. One of the most powerful figures of the previous administration, Santiago Levy, was appointed head of the Mexican Institute of Social Security (IMSS) and retained considerable influence in the new administration, particularly in the area of social policy. At the same time, however, the country's most important conglomerates appeared to have obtained even greater access to top policy makers and particularly to the president. An unprecedented number of cabinet appointments (nine) went to individuals with experience in the private sector.[48] In addition, Fox has been personally linked to precisely those entrepreneurs who had benefited from the questionable bank rescue operation implemented by the previous PRI administration[49]—an operation that his own government made no attempt to investigate. Fox's business support remained selective and narrowly based.

President Fox proved himself unable to build a coalition in congress capable of getting his most cherished pieces of legislation passed. Indeed, the most innovative pieces of legislation addressing some of the main social challenges facing the country, passed during his administration, did not come from him at all. The Law for Social Development, which establishes independent evaluation for all social policies and restricts reductions in social spending, was instigated by the opposition parties in congress. The Law for the Support of Civil Society Organizations seeks to strengthen civil society by providing a legal framework and access to financing for civil society organizations. It originated in the civil society organizations themselves. And his flagship poverty alleviation program, Oportunidades (see below), originated in the previous PRI administration.

Fox failed to get congressional agreement to his tax reform proposal, and he resisted a compromise solution. On the one hand, the private sector fiercely resisted reforms that would have increased its revenue contribution, causing Fox to abandon an early proposal for a tax on wealth and property taxes.[50] Looking for a tax arrangement that would be palatable to business, Fox proposed a 15 percent value-added tax (VAT) on all goods, including food and medicine, despite the fact that these latter had previously been exempt. This new proposal was supported by the private sector but was defeated in congress, where the opposition spoke out strongly against the taxation of such essential items. Nevertheless, the president continued to insist on a VAT on food and medicine. Another policy goal pursued persistently despite the fact that nationalist elements in congress remain intractably opposed was the opening up of the energy sector to foreign capital investment.[51] Even though all parties agree on the need for reform of a highly inequitable and expensive social security system, the administration, refusing to budge from its commitment to an entirely privatized system, failed to initiate negotiations with congress, where the opposition PRD and PRI congressmen supported a mixed system.[52]

In addition, Fox's purported openness to the participation of civil society groups was questionable when it came to allowing actual influence on policy. This is particularly apparent in the way the government's Oportunidades program evolved. The program claimed to eliminate the political use of social programs in rural areas through a reliance on technocratic criteria for the handing over of small sums of money to the female heads of households in exchange for children's regular attendance at schools and at health clinics. In the years leading up to the 2000 election campaign, the program had generated enormous criticism; opponents alleged, for example, that the program omitted large numbers of poor both within and outside of targeted communities and that it generated intracommunity conflict and even violence. Leaders of civil society organizations were particularly critical of the fact that the program failed to allow any role for the community in the design of the program or in the distribution of resources, favoring instead a direct relationship between the federal government and the individual recipient.[53]

Mexican civil society organizations take the position that a viable strategy to overcome poverty and inequality must include the organization and strengthening of civil society groups and their involvement in policy. The proposals made by the Fox social policy transition team, emerging out of the broadly consultative process, reiterated these criticisms of Oportunidades and emphasized the importance of civil society participation and evaluation of the program.[54] Not only were most of these recommendations ignored, but the Fox administration rejected the World Bank's offer of $20 million to carry out a civil society consultation. The Fox administration also refused to accept Ford Foundation support for the same purpose. The stiffest resistance to civil society consultation came from the Finance Ministry.[55] Changes in Oportunidades were made by the Fox administration,[56] but these alterations did not include the incorporation of civil society groups in the evaluation or monitoring of the program, nor did the changes contemplate community involvement in the selection of beneficiaries—all demands made by civil society organizations. Further, none of the individuals on Fox's social policy transition team were later named to top government posts.

Even when civil society consultation was carried out, the president used his executive power to veto the negotiated agreement. The Intersecretarial Commission for Human Rights had been created in 1999 as a consequence of UN criticism of Mexico's human rights situation. This organization created working groups where extensive civil society consultations occurred. These extensive discussions produced, by early 2004, a consensus on a new human rights bill that included a number of key civil society demands such as an expanded concept of human rights (including the right to food, housing, health care, and labor rights) and the prohibition of discrimination against women. Before being sent off to congress, however, the president's legal office, which is supposed to confine its activities largely to the wording of bills, removed the new social rights that had been negotiated. Civil society leaders were deeply distressed by this turn of events; to them it indicated that although the president might be willing to go through the motions of civil society consultation, his heart was not in it. They concluded there was in fact no avenue through which they could effectively influence policy outcomes.[57] Congressional involvement in policy, on the other hand, expanded, as is illustrated by the passage of the two new laws on social policy and civil society organizations. But the effectiveness of these new pieces of legislation remains to be seen. Critics say that the executive continued to define social policy throughout the Fox years.[58] And although civil society organizations became stronger lobbying forces, they were not necessarily listened to.

CONCLUSIONS

Historical context and institutional development have shaped the evolution of leadership styles and forms of decision making in Latin America. Presidentialism—heavy concentration of political power in the hands of the president—is a common feature of Latin American countries. Moreover, it has often been supplemented by informal power arrangements—in particular, by Latin America's form of patrimonialism, known as *caudillismo.* In the two cases examined here, the experience of first-phase market reform involving sharp reversals of earlier statist arrangements (trade liberalization, privatization, and deregulation) entailed both institutionalized and informal mechanisms of power concentration, producing highly authoritarian and exclusionary forms of leadership and decision making. More striking, perhaps, are the similarities in leadership and decision-making styles between regimes that are otherwise distinct (military and one-party authoritarian). In both cases, strong leadership and concentrated forms of decision making undoubtedly facilitated the economic reform process by blocking the access of opposition critics to that process.

However, this analysis has pointed to ways in which such forms of decision making can be counterproductive, insulating decision makers from pressures and decisions that might mitigate the depth of economic crisis. Such concentrated and personalistic forms of decision making facilitated cronyism and corrupted the reform process. Moreover, market-liberalizing reforms have left in their wake social problems (poverty in the case of Mexico and ongoing inequality in both Mexico and Chile) that the market alone has not been able to solve. Policy solutions to these problems cannot be addressed without the building of a broad societal consensus around policy, because addressing such problems involves important redistributive measures (both taxation and spending) and therefore is likely to spark conflict that government must mediate. Leaders with authoritarian predispositions, or ones unduly influenced by groups that are already very powerful, are not in a position to resolve such disputes to the satisfaction of the general public. At the very least, such leaders and governments are in danger of losing legitimacy because of the appearance of bias. Moreover, it has become increasing clear that the involvement of civil society is important to the effectiveness of policy outcomes, particularly of social policy outcomes. More important, however, is the recognition that continued resistance to the increasing pressure for civil society involvement in policy is likely to erode both the support for and the effectiveness of government leadership. At the same time, it must be acknowledged that even the most well-meaning of Latin America's leaders face tough dilemmas. They usually rule deeply divided polities and have relatively scarce resources to distribute. In such contexts, mediating political solutions can be extremely difficult, even for strong, conciliatory, and flexible leaders.

NOTES

1. Comisión Económica para América Latina (CEPAL), *Panorama social en América Latina, 2002–2003: Anexo estadístico* (Santiago: CEPAL, 2003), 282.

2. United Nations Development Program (UNDP), *Human Development Report 2004: Cultural Diversity in Today's Diverse World* (New York: UNDP, 2004), 188–189.

3. On the interplay between various types of personal politics and formal institutions across regions, see Gretchen Helmke and Steven Livitsky, "Informal Institutions and Comparative Politics: A Research Agenda," *Perspectives on Politics* 2, 4 (2004): 725–740. Although they have specific historical contextual origins, similarities in the modern manifestations of specific types of informal politics are well documented, and it is widely recognized that patrimonialism and clientelism have had unhappy political and economic consequences in most countries of the global South. One of the classic works on this topic is Joel Migdal, *Strong Societies and Weak States: State-Society Relations and State Capabilities in the Third World* (Princeton, NJ: Princeton University Press, 1988). The exception to the generalization about the negative impact of personal discretionary politics is East Asia. In South Korea, for example, personalism and rent seeking were manipulated by an astute leadership to induce business to invest in export-led growth. On this see Yoon Je Cho, "Government Intervention, Rent Distribution and Economic Development in Korea," in Masahiko Aoki, Hyung-Ki Kim, and Masahiro Okuno-Fujiwara (eds.), *The Role of Government in East Asian Economic Development: Comparative Institutional Development* (New York: Clarendon Press, 1997), 208–231.

4. Caudillismo is usually traced to the experience of Spanish colonial rule, which was characterized by an omnipotent and absolutist monarch who exercised arbitrary authority and allowed access to unlimited wealth in exchange for loyalty. On this see Jacques Lambert, *Latin America: Social Structures and Political Institutions* (Berkeley: University of California Press, 1967), 149–166.

5. Julio Faundez, "In Defense of Presidentialism: The Case of Chile," in Scott Mainwaring and Matthew Soberg Shugart (eds.), *Presidentialism and Democracy in Latin America* (Cambridge: Cambridge University Press, 1997), 300–320.

6. Paul E. Sigmund, *The Overthrow of Allende and the Politics of Chile, 1964–1976* (Pittsburgh, PA: University of Pittsburgh Press, 1977), 206.

7. The term *Chicago Boys* refers to Chilean market reform proponents who studied economics at the University of Chicago as a consequence of an agreement signed between the University of Chicago and the Catholic University of Santiago.

8. On this see Eduardo Silva, *The State and Capital in Chile: Business Elites, Technocrats and Market Economics* (Boulder, CO: Westview Press, 1996).

9. Ibid.

10. Pamela Constable and Arturo Valenzuela, *A Nation of Enemies* (New York: W.W. Norton, 1991), 58.

11. Ibid.

12. Judith A. Teichman, *The Politics of Freeing Markets in Latin America: Chile, Argentina and Mexico* (Chapel Hill: University of North Carolina Press, 2001), 72.

13. Laura A. Hastings, "Regulatory Revenge: The Politics of Free Market Financial Reforms in Chile," in Stephan Haggard, Chung H. Lee, and Sylvia Maxfield (eds.), *The Politics of Finance in Developing Countries* (Ithaca, NY: Cornell University Press, 1993), 210–229.

14. Osvaldo Larrañaga, J. and Jorge Marshall, R., "Ajuste macroeconómico y finanzas públicas, 1982–1988," Programa de post grado de economía, ILADES (Georgetown: Georgetown University, 1990), 17.

15. The constitutional provision for the appointed senators was removed in June 2005.

16. Mario Vargas Llosa, quoted in Dan A. Cothran, *Political Stability in Mexico: The Perfect Dictatorship* (Westport, CT: Praeger, 1994), 55.

17. Jeffery Weldon, "Political Sources of *Presidencialismo* in Mexico," in Scott Mainwaring and Matthew Soberg Shugart, op. cit., 225–258.

18. A classic work on this topic is Frank Brandenburg, *The Making of Modern Mexico* (Englewood Cliffs, NJ: Prentice-Hall, 1964).

19. John Bailey, *Governing Mexico: The Statecraft of Crisis Management* (London: Macmillan, 1988), 78.

20. The author who has written most extensively on Mexican camarillas is Roderic Camp. See references below.

21. Peter Smith, *Labyrinths of Power* (Princeton, NJ: Princeton University Press, 1979), 14, 123.

22. Roderic A. Camp. "The Political Technocrat in Mexico and the Survival of the Mexican Political System," *Latin American Research Review,* 20 (1985): 97–119; and "Camarillas in Mexican Politics: The Case of the Salinas Cabinet," *Mexican Studies/Estudios Mexicanos* 6, 1 (1990): 85–107.

23. Ibid.

24. Judith A. Teichman, *Privatization and Political Change in Mexico* (Pittsburgh, PA: University of Pittsburgh Press, 1996), 77.

25. Teichman, *The Politics of Freeing Markets in Latin America,* 145.

26. Teichman, *Privatization and Political Change,* 187.

27. The initial, most important trade liberalization had occurred in 1985 and under the previous administration, when quantitative restrictions and tariffs were reduced.

28. Confidential author interviews with two former senior-level government officials in Mexico, 1999.

29. The most important parties in the Concertación alliance are the Christian Democratic Party (PDC) and two socialist parties: the Socialist Party (PS) and the Popular Party for Democracy (PPD).

30. Whereas the percentage of poor families stood at 28.5 percent in 1970, that figure reached 56.9 percent in 1980 and 48.7 percent in 1987. Income distribution also became more unequal, and private consumption dropped. See Sebastian Edwards and Alejandra Cox Edwards, *Monetarism and Liberalization: The Chilean Experiment* (Cambridge: Ballinger, 1987), 162; and Eugenio Ortega R., "Los pobres y la sobrevivencia," in Eugenio Ortega R. and Ernesto Tironi B. (eds.), *Pobreza en Chile* (Santiago: Centro de Estudios del Desarrollo, 1988), 25–47.

31. For a discussion of this process as it pertained to tax reform, see Delia Boylan, "Taxation and Transition: The Politics of the 1990 Chilean Tax Reform," *Latin American Research Review,* 31 (1996), 7–36.

32. Confidential author interviews with three senior-level government officials in Santiago, 1996.

33. Patricio Silva, "Technocrats and Politics in Chile: From the Chicago Boys to the CIEPLAN Monks," *Journal of Latin American Studies* 23 (1991), 385–410.

34. Confidential author interviews, Santiago, 1996.

35. Philip Oxhorn, *Organizing Civil Society: The Popular Sector and the Struggle for Democracy in Chile* (University Park: Pennsylvania State University Press, 1995).

36. James Petras and Fernando Ignacio Leiva, *Democracy and Poverty in Chile* (Boulder, CO: Westview Press, 1994), 92.

37. Julia Paley, *Marketing Democracy: Power and Social Movements in Post-Dictatorship Chile* (Berkeley: University of California Press, 2001).

38. "Gobierno envía proyecto que regula pago de horas extras," *La Tercera,* Martes 5 de octubre de 2004, http://www.tercera.cl.

39. Gonzalo Ibañez, "El problema de la salud es de gestión y no de financiamiento," *Estrategia,* 10 de abril de 2002, http://www.estrategia.cl. "Plan Auge: de la teoría a la práctica," *La Tercera,* 30 de agosto de 2004, http://www.LaTercera.cl.

40. Confidential author interviews with three senior government officials and four leaders of NGOs, Santiago, 2003.

41. Confidential author interviews with four civil-society leaders, Santiago, 2003.

42. As a consequence, between that election and the national election of 2000, economic policies were tampered with in ways that were unheard of in the past. Interfering in the executive's budget by legislating a tax cut; refusing to support the executive's bank rescue operation and demanding that it be audited; and refusing to agree to further privatizations are some of the ways in which congress thwarted executive wishes under the last PRI president.

43. An important social policy developed under President Zedillo, Progresa (Education, Food and Health Program), was renamed Oportunidades and expanded under Fox. The program was developed by a small group of technocrats and imposed by Zedillo upon a very reluctant Social Policy ministry.

44. Under Fox, no party controlled either house.

45. Cecilia González, "ONG, Entre el escrutinio y el acceso a recursos," *Reforma,* 13 Noviembre 2000, http://busequedas.gruporeforma.com.

46. Both later resigned.

47. Cecilia Loria, senatorial candidate for the left PRD in 1997 and an activist on NGOs involved in women's issues, was appointed head of INDESOL, the government agency responsible for allocating funds to NGOs. The former

head of the NGO Alianza Civica, Rogelio Gomez Hermosillo, was appointed head of Oportunidades.

48. Judith Teichman, "Private sector power and market reform: Exploring the domestic origins of Argentina's meltdown and Mexico's policy failures," *Third World Quarterly* 23, 3 (2002), 491–511.

49. Juan Manuel Venegas y Enrique Méndez, "No se indagaraon los antecedentes de invitadosa la gira de Fox: Sahagún, *La Jornada,* 4 de agosto 2000, http://www.jornada.unam.mx.

50. Currently in Mexico, fiscal revenue represents just 11.6 percent of GDP, far below the 20 percent collected in Chile and Argentina; in the United States, the figure is 30 percent of GDP. Tim Weiner, "Roadblocks Right and Left for Mexico's President," *Information Services Latin America, Mexico,* January 22, 2001, 1.

51. The issue is more complicated than might appear on the surface and involves other issues where negotiation and compromise might help alleviate the situation. Seventy-seven percent of the earnings of the state petroleum company, PEMEX, goes to the government in taxes, a fact that has contributed enormously to its current liabilities. The ability to impose other sources of tax revenue would obviously make possible a reduction of PEMEX's tax contribution and free up revenues for its own investment.

52. Confidential author interviews with four members of congress, Mexico City, 2004.

53. See, for example, Julio Boltvinik and Fernando Cortés, "La indentificación de los pobres en el Progresa," in Enrique Valencia Lornelí, Mónica Gendreau, and Ana María Tepchín Valle (coords.), *Los dilemas de la política social. ¿Cómo combatir la pobreza?* (México D.F.: Universidad Iberomericana, 2000), 31–59; and Manuel Canto Chac, "Política social y sociedad civil: La participación de los organizaciones civiles en la política social," ibid., 369–380.

54. Confidential author interviews with two members of the Fox transition team, Mexico City, 2004.

55. Fear of "populist pressures" was one important reason. Continued opposition also stemmed from the fact that the Finance Ministry wished to maintain its exclusive position as interlocutor with the bank. Confidential author interviews with two senior-level officials and two NGO leaders, Mexico City, 2004.

56. The program was maintained largely because of a very positive evaluation from the International Food Policy Institute based in Washington. Changes in the program under Fox include expansion of the program to cover all qualified candidates in the rural sector and expansion into the urban sector with a large loan from the Interamerican Development Bank to do so.

57. The information in this paragraph comes from three confidential author interviews with leaders of civil-society organizations, Mexico City, 2004.

58. There is some fear, for example, that the definition of what constitutes "social" expenditure might be manipulated by the executive in order to get around the limit on reducing social expenditure. Confidential author interviews with two opposition members of congress, Mexico City, 2004.

8

BACKWARDS AND IN HIGH HEELS:
NGO LEADERSHIP IN ASIA

Ian Smillie

The Asian nongovernmental organization (NGO) movement has grown dramatically in the last thirty years, from a limited number of welfare-type operations to tens of thousands of organizations, some of them today the largest and most dynamic in their field. Some of these NGOs have been intimately involved in the democratization movements of the Philippines, Indonesia, and Thailand. NGOs initiated the women's movement in Asia, especially in Muslim countries such as Indonesia and Bangladesh; they have been at the forefront of the environmental movement; and they have challenged governments on a wide range of governance issues, from human rights and democracy to basic understandings of effective service delivery. Asian NGOs pioneered micro-credit, today an accepted worldwide approach to poverty reduction. They have been at the forefront of innovations in basic education, public health, and experiments in the production of generic pharmaceuticals.

They have challenged some of the largest bilateral and multilateral development projects in their countries: the Narmada Dam project in India and the Pak Moon Dam project in Thailand. Though not always successful in these challenges, NGOs have caused governments and donors to reappraise their efforts with a more critical eye. Much admired, frequently vilified, and usually misunderstood, NGOs are often confused with the larger phenomenon of "civil society," and the more visible among them are identified solely with their leadership—in particular with the founder-leader.

This chapter explores the leadership phenomenon in Asian NGOs. Leadership is frequently discussed from a here-and-now perspective. A snapshot is taken of the institution in question, and it is then given a forensic analysis, often with little appreciation of history and context. This chapter is written almost exclusively from the perspective of history and context, because it is time and events, culture, economics, external influences, and politics that have shaped the quite remarkable Asian NGO phenomenon and its leadership.

HISTORICAL CONTEXT

Much ink has been spilled in recent years on the subject of Asian NGOs, although considerably less has dealt with their leadership. Until the mid-1980s, NGOs were seen largely as do-gooders: social service agencies that acted as a substitute for or alternative to government, or even to the market. From a theoretical point of view, NGOs are viewed as a product of governmental absence or failure, and/or of the failure of the market to fill in gaps. Nongovernmental organizations, for example, might build schools where there are none. They might also develop curriculum, and they might find, manage, and pay teachers. This was as true of community groups on the American prairie in the nineteenth century as it is of a more formalized NGO in today's Philippines.

NGOs, in Asia and anywhere else in the world, often begin through community-based voluntarism, small inchoate self-help activities, frequently of a welfare nature. In time, the effort may become institutionalized, often out of necessity. In the school example, government may standardize the curriculum. It may demand a degree of professionalization, setting criteria for teachers, and it will sooner or later become involved in some aspects of funding the educational system. In a welfare state, government may take over all aspects of education: schools, curriculum, teachers, and funding. In some cases, however, it may allow a degree of nongovernmental participation, on philosophical or ideological grounds, or because the cost of running an entire educational system is beyond the financial and managerial resources of the state.

Theoreticians have created typologies of NGOs flowing from this sort of model. In the first rank are those that form to provide a welfare service, often in a single community: the one-room school in the Old West, a poorhouse in medieval France, a village fund for widows and orphans in Taiwan. There are tens of thousands of organizations such as this, all over the world. They are not a new phenomenon; they find their wellspring in human nature and in the teachings of almost every religion. The Babylonian Code of Hammurabi spoke of justice for the poor; the Confucian code of ethics, based on goodness, benevolence. and love for all, dates from the sixth century B.C. A core value of Buddhism is the reduction of greed; Hinduism teaches that doing good works leads to salvation and release from the endless cycle of rebirth. Jewish law, Greek philosophy, Christianity, and Islam all encourage good works and giving.

Historically, however, the religious ideal of *help* was largely personal and individual, as in the tale of the Good Samaritan. It rarely involved organizations, and this is one of the great challenges in moving from traditional to modern philanthropy.

Charity and *ad hoc* activities, of course, are not enough to deal with the problems that some communities face, especially in developing countries. Some community-based organizations discover in time that there are others like them and that the problems they face are systemic rather than village-based. With the right kind of leadership, an organization can grow from a simple idea, or something originally bound by time and geography, into a wider enterprise. A Quaker group in Britain organized something called the Oxford Famine Relief project, sending food to Greek famine victims during World War II. Its organizers realized that famine was not unique to Greece, however, and, shortening the name, they became Oxfam. Oxfam soon learned that the need for the relief of famine might be reduced if famine could be prevented in the first place. And so it began to work in *development*—teaching people to fish rather than the proverbial handing out of fish. All of today's big international NGOs started as relief operations: Save the Children, CARE, Foster Parents Plan, World Vision. And all moved on to much greater investments in development.

So it is with many of today's development NGOs in Asia. Many of the most professional began as small welfare initiatives, or temporary relief operations, following an earthquake or a civil conflict. Many of the strongest health, education, and women's NGOs in Bangladesh, for example, emerged directly from the 1970 cyclone and the liberation war with Pakistan.

State and market "failure"—or, rather, the absence of the state and weaknesses in the market—supply one explanation for the creation of NGOs. Another emerges from what might be called "*voluntary* failure." A weak voluntary ethic can allow the state to co-opt or bypass what might otherwise be—or what might otherwise have become—a vibrant nongovernmental community. When the state falters, however, organizations form. Some of them live and work as a kind of underground, as was the case during the waning years of the Marcos regime in the Philippines. In other cases they simply fail to develop. Indonesia's anti-Communist bloodletting took the lives of between 150,000 and 500,000 people in 1965 and 1966 and led to the creation by the Suharto government of what was called the "New Order" and a state ideology called *Pancasila*. *Pancasila* was based on five principles: one God, a just and civilized society, national unity, democracy, and social justice. With the exception of the first, each of these principles bore a unique Indonesian stamp, characterized by an absence of most of the basics of a democratic society. With the benefit of oil money, Suharto was able to impose his New Order in ways that integrated all forms of social and political endeavor under state control, leaving little room for NGO development activity and no room whatsoever for a discussion of alternatives.

This "discussion of alternatives" represents a second dimension to the NGO phenomenon and, more widely, to civil society itself. "Civil society" comprises the bodies that lie between the state and the market: professional associations, trade unions, advocacy groups, consumer organizations, and organizations that provide welfare and development services. The term *civil society* derives from the writings of Hegel, Gramsci, and de Tocqueville and had been used by more recent writers,[1] but it was not until the publication of Robert Putnam's 1993 study of governance in Italy that ideas about civil society's role in the promotion of democracy and good governance began to gel. *Making Democracy Work: Civic Traditions in Modern Italy* found, through a detailed analysis of five hundred years of documented Italian history, that it was civic institutions and what Putnam called "social capital" that made the difference between democracy and good governance in the north of the country, and their absence in the south.

The idea quickly resonated with development writers and practitioners concerned about governance and democracy in poor countries. Soon books, studies, and tracts on civil society had become commonplace. Courses on civil society sprang up at the London School of Economics, Johns Hopkins University, Yale, and dozens of other universities. Definitions and descriptions proliferated, grouping civil society organizations into various conceptual clusters: civil society as a collective noun, civil society as a space for action, civil society as a historical moment, civil society as anti-hegemony, civil society as an antidote to the state.[2] Civil society was *expected* to speak out and to hold governments accountable for their action or lack thereof. *Give a man a fish; teach a man to fish*—the old saying has a nice ring to it, but teaching a man to fish may not be enough. He may have no access to equipment or credit; he may be unable to compete with commercial firms; he may not be able to sell what he catches, or he may catch nothing at all because the fishery has been destroyed by overfishing or pollution. "Teaching" may not be enough. Who will *speak* for the fisherman? Who will organize fishing families to speak for themselves?

These new ideas about civil society cast Asian NGOs in a fresh light, one characterized by deepening discord and protest across the region. The idea of civil society advocacy, of course, is not new. Nor is it new even to the more narrow types of organizations defined here as NGOs. The Anti-Slavery Society, founded in 1787, provided a wide variety of welfare services for freed slaves, but its lasting legacy is the work it did to end slavery entirely. European and North American organizations working with the handicapped provide a wide variety of services to their clientele. But a large part of their work has to do with advocacy: pushing, campaigning, lobbying for the rights of the blind, the deaf, and those who are otherwise physically or mentally challenged. This is not a new idea in the West. And although such campaigning has included moments of real violence—around labor issues, for example, and the women's movement—it is not usually regarded in the West today as especially threatening, even when civil society comprises organizations such as the National Rifle Association.

But in Asia it has been different. The Suharto regime, pushed to the economic wall by the Asian economic meltdown of 1997, collapsed unexpectedly under the weight of its own corruption. Until then, the space for an NGO voice was highly constrained. In Malaysia, a quasi-democratic regime managed to co-opt much of the NGO voice and to characterize those venturing beyond welfare activities as political and even anti-state activists. In Singapore the state was even more constraining of NGOs until recently. Even now, NGO activity is guided by a Societies Act that requires organizations to register under, and comply with, the government's highly discretionary interpretation of peace, welfare, and good order. Foreign funding may be denied to NGOs deemed by government to be "political associations," a tricky situation for environmental and human rights organizations, and even for those that might be inclined to speak out on behalf of society's weaker elements.

In Thailand, the space for NGO and civil society advocacy has grown, but not without a series of violent incidents, beginning with a student uprising against the country's authoritarian regime in 1973, a period of continuing violence, and a return to authoritarianism in 1976. Violence erupted again in 1992 and was followed by the creation of a constitutional government and greater space for legitimate dissention. In Thailand, Indonesia, and the Philippines, governmental fear of protest during the 1970s was very much rooted in a fear of Communism. The Cold War, in its grave now for the better part of a generation, may seem like a quaint historical relic, but the violence used to suppress the Communist Party of Indonesia was far from quaint. Fear of the Communist Party of Thailand was alive and well through the 1960s and 1970s, when the government there foresaw the very real possibility of Thailand's becoming one more in a series of tumbling dominoes.

In the Philippines, the Maoist New People's Army (NPA) had 1,000 regulars in 1972, and Maoist youth groups were thought to have as many as 100,000 members. It is not surprising that President Marcos, never a great proponent of democratic dissent, could not distinguish—or did not bother to distinguish—between the voice of reasonable dissent and that of its growing and much more radical sibling. Things did not change much until 1986, however, when the blunt instruments of police violence, assassination, mass arrest, and martial law finally encouraged the Catholic Church to side openly with street protestors. Dorothea Hilhorst discusses in painful depth the radicalization of small Philippine NGOs in the country's northern Cordillera region around protests, in the mid-1970s, over a series of proposed hydroelectric dams on the Chico River.[3] Here the issue was one of NGO co-optation not by government but by the underground National Development Front, the Communist Party of the Philippines, and various affiliated hard-left organizations. Their influence was carried forward with considerable success into the women's movement in the 1980s and beyond. Even with the flight of Marcos and the advent of constitutional democracy, it would take years for an ideologically fractured civil society to come to terms with a reality in which providing services to the poor, for example, was not seen by some NGOs as selling out to government or to "imperialistic" foreign donors.

In a completely different context, it is perhaps not surprising that the government of Vietnam has allowed few societal organizations beyond the control of the state and the party, nor is it surprising that the Myan-mar generals have done the same. Further west in South Asia, however, despite often draconian government efforts to control NGOs and civil society, there has been a flourishing over the past four decades that is lit-tle short of remarkable. In Sri Lanka there are said to be as many as 60,000 NGOs. Pakistan, a late bloomer, has nevertheless developed a respectable cadre of NGOs, mostly since the 1980s, working on a wide range of issues: the environment, economic development, women's is-sues, and human rights. IUCN, one of the largest international envi-ronmental organizations, has its biggest program in Pakistan, devised and managed exclusively by Pakistanis. The Aga Khan Rural Support Program in the Northern areas has spawned a variety of independent clones throughout the country, and despite Pakistan's conservative reli-gious background and its poor record on democracy and human rights, its women's movement has made considerable strides.

There is no simple or reliable way to report the numbers of Asian NGOs. Each country has different registration procedures and defini-tions. In Korea, where the growth has been tremendous since democra-tization in 1987, there were more than 11,000 registered "third sector organizations" by 1998, including civic groups, cultural institutions, en-vironmental NGOs, and foundations. The Korean NGO directory listed 730 nationwide organizations, although this number contains no breakdown as to size or activity.[4] Similar problems prevail in other countries, with aggregate numbers saying little about size, quality, or areas of work: Thailand, 18,000 organizations; Philippines, as many as 100,000, of which one-third are cooperatives; Taiwan, 12,825 "mem-bership organizations" listed in 1997, up from 4,217 in 1981.[5] Indone-sian lists speak of tens of thousands of cooperatives and community organizations, along with thousands of "self-reliant organizations" and "nonprofit organizations."

The Official Website of the Malaysian Registry of Societies wel-comes the visitor, instilling the hope that the site will be informative. It is not. The most recent information dates from 1998, when there were 29,574 "societies" registered. "This," the registrar says, "imposes a tremendous strain on the limited resources that are at the disposal of the Department." He goes on to conclude his welcome by saying that "Peace, security, public order, good behaviour and morality must be maintained at all times, without compromise."[6]

Huge numbers of NGOs are cited for India. A 2005 study found that there were between 20,000 and 30,000 working in some way on development with the poor and marginalized,[7] but the Planning Commission of India lists a smaller number on its website: 16,430.[8] Although each one of them has a searchable entry, many contain little or no information beyond the organization's name. This paucity of concrete information would be true of most other Asian countries, if one were to dig into the numbers. Many of the organizations are small, village-based efforts. Some have been formed to gain access to a particular state funding initiative; many are probably dormant, and others plug along as best they can with limited means and experience. In all countries the numbers of those that work in more than a handful of villages are a tiny fraction of the whole, and those that might be considered "national" in scope would probably number in the tens rather than the hundreds.

It is Bangladesh, however, that has been most surprising in the growth of NGOs. From a time before 1970 when there were virtually no NGOs of a recognizable modern hue, today there are, as in India or the Philippines, thousands. In fact the estimates range from 200,000 to an almost astronomical 770,000.[9] Several are national in scope, and a few have become very large, counting their village initiatives in the thousands and their beneficiaries in the millions. The Asian Development Bank estimates that during the 1990s, Bangladeshi NGOs working in the field of micro-credit made loans of a billion dollars among 3.5 million people, 80 percent of whom were women.[10] It is here in Bangladesh that the discussion of leadership will start, because Bangladesh, an impoverished country fraught with political turmoil for much its brief life, has in many ways become the leader in Asian NGO development.

THE GURU SYNDROME AND
ORGANIZATIONAL CULTURE

Many of the largest and most successful Asian NGOs today are associated in the public mind almost exclusively with the founder-leader: Sarvodaya's Ariyaratne in Sri Lanka, Muhammad Yunus, founder of the Grameen Bank in Bangladesh, Mechai Viravaidya of the Population and Community Development Association in Thailand. These individuals, and many others like them, are often described as "charismatic" leaders who benefit from a traditional Asian deference to authority. Their style is sometimes described by observers as guru-like, and some of them have been accused of encouraging personality cults, of dominating their organizations, and of failing to adapt to changing circumstances.

These characteristics certainly exist in some NGO leaders, and not only those in Asia. Similar characteristics can also be found in the business world, but they are seldom associated with sustained commercial success if they are the sole attributes of the leader. The same is true in the Asian NGO world. In fact, the "guru syndrome" is little more than a caricature. Successful Asian NGOs could never have grown up in the harsh national political climates of the 1970s, 1980s, and 1990s on the basis of mercurial leadership alone. Poverty-stricken villagers do not long remain in thrall to organizations that offer little more than charismatic leadership. And contrary to the perceptions of some critics, money—whether it comes from Northern NGOs or from bilateral, multilateral, or local government agencies—does not grow on trees and cannot be conjured up or long sustained by charisma alone.

In fact the guru syndrome is largely a fiction imagined by outsiders, most of them Northern donors, journalists, and academics who promote the guru idea through their own behavior. Many engage almost exclusively with the executive director of the NGO in question and with a very limited number of others at the top of the organization. One of the reasons for this is that they want to communicate with the leadership directly. From a management point of view, this may be important; from a financial point of view, if you are a donor, it may be essential. Another reason is simple practicality: it is often only those at the top who are fluent in English, the language of international donorship and much development writing. And the leader, after all, *is* the spokesperson for the organization.

Outsiders, however, are rarely privy to internal management systems, debates, and ructions. They cannot always be expected to understand the political, cultural, and managerial pressures an NGO leader faces. They usually encounter a fully formed organization, and unless they have had a long-time acquaintance (almost never the case among those who work for donor organizations), they have seen little of the NGO's evolution or the transformation of its leader from social entrepreneur to apparent guru. This is not to say that successful Asian NGO leaders have no charisma, but charisma develops with the organization and with organizational culture. And organizational culture develops over time, in the way people work together and in the shared experience of the struggle to help a project or the organization itself succeed. Organizational values are important to the development of a shared culture. For most NGOs and their staff, these have their basis in ideas about human rights, equity, and justice. They may be articulated in a mission statement—almost *de rigueur* in recent years—but they are most often and best espoused in what the staff of an NGO believe. This in turn may be articulated not so much in words as in the way staff members are treated, and in the way they are expected to treat the organization's intended beneficiaries.

Organizational symbols, ritual, and stories are an important part of organizational culture. They can be the glue that holds an organization together, they serve an orientation function for new staff, and they may contribute to perceptions of charisma in the leadership. As noted earlier, many Asian NGOs grew out of conflict—the liberation war in Bangladesh; the democracy movements in Indonesia, Thailand, and the Philippines; the women's movement; and environmental struggles such as the Pak Moon and Narmada Dam projects in Thailand and India. Sometimes the "stories" are more personal. After visiting an Indian NGO in the 1940s, Ghandi insisted on an invoice for his meal and accommodation, a story the NGO tells to this day as a message about responsibility and free rides. Building Resources Across Communities (BRAC) employees tell a similar story about the founder of their organization, Fazle Hasan Abed, who once arrived home from a field trip to a fisheries project to find the gift of a large fish in the trunk of his car. He sent a strong note back, insisting on a bill. BRAC staff tell stories of the first time its women field workers drove motorcycles, then a culturally daring and possibly even dangerous undertaking. And they recall the time when President Clinton's visit to a BRAC village was canceled on security grounds at the last moment, requiring half the village to be bussed to the American embassy instead. Struggle, admonishment, risk, humor—all have a part to play in the evolution of organizational culture and in perceptions of leadership.

Few of today's large and successful NGOs, in Asia or anywhere else, sought to become large or famous. All, of course, wanted to succeed, but size and fame were rarely part of the motivation. The Red Cross, first conceived amid the carnage on the battlefield at Solferino in 1859, did not foresee its becoming a global movement for many years. The first Oxfam shipments to Greece in 1942 did not look like the start of a major international NGO, any more than the first CARE packages to Germany did in 1946. The small group of Bangladeshi activists who started BRAC in 1971 saw it as a temporary activity, dealing only with a short-term emergency. None, not even the organization's founder-leader, Fazle Hasan Abed, envisioned an organization that would have a 2004 income the equivalent of US$173 million, 75 percent of it self-generated.

In financial terms, BRAC is certainly the largest NGO in Bangladesh. It is almost five times bigger than Grameen Bank (which in any case insists that it is a bank, not an NGO), and its lending portfolio alone is 20 percent larger than Grameen's.[11] In financial terms BRAC is also undoubtedly the largest NGO in the developing world, and in real terms its income is comparable to many of the biggest international NGOs. It has expanded its operations to Afghanistan and East Africa and has provided technical assistance to organizations and governments as diverse as Vietnam and UNICEF. In 2004 its income was almost the same as that of the International Federation of Red Cross and Red Crescent Societies, and although its budget is smaller than those of several large transnational NGOs, its spending power is probably comparable to most.[12]

SPECIFIC CONTEXT

It is perhaps worth considering why so many NGOs and community-based organizations have developed in Bangladesh, and why a handful have risen to such regional and international prominence. Where NGOs are concerned, Bangladesh began with the same history as Pakistan, yet within ten years of its independence in 1971, the old-fashioned welfare organizations that characterized the *ante bellum* Pakistani voluntary sector had been left behind by a throng of vibrant young activist organizations. It took another two decades for a similar generation of Pakistani NGOs to emerge. In India, the NGO sector is large, and its roots are deeper than those in Pakistan and Bangladesh, but Indian NGOs have generally been overshadowed by the achievements and growth of their Bangladeshi counterparts, despite the fact that India has eight times the population.

One possibility might be the national Bangladeshi character, but this was not significantly different before and after 1971. Nor is the answer likely to be cultural, given that India's 85 million Bengalis have not created anything like a BRAC, a Proshika, or a Grameen Bank. Nor is the answer to be found in religion, at least not in a comparison between Pakistan and Bangladesh. Most of the answers have to do with context. In the early 1970s, the needs in Bangladesh were great, and they have not significantly diminished. As many as a million Bangladeshis died in the war that gave the country birth. Ten million more became refugees, and when they went home, they returned to lives of destitution. Neither the new government nor the hundreds of international aid agencies that arrived with unprecedented levels of funding were even remotely able to meet the challenge. Not surprisingly, the independence movement had spawned a cadre of young activists who wanted to help rebuild their communities or in some way contribute to the creation of their new country. The drive and energy of the young people who formed the core of the first NGOs—after independence NGOs—were striking.

Donor funding was, of course, available, but not in great amounts for untested Bangladeshi NGOs. In fact the idea of funding local NGOs in developing countries anywhere was still in its infancy at that time. Organizations such as BRAC, Gonoshasthaya Kendra, and Proshika were, however, able to obtain funding in the early 1970s, in part because they proved their bona fides quickly, but also because the international agencies that supported them had no grassroots programming capacity in a country that had—as a part of Pakistan—been largely ignored.

As the new NGOs began to prove themselves, funding possibilities grew, as did they themselves. The sheer volume of donor funding, therefore, does set Bangladesh apart from India and Pakistan. There are other factors, however. One is the unified nature of the Bangladesh government. The federal structures in India and Pakistan add a layer of governmental bureaucracy and control that has undoubtedly been inhibiting to NGO growth. And despite its efforts to control NGOs, the Bangladesh government has, with the occasional lapse, never imposed the draconian generic constraints that have occasionally characterized state, provincial, and national behavior in India and Pakistan. The size of the country is also a factor: Bangladesh is relatively small, and despite serious communications problems, most areas are accessible from Dhaka in less than a day. Another, more important factor is related to cultural and economic homogeneity. Over 90 percent of the population shares the same language, the same religion, the same traditions. And although there are great economic disparities between the haves and the have-nots, the wide feudal disparities inherent in Indian or

Pakistani society are largely absent. In Bangladesh, only 7 percent of the population own more than two hectares of land, and owning four hectares defines a major landholder.

Finally, because poverty is so deep and so widespread, and because it is not greatly dissimilar from one part of the country to the next, it has been possible to replicate health or education or agricultural programs from one village to the next without having to alter them dramatically in response to linguistic, cultural, religious, or social considerations. The process of group mobilization can be similar throughout the country, an impossibility in either India or Pakistan.

MANAGING THE EXTERNAL ENVIRONMENT

An essential quality in the leadership of any Asian NGO that hopes to survive is an ability to understand, manage, and endure in the external environment. Some Bangladeshi leaders have done this well, but others have not. The paragraphs above provide an overview of the historical context, but they give few specifics of what this might mean to an NGO. A constant challenge for most Asian NGOs is deciding how close a relationship they want with government. In Thailand and the Philippines during the 1970s, some were distinctly anti-government, whereas Indonesian NGOs that hoped to survive during those years had to work overtly *with* government, regardless of the personal views of the leadership.

Defying logic and prediction, Bangladesh—which had a 10-million-ton annual food deficit in the 1970s—has today become largely self-sufficient in rice and wheat, even though the population has doubled. Bangladesh has reduced child mortality, has eradicated polio, and enjoyed annual GDP growth rates averaging 5 percent during the late 1990s and early 2000s. Despite a stormy political history, the country has been governed by a parliamentary democracy since 1990. Emerging from a conservative Muslim tradition, women have taken an increasingly important role in society, and both prime ministers since 1991 have been women. These are remarkable achievements that few among even the most optimistic would have dared to predict thirty years before.

But there is another side to Bangladesh. It is the most densely populated country in the world. Half of the population lives in abject poverty, and despite its remarkable agricultural track record, the prospects for the 240 million people who are likely to live in Bangladesh by 2020 are not hopeful. Donors optimistically say that with good public policies, strengthened institutions, and sustained levels of growth, some of the UN's Millennium Development Goals could actually be met in Bangladesh by 2015.

But Bangladesh does not have good public policies, strong institutions, or the level of growth that will be needed. The parliamentary democracy that followed twenty years of coups, countercoups, and military government is fragile. Each of the two main parties makes it as difficult for the other to govern as possible. The general strike, or *hartal,* initiated by Gandhi as a demonstration of peaceful resistance to British rule has become the order of the day, disrupting and paralyzing government on a regular basis. Between 1990 and 2002 there were 827 hartals, estimated to have cost the economy between 3 and 4 percent of GDP.[13]

All donors recognize that poor governance threatens everything in Bangladesh: growth, security, human rights, and democracy. In August 2005, more than three hundred small bombs were set off within minutes of each other in Dhaka, causing panic in the streets and even greater panic in the corridors of power. Leaflets found at bombing sites called for the imposition of Islamic law. And more bombs were to follow. The erosion of what few democratic processes remain is rampant; communal violence is largely ignored as a concession to increasingly militant fundamentalist parties; and Bangladesh, along with Nigeria and Haiti, now finds itself at the very bottom of Transparency International's corruption index.

Bangladeshi NGO leaders must decide how to relate to government under such circumstances—and not just in a generic sense, but on a day-to-day basis. The most adept will make choices about when and where to work with government, and where self-reliance makes more sense. BRAC has collaborated with government in programs to immunize children and pregnant women. It has worked with government on disaster preparedness and flood relief efforts. It has initiated a training program to build the capacity of women leaders in local government. It has a joint nutritional program with government and works closely with government in a tuberculosis control program. But many of its initiatives, such as its non-formal primary education program (NFPE), function largely outside the government sphere of influence. BRAC's primary and adolescent primary schools aim to get dropouts back into the formal system, and although some criticize the effort as a parallel educational system, BRAC sees that as a complement. A project that began with 22 one-room schools in 1985 had grown to more than 49,000 primary and pre-primary schools by 2004, with an enrollment of over a million children, 65 percent of them girls.

BRAC has a variety of programs that promote human rights. It holds human rights training programs, runs a legal aid clinic, and helps to organize villagers into lobby groups to demand local government services. It has given voice to the voiceless and has organized them in ways that give them real political strength. But it has assiduously avoided the temptation to engage in partisan politics. Others have not, and too often the story has ended badly. Omar Asghar Khan, the mercurial founder of Sungi, a successful Pakistani NGO, accepted the job of minister of environment, local government and rural development from the Mussharaf government in 1999. In 2001 he resigned to create his own political party, but six months later he was found dead, hanging from a ceiling fan in a Karachi bedroom. "Suicide," was the official verdict, but few believed it. There may be no lesson here. Or it may be that NGOs and politics make bad bedfellows.

In Bangladesh, Faruque Ahmed, the founder-leader of Proshika, also took an overt approach to politics, calling openly for the resignation of the quasi-military Ershad government in 1990, and then of the BNP government in 1996. This endeared him to the Awami League government that succeeded the BNP in elections that year, and for a while, the sun shone on Proshika. But the BNP returned to power in 2001, and things soon changed. Three weeks after the election, Prime Minister Khaleda Zia made a speech in which she mentioned NGOs:

> During the last 30 years, the NGOs worked hand in hand with the government in poverty alleviation, removal of disparity, and social development. We want to maintain this course. But, there has been widespread reaction in society regarding a handful of NGOs, as they have involved themselves in party politics and views. Adverse and hostile attitudes have been created among the common people. Using foreign aid for party activities is a serious crime. Proper investigations into the misdeeds of such NGOs will be made and action under the law of the land will be taken. No one should be allowed to do whatever they like whilst violating the laws of the Republic.[14]

The speech seems to have been a signal to target Proshika. Five months after the election, two Proshika staff members were arrested on charges of sedition. The following year a number of Proshika project funds were frozen, and early in 2004 the youth wing of the BNP laid siege to the Proshika office in Dhaka. In April, 72 Proshika staff were arrested, and in May a police raid on the Proshika office resulted in the arrest of Faruque Ahmed and several other senior staff members on charges of financial mismanagement. It was sixty-six days before a bail hearing could be arranged for their release, and since then Proshika has been unable to access international funding, despite interventions from many of the donors that had been supporting Proshika, and despite the fact that the implausible charges against Proshika staff members were never brought to court.

MONEY AND DONORS

Without money, an NGO will cease to exist. There are essentially four sources of funding for Asian NGOs: domestic philanthropy, government assistance, funding from international donors, and earned income. Some Asian NGOs have tapped domestic philanthropy for emergency relief efforts, but giving for long-term development in most countries is still in its infancy. Several Asian governments have funding mechanisms to support voluntary efforts, but these focus to a large extent on cooperatives and village-based organizations, and many are one-off (ad hoc) arrangements that provide little in the way of institutional sustenance.

Finding, managing, and keeping international donors is therefore a principal responsibility of NGO leadership. During the 1970s, coincident with the growth of Asian NGOs, many of the Northern NGOs that once devised and managed their own development projects began to change. They saw that local organizations could, with support and capacity building, do things better and more cheaply than outsiders. The locals knew the history, the culture, and the language; they could get around the countryside more easily; and their salaries were a fraction of international levels. It was this trend, initiated by Oxfam and some church-based organizations, that gave many Asian NGOs their start. During the 1980s, some bilateral and multilateral agencies began to join the trend. As organizations such as BRAC, Proshika, and Sarvodaya grew larger, the burden of managing twenty or thirty different projects, funded by as many donor organizations, became increasingly difficult.

In addition, the shift from relatively small partnerships with like-minded Northern NGOs to contractual arrangements with bilateral or multilateral agencies is, for most Asian NGO leaders, a leap of quantum proportions. One development that made the change workable was a gradual move on the part of some donor agencies away from projects to more holistic funding arrangements. Projects tend to reflect donor priorities and time frames more than those of the recipient or the people with whom the projects work. And they take activities out of the context in which they function. But farmers do not plant according to a donor funding cycle, and a preventive health program may not function unless it is combined with curative services. By the mid-1980s, some of the larger Asian NGOs were balancing a broad portfolio of projects, some well funded and some badly funded, while many necessary ancillary activities and support functions were not funded at all.

One innovation was the creation of donor consortia that took a programmatic approach to the broad spectrum of an organization's activities. Pioneered by Sarvodaya in Sri Lanka in the mid-1980s with Canadian International Development Agency (CIDA), Norwegian Agency for Development Cooperation (NORAD), U.K. Department for International Development (DFID), and Netherlands Organization for International Development Cooperation (Oxfam Novib), consortia have several advantages for both donors and recipients. First, everything is included. The NGO prepares a comprehensive plan and budget covering, say, three years. A group of donors meets, discusses that plan with the NGO, and refines, adds, or subtracts, and then funding is provided in accordance with a donor's level of interest or capacity. Because each donor supports a percentage of the overall program, each donor has the advantage of seeing the overall effort and of knowing that the whole enterprise is being adequately supported. From the NGO's point of view, in addition to providing a holistic form of financial support, a consortium can reduce the amount of time required to service donors. In the donor consortium established for BRAC in the 1980s, for example, there was one set of reports, one set of donor monitors, and one set of evaluators.

The challenge for the NGO leader, of course, is to make sure that the organization meets expectations and lives up to commitments. This is not as simple as it might seem. Donors can be fickle, interests and priorities can change quickly, and donor personnel turnover is high. And although a consortium may reduce the transaction costs for both giver and receiver, it requires greater transparency on the part of the NGO, it reduces opportunities to build Chinese walls between donors, and it is easier for donors to "gang up" on the recipient—for good reasons or bad.

One technique that leaders have developed for dealing with donors is what Alnoor Ebrahim calls "buffering strategies": techniques that help to protect core activities from undue outside interference and from the inherent instability of the funding regime. Ebrahim examines this buffering under the headings of "symbolism," "professionalization," and "selectivity." "Symbolism" is used to mean the formal gathering of the information—through monitoring, evaluation, and research—that is necessary for building donor confidence, even if it is sometimes irrelevant to the way an NGO actually makes decisions. "Self-criticism," he says, "when present at all, is minor, and there is a tendency to highlight success while downplaying negative events."[15] Failures may be well known by the NGO and may be incorporated into future planning, but Ebrahim argues that these are seldom volunteered in the formal reporting systems established for donors.

Ebrahim's second buffering strategy is "professionalization": the hiring of engineers, social scientists, managers, and computer experts. This is a universal trend among NGOs, required not so much by donors as by the needs that NGOs seek to address. It does, however, serve an additional purpose: to smooth communications between NGOs and funders. "These professionals share with funders a common development language—terms such as participation, sustainability, cost-benefit analysis, impacts, indicators and so on. Thus, the professionals are able to communicate their activities in terms acceptable to funders. By justifying their work in terms of a dominant currency, the NGOs are able to deter probes into their work."[16]

This may sound devious, but it is no less so than the behavior of donor agencies that permit few insights into their own inner workings, providing few explanations for late funding, delayed decisions, policy and staffing discontinuity, and a propensity for cherry-picking. One Asian NGO leader talks about the problem of balancing two sets of constituencies, one demand based, and the other supply based.

> The demand-based constituency is the one to whom we must deliver our services—government, NGOs, the people for whom we work; the supply side is the funding agency or donors. The real challenge is to try to balance these two, matching demand with supply and still maintaining the integrity of purpose in terms of one's own organization, mission and strategy . . . especially when you realize that your financier has totally different agendas and objectives.[17]

Ebrahim's "selectivity" refers to the donor desire for, and the NGO willingness to supply, "product data" rather than "process data." Donors have a tendency to focus on the quantifiable: how many schools, how many tubewells, how many children vaccinated. These may or may not be tied to a longer-term result such as reduced poverty or improved health. But the *process* of getting to schools and tubewells and vaccinated children, or to reduced poverty and improved health, is usually missing from the discourse. This can reduce the analysis of outcomes to a financial calculation—for example, one NGO's tubewells are more expensive than another's—ignoring the importance, for example, of enthusiastic village participation to the sustainability of the product. The danger lies not so much in donor-recipient misunderstandings (although that is a real possibility) as in the risk that product will simply overshadow process: output trumping outcome.

Many donors have begun to move away from output targets, placing greater emphasis on "results." This too can be problematic, however, especially where the intended result—such as a demonstrable correlation between better health or education and poverty reduction—falls outside the donor time frame. The insatiable donor desire for concrete measurables may also serve to devalue some of the fundamental NGO hallmarks, such as innovation, experimentation, and risk taking. And it could move NGOs away from poorer people and communities where success is more difficult, more expensive, and more time-consuming. When there are so many tradeoffs to be made between getting the money and spending it wisely, an essential NGO leadership function revolves around keeping the organization's vision clearly in mind.

MONEY: INCOME EARNED

In a climate where governmental relations are fraught with peril and where even limited government funding is likely to come with strings, if not intrusion, alternatives are essential for NGO leaders who want to maintain their organization's independence. International donors—first

NGOs and then bilateral and multilateral agencies—have provided the major funding for most Asian NGOs over the past two decades. But another avenue has been developing, and for some Asian NGOs it provides a clear answer to independence and long-term sustainability: earned income.

Earned income is not a new phenomenon. Northern NGOs have run bake sales, sold Christmas cards, and run thrift shops for years. Usually, however, the proceeds are a small adjunct to their philanthropic income and government support. Among Asian NGOs, and increasingly in other parts of the world, microfinance operations have been one source of financial sustainability. Although Grameen Bank gets the credit, BRAC pioneered microfinance in Bangladesh and was soon followed by others across Asia. The essence of micro-credit in financial terms is that the borrower repays the loan and covers the cost of the lending operation. For organizations that received early donor support for microfinance in the form of grants, successful management of the loan portfolio has become a wholly owned, sustainable nest egg. If all else failed and no income was available from any other source, the revolving loan fund could continue. For some organizations this nest egg is small, and for some, poor decisions and weak management have made it a sinking, rather than a sustaining, fund. For others, however, it has become the foundation of sustainability. In 2004, more than half of BRAC's assets were described as loans to its village organization members, totaling more than $200 million. This contrasts sharply with typical Northern NGO financial statements. Save the Children UK, for example, had a gross income 33 percent higher than BRAC in 2005, but its net assets, at about $78 million, were significantly lower and significantly less tangible.[18]

BRAC's idea of earning money began before the organization was five years old, perhaps because its founder-leader, Fazle Hasan Abed, came from an accounting background at Shell Oil. One of the first "businesses" was a handicraft shop—Aarong—not unlike an NGO thrift or fair-trade shop in Europe. The handicrafts were produced by members of BRAC village organizations, and the Dhaka shop was an effort to create a domestic market as an alternative to the fickle behavior of buyers from Northern NGOs. The shop was a success and more were opened. Today, Aarong provides income for 35,000 artisans, 85 percent of whom are women. Sales in 2004 grew by 17 percent over the previous year, and profits grew by almost 20 percent.

Parallel with the beginning of Aarong, BRAC set up a print shop, buying used presses from Europe to print textbooks and other educational material for schools and health programs. This saved the organization money, improved on quality, and enabled it to take on outside work that helped to pay core costs. Today BRAC Printers is well known in Bangladesh for the quality and variety of its work. BRAC, in fact, now has a wide array of income-earning projects that, not counting income from lending operations, return more income to the organization than external donors. In 2004, the combined revenue from commercial and program support enterprises was $59 million (whereas donor income was $52.61 million) representing about 30 percent of the organization's total income for the year.[19]

Where earned income is concerned, BRAC is undoubtedly unique in terms of both volume and scope, but the trend to greater earned income is growing among Asian NGOs and could provide the answer to long-term sustainability if donors are willing to support it. Oddly, despite constant refrains about dependency avoidance and sustainability, many are not.

OPPORTUNISM AND THE SOCIAL ENTREPRENEUR

One of the most important characteristics of the successful Asian NGO leader is an ability to take advantage of opportunities as they arise. Another is the ability to *create* opportunity where others see none. Rural poverty is the defining feature of many Asian countries, and rural poverty pushes people toward cities, where urban poverty can often be much worse. The challenge in rural development is the creation of new livelihoods. Microfinance, or a stripped-down approach with micro-credit as the centerpiece, has been held up as the salvation of the rural poor. Certainly, if a borrower can turn a small loan into a successful commercial investment, that is a good thing. Many undoubtedly do. But the interest rates on micro-credit, if it is to recoup its costs, are high—usually between 25 and 30 percent. That means borrowers have to be able to make at least that much in fairly short order, if they are to repay the loan with the return on their investment. Realistically (that is, in the real world), a 25–30 percent return on any investment would be little short of miraculous.

Most micro-borrowers do what they see others doing: they set up a small retail operation, buying low and selling high; they invest in rice husking, cattle fattening, backyard poultry, and whatever else looks like an opportunity. The problem is that most of these things were already being done in the village. The demand for husked rice and chickens will not change just because new people are providing them. The enterprise may shift from whoever was doing this before to the clients of the micro-banking institution, and they may well make their 25–30 percent return. But nothing new has been created in the village: no new production and no incremental livelihoods, apart, possibly, from a slightly expanded kiosk economy.

BRAC leaders saw long ago that credit alone, or even credit with savings and other banking facilities, would never make much difference to the rural poor unless new opportunities could be created. Where chickens were concerned, for example, they saw that there was a growing urban demand for poultry and eggs, but only if village borrowers could find a way to produce better chickens. Instead of a problem, they saw an opportunity. The higher-quality day-old chicks they introduced to village women soon died, however. And in any case, in an economy where the market barely functions, rounding up chickens and getting them to city markets posed a problem. The eventual solution, after a great deal of testing, was a complete, integrated poultry system, where women at each stage in the chain could finance their operations through small loans. The chain consisted of hatcheries, chick rearers, vaccinators, cage rearers, and egg collectors. BRAC developed the system and provided the credit; the borrowers did the rest. To give an idea of the size of the operation, in 2004 BRAC hatcheries distributed 12 million day-old chicks, and its three feed mills produced 35,000 metric tons of balanced feed.

BRAC has used the same approach with fish, prawns, vegetables, and silk production. The best example of its opportunism—its social entrepreneurship—came when the European Union reduced subsidies on dairy products. Suddenly the cheap imported milk powder that had been making local dairy production uncompetitive beyond the village vanished, and BRAC saw an opportunity that could be translated into more rural livelihoods. In 1998 it opened a dairy in Dhaka, supported by twenty-nine chilling plants around the country and a modest transportation system. The dairy project, which today involves more than 30,000 farmers, produces 70,000 liters of milk every day.

Each of the BRAC examples is striking for its size and ingenuity, and many observers are daunted by the scale. Bangladesh, however, demands scale if there is to be any impact on poverty, and the same is true elsewhere in Asia. What BRAC has shown with each of its projects is almost more striking because of the common sense approach that has been applied to learning and testing before new ideas are put into action.

CONCLUSION

There is a very telling point made by feminists about the 1930s American dance team of Fred Astaire and Ginger Rogers. Astaire, the man, was of course the leader, the teacher, the one to watch. Ginger Rogers was the student, the follower, the subordinate part of the team. The truth was, however, that Ginger Rogers had to do everything Fred Astaire himself did, and *she* had to do it backwards and in high heels! Her situation is a bit like that of Asian NGOs and their leaders, who must always be able to look over their shoulder as well as forward, and who must keep their balance in a fast-moving environment with very fragile supports. They are expected to run organizations with plans, budgets, and governance structures like those of their Northern counterparts. They are expected to maintain high financial standards, to employ, train, and manage a professional cadre of workers, and to report to each donor on time and in good English. They are expected to reach the poorest of the poor in meaningful ways in which most donors and governments cannot, and do not, reach them. They are expected to be innovative, and their innovations, when successful, are expected to be replicable. They are expected to be gender-sensitive and to speak out about human rights and injustice, but to do so in a way that does not incur the wrath of their governments and of passing religious fundamentalists.

They must do all this in a climate fraught with peril, where a small political misstep can put a leader in jail and jeopardize an entire generation of work. Unlike Northern NGOs, they have no local philanthropic base of support, and the funding they receive from international supporters can be fickle and unpredictable. The leadership must be entrepreneurial and willing to take risks. But in a climate where any kind of exposure is risky, and where the cost of failure can be high, this requires a great deal of self-confidence, nerves of steel, and an ability to motivate staff members for whom the perils are equally grave.

This chapter has focused to a large extent on BRAC, not because it is big and successful, but because, despite its size and success, it, like every single extant Asian NGO, was once small and uncertain. Many look at BRAC today and see a huge nonprofit conglomerate, something that few could aspire to and something that is no longer representative of the NGO category. "It isn't an NGO," they say, "it's a parallel government."

There is another way of looking at it, however. Sheldon Annis once said of NGO efforts to end poverty that "small scale" can merely mean "insignificant," "politically independent" can mean "powerless or disconnected," "low-cost" can mean "underfinanced" or "poor quality," and "innovative " can mean simply "temporary" or "unsustainable."[20] BRAC has shown that none of this has to be the case. And it is not alone; the rise of the NGO has been faster, and they have become more prolific, in Bangladesh than in other Asian countries, but there are now many successful NGOs across the region, led by men and women who are as talented and as entrepreneurial as BRAC's Fazle Hasan Abed. Like BRAC, they are setting new standards for what NGOs can and may well be in the years ahead.

NOTES

1. See, for example, Adam Seligman, *The Idea of Civil Society* (Old Tappan, NJ: Free Press, 1992). The term *civil society* was widely used at the 1992 Earth Summit in Rio, notably by representatives of organizations from countries emerging from Communism, who said that those organizations represented something that was not controlled by party, military, or the state—they represented "civil society."

2. There have been many books written in recent years on civil society. A good historical and theoretical overview can be found in Alison Van Rooy, *Civil Society and the Aid Industry* (London: Earthscan, 1998).

3. Dorothea Hillhorst, *The Real World of NGOs* (London: Zed Books, 2003).

4. http://www.asianphilanthropy.org/countries/korea/size.html.

5. http://www.asianphilanthropy.org/countries/taiwan/size.html.

6. http://www.jppmros.gov.my/speech01.htm.

7. Neema Kudva, "Uneasy Relations, NGOs and the State in Karnataka, India," Cornell University, June 2005, http://www.isec.ac.in/Karnataka_Kudva 17.5.05_aligned.pdf.

8. Planning Commission of India, Voluntary Organization Data Base, http://164.100.97.14/ngo/default.asp, December 27, 2005.

9. http://www.asianphilanthropy.org/countries/bangladesh/size.html.

10. Asian Development Bank, "The State of NGOs in Nine Asian DMCs," Manila, 1999.

11. In 2003, Grameen's lending totaled Bangladeshi Tk21.4 billion; BRAC's in 2004 was Tk25.9 billion. Source: *Annual Report,* Grameen Bank 2003; *BRAC Annual Report,* 2004. There are several other large micro-credit NGOs in Bangladesh. One of the most prominent is ASA, which had an outstanding loan portfolio at the end of 2004 of Tk11.9 billion.

12. In cash terms, World Vision is probably the largest transnational NGO. Its collective 2004 cash income was more than $1 billion, according to its 2004 annual report.

13. UNDP, "Beyond Hartals," Dhaka, March 2005.

14. Speech by Prime Minister Khaleda Zia, October 19, 2001, quoted in Amnesty International, "Bangladesh Human Rights Defenders Under Attack," London, August 23, 2005.

15. Alnoor Ebrahim, *NGOs and Organizational Change: Discourse, Reporting and Learning* (Cambridge: Cambridge University Press, 2003), 97.

16. Ibid., 99.

17. Ian Smillie and John Hailey, *Managing for Change: Leadership, Strategy & Management in Asian NGOs* (London: Earthscan, 2001), 39.

18. Figures are taken from the Annual Reports of BRAC (2004) and Save the Children UK (2005); the exchange rate was what prevailed in February 2006.

19. All figures are taken from *BRAC Annual Report 2004,* Dhaka, 2004

20. Sheldon Annis, "Can Small-Scale Development Be Large-Scale Policy?" in Sheldon Annis and Peter Hakim (eds.), *Direct to the Poor: Grassroots Development in Latin America* (Boulder, CO: Lynne Reinner, 1988).

9

LEADING CHANGE BY EXAMPLE AND SPIRIT:
LEADERSHIP STYLES AND PATTERNS RECOGNIZED BY THE MAGSAYSAY AWARDS

Rosemary Morales Fernholz

Serious public-welfare concerns in Asia result in a wide variety of development challenges. Despite impressive economic growth, especially in East and Southeast Asia, more than 700 million people are still considered poor by international standards.[1] Large pockets of poverty remain in some South Asian countries, where gross domestic product per capita was estimated in 2003 to be even lower than that of sub-Saharan Africa.[2] Although countries such as China and India have made big improvements in poverty reduction, some others have stagnated, and still others are fighting for basic freedoms and for human survival through various crises.

Leaders in the region need to take a major role in addressing twenty-first-century challenges with their ideas and strategies, and they need to gather support and resources in order for development strategies to be effective. Development literature and experience show clearly that this leadership has to come from many sources and that public sector leadership is often not enough nor well directed. Momentum for reform or innovative changes may start in small ways. Muhammad Yunus, for example, worked many years on his concept of sustainable micro-loans in Bangladesh before micro-credit was translated into policies and a movement. Mechai Viravaidya likewise initiated many activities to promote responsible sexual behavior before his approach became accepted as a national program in Thailand. Both strategies have since gained more universal acceptance and have been replicated widely. Mr. Yunus has been a leader from civil society, whereas Mr. Viravaidya has had leadership roles from within and outside of the government.

This chapter discusses the behavior and strategies used by persons such as Yunus and Viravaidya who have worked to bring about positive welfare changes in Asia. It is based on the experiences of a set of transformational leaders who have been recipients of the Magsaysay Awards, which have been given annually for almost half a century to recognize men and women in Asia who demonstrate concern and leadership and who act successfully to improve the welfare of people. Some of these leaders are publicly acclaimed, but many are less well known. Many of the leaders do not hold official positions of authority, and yet they have been able to inspire or effect positive change. Reviewing the experience of the awardees, this chapter highlights the behaviors that have made for their leadership success and examines the approaches they have taken.

AWARD PROGRAMS AND LEADERSHIP

Well-designed and well-executed award programs are good ways to recognize, encourage, and support leaders. Some programs recognize outstanding past achievements. For more than a century, for example, Nobel Prizes have recognized contributions and leadership in specific fields, such as peacemaking, and awards have gone to those "who, during the preceding year, shall have conferred the greatest benefit to mankind."[3] Other awards are given to recognize and encourage leaders and, by publicizing their accomplishments, to inform and motivate others. Public policy award programs are examples, and they are supported by international organizations, national governments, and civic organizations. Some awards are made specifically to identify change agents and provide them with resources because, in the experience of the Ashoka Foundation, for example, "to be effective, resources had to be placed in the hands of people who would really use them well."[4] Although many award programs focus on the best practices or innovations rather than on the leader or innovator, inevitably there is a leader or group of leaders who have made the innovative change happen. The ultimate goal of these award programs, therefore, is to reward and encourage positive change, directly or indirectly to identify and recognize the leadership that has made this happen, to provide role models, and to create channels for expanding the good work. The list of awardees is a list of leaders in relevant spheres of endeavor, geography, and time.

This chapter discusses Asian leadership in the context of the Magsaysay Awards. It first focuses on this enduring and prestigious award program and on the foundation that sets policies for and manages it. It then explores the leadership attributes and behaviors of leaders and their strategies, providing insights into their experience and their capacity to be effective in changing times and conditions in Asia. Finally, it shows that even though the leaders are selected on the basis of attributes and behaviors that are considered universal, their leadership strategies reflect sensitivity to what is most relevant in their times and cultures.

THE MAGSAYSAY AWARD PROGRAM

The Magsaysay Awards were designed as living memorials to a Philippine president admired for his selfless efforts to improve the welfare of people. Shortly after President Ramon Magsaysay died in an airplane crash in 1957, John D. Rockefeller III, on behalf of the Rockefeller Brothers Fund (RBF), wrote a letter to the subsequent Philippine president suggesting that an award be created in his name to honor people in Asia whose "demonstrated leadership is motivated by a concern for the welfare of people comparable to that which characterized the life of Ramon Magsaysay."[5] The suggestion was accepted and endorsed by the Philippine president and by the family of the late president Magsaysay.

Colleagues of the late President Magsaysay and representatives of the RBF set up a foundation, the Ramon Magsaysay Award Foundation

(RMAF), in 1957 to administer the proposed award program. Although they provided much of the financial support for the program, members of the Rockefeller family who were involved and other leaders of the RBF entrusted the formation of the program to a carefully selected and all-Filipino Board of Trustees. This board included family and friends of the former president who themselves were known for their prominence and integrity. The board, in close consultation with the Magsaysay family, decided on some fundamental policies:

1. The awards, given annually, would recognize leadership linked with selfless service for others in Asia.
2. There would be five categories for the awards, each in recognition of a characteristic of Magsaysay: government service; public service; community leadership; journalism, literature, and creative communication arts; and international understanding (peace was added later). In recent years a new category, emergent leadership, was also added.
3. The foundation would function as an independent organization that would set its own policies and procedures.

This institutional framework and these policies have provided the award program with much stability; indeed, many initial policies have remained in place for decades. Over a period of almost fifty years, the foundation has had only four executive directors. The Board of Trustees, originally composed of Filipinos who knew the late president, is now composed of eminent people chosen for their own sense of service and integrity, who as a group represent a diversity of perspectives, and who serve on an unpaid and voluntary basis. The nine trustees (originally there were seven) serve for four years, with members' terms ending on a rotation basis. Trustees can serve for several terms, though not consecutive terms. The decision to retain an all-Filipino board has been examined and sustained, and the consensus is that this decision has served to ensure that the ideals of the late president are preserved and that the board can convene effectively. Keeping the prestigious awards recognized as a respected independent process remains a high priority.

Awardee Selection

A major concern for the foundation is maintaining the integrity of the selection process. A Code of Procedures prepared in 1957 guides this process. The selection process involves three stages: first, casting a wide net in making nominations; second, investigation and first-level evaluation; and third, final selection by committees and the Board of Trustees. To ensure that this process would be done well, the first executive trustee visited the Nobel Prize Foundation and the award ceremonies in Sweden and also reviewed the experience of other prestigious award programs such as the Pulitzer Prize.

Selection of the individuals who nominate the candidates is an important and continuing challenge for the foundation's management. Selected people based in, or with expertise on, various Asian countries and chosen for their own integrity and distinguished qualities, along with previous awardees, make the initial nominations. The nominators are cautioned not to inform the candidate. The next stages are also challenging and confidential. The executive director, mainly, does a careful first-level investigation and evaluation of the pool of nominees and does so with much care and discretion. There is a wide range of countries and categories for the awards, so the process takes place over several months and includes interviews with the unknowing candidates.

This stage results in a compilation of information and a list of some one hundred nominees each year for consideration of committees formed with members of the Board of Trustees. Because the awards are made on the basis of quality of spirit and motivation toward service, the challenge to the team handling first-level selection and research is to assess the candidates on these elusive qualities, to express their assessments in their reports, and to bring to life this nobility of spirit for people who may not be well known. New technologies are now making this process easier and more productive. The Internet makes it possible to gather much more background information early in the process, and new technologies enable the investigators to videotape some of their observations to benefit the board in its final selection.

Committees formed with the participation of individual members of the board continue the selection process until the Board of Trustees compiles the final list of awardees—usually five to seven people or organizations. In some categories, two people can share a prize; in any category no award is given unless a suitable candidate is found. The awards are presented on Magsaysay's birth date, August 31. The ceremonies in Manila are conducted with much dignity and often with members of the Magsaysay family in attendance. Awardees are encouraged to give public lectures or to share their craft with a wide audience. Awardees are given a certificate, a symbol trophy, and a stipend—the amount of which has been adjusted over the decades. In all of this, the documentation—such as the citations, the biographies, and the books—are written with precision, clarity, and care to create a timeless record.

A Partnership Built on Respect: The RMAF–RBF Partnership

A distinctive feature of the Magsaysay awards is a close partnership between the RMAF and the RBF. The Rockefeller brothers, John D. III and Nelson, had known President Magsaysay personally. It was they who proposed this living memorial to honor the late president. Unparalleled in RBF history, the constancy of support for both the awards program and the foundation has spanned close to half a century. From the start, the RBF has recognized the professionalism and dedication of the Boards of Trustees and executive directors and has delegated full direction of the program to them.

The Rockefeller Brothers Foundation support has taken various forms. The financial support has been substantial, continuing, and innovative. The award program and foundation administrative costs were initially and fully underwritten by the RBF. During the first awards ceremony, Justice Pedro Tuason, chairman of the Board of Trustees of the Ramon Magsaysay Foundation, noted that the foundation "was conceived through the generosity and practical idealism of the Rockefeller Brothers Fund of New York, which made a money grant out of which the Awards are to be distributed yearly."[6] Subsequently, the RBF extended a loan supplemented by a grant, to cover construction costs of a building, the Ramon Magsaysay Center, that would house the foundation and library, and bring in revenues to support future foundation and award activities. Equally important has been other direct and indirect support that helped elevate the award program to a high level of prestige in the region.

The RBF has provided technical assistance and advice, in addition to support for new initiatives. The foundation has supported conferences and workshops to bring together the awardees to share ideas and to address regionwide issues such as food security. In 1987, the RBF and RMAF announced the companion grants program, a Program for Asian Projects, in response to requests from participants at the Magsaysay Awardees Assembly in Bangkok, Thailand, for support of their current work or new projects. The awardees recommended four areas for the grants: rural environment, urban environment, education and religion, and peace and security. Under this program, previous Magsaysay awardees (individually or in collaboration) could send in proposals for funding for collaborative projects. The screening and evaluation of nominees would be done by the Board of Advisers for the grants program. Final selection would be done by RBF, and the grants would be administered by the RMAF.

The grants program has evolved over the years on the basis of growing experience in grant administration and feedback from the awardees. Two important changes have come about: (1) The RMAF provides more help to awardees to select, frame, and write proposals; and (2) the grant framework was broadened to fund a diversity of activities important to the awardees, including travel, reunions to promote the cross-fertilization of ideas, workshops (for example, on financial sustainability), conferences, documentation, social enterprise, and emergency assistance (necessitated, for example, by persecution).

ASIAN LEADERS AND THE MAGSAYSAY AWARDS

Magsaysay awardees are a set of public-welfare-oriented leaders selected for their impact and potential as role models. The award program annually selects men and women who have "quietly helped others, serving selflessly and without expectation of public recognition." The awards highlight service and leadership in Asia and seek to "place living examples of exceptional service before the public."[7]

From the start, there were five categories of awards: (1) *government service* recognizes leadership from any sector of government service, (2) *public service* honors outstanding service for the public good by a private citizen, (3) *community leadership* cites leadership of a person or community to improve social welfare, (4) *journalism, literature, and creative communication arts* focuses on leadership in the use of these different art and communication forms for the public good, (5) *peace and international understanding* marks outstanding contributions to improve the foundations for peace and sustainable development. These awards were meant to encompass "the fields of influence which vitally interest and affect the vast majority of humanity."[8] In 2001, with support from the Ford Foundation, a new category was added; (6) *emergent leadership* highlights outstanding work of an individual forty years of age or younger to bring about social change.

A summary of the awardees by category and gender is presented in Table 1.

Although there have been women awardees from the start, the summary shows that in all the traditional categories, men outnumber women. Among the few emergent-leader awardees, however, about half of the awardees are women. The awardees were chosen from 12 countries when the program started in 1958. Subsequently, the number of countries from which leaders are selected has more than doubled. By 2005, 249 awards had been given to 210 Asians and 24 foreigners living

Table 1 Magsaysay Leadership Awards, 1958–2005

Category	Male	Female	Total
Government Service (GS)	40	7	47
Public Service (PS)	35	18	53
Community Leadership (CL)	37	16	53
Journalism, Literature, and Creative Communication Arts (JLCCA)	42	4	46
Peace and International Understanding (PIU)	24	5	29
Emergent Leadership (EL)	3	3	6
TOTAL	181	53	234

Source: Ramon Magsaysay Award Foundation

and working in 21 countries of Asia, and to 15 organizations.[9] A list of the countries represented appears in Table 2, and as it shows, these leaders have been chosen from a cross section of countries in Asia. Five countries—the Philippines, Thailand, and Indonesia in Southeast Asia, India in South Asia, and Japan in East Asia—account for more than 60 percent of the Asian awardees. The nationality that has received the most awards (one-fifth of all) is Indian. Awardees represent a diversity of cultures and religions.

LEADERSHIP ATTRIBUTES AND BEHAVIORS

The Magsaysay awards are made to men and women who have demonstrated concern for public welfare through unassuming and selfless service on behalf of others. Five attributes or behaviors can be related to individuals who meet these criteria: They are people who are self-motivated, credible, caring, humble, and courageous. In the following list, these attributes are discussed in relation to several specific awardees.

1. *Self-Motivation.* These leaders who serve others are mainly motivated by their own belief system and values. Several of the

Table 2 Magsaysay Awards by Country

	First Awardee	Number of Awardees (1958–2005)		First Awardee	Number of Awardees (1958–2005)
ASIA					
Afghanistan	1994	1	Malaysia	1960	11
Bangladesh	1978	7	Nepal	1977	2
Burma	1959	3	Pakistan	1963	9
Cambodia	1998	2	Singapore	1965	2
China	1958	8	Sri Lanka	1969	7
Philippines	1959	29	Taiwan	1960	9
India	1958	41	Thailand	1961	19
Indonesia	1958	18	Tibet	1959	1
Japan	1964	21	Timor	2003	1
Korea	1962	14	Vietnam	1964	3
Laos	1967	2	Subtotal		210
NON-ASIAN IN ASIA					
US	1961	9	France	1976	1
Argentina	1994	1	Ireland	1975	1
UK	1958	10	Spain	1959	1
Denmark	1976	1	Subtotal		24
			TOTAL		**234**

Source: Ramon Magsaysay Award Foundation

awardees are members of religious organizations, belong to spiritual sects, or are persons of deep conviction. Their belief in the need to improve life for others is the wellspring of their action and the source of their optimism that it can be done. Prayong Ronnarong of Thailand had a sense of "the value of serving others and the respect it confers,"[10] learned from his grandfather, a revered local healer, and his parents. Mechai Viravaidya's mother gave him advice that guided him for life: "If you work for a company and make some money, that is fine. But who will work for the poor? If people like you, with an education, don't work for the poor, who will?"[11]

Seiei Toyama was drawn by his Buddhist faith and sense of "green atonement." In his words, "I believe that mere existence is meaningless, and that human beings must serve society in order for their lives to have meaning. I therefore believe that I must work for society, even if I have to take personal sacrifices. Otherwise, mine will be a meaningless life."[12] Toyama from Japan was ninety-six years old and still working, using his professional skills to help Chinese scientists battle severe desertification exacerbated by seasonal floods, when he got his award. For Hye-Ran Yoon it was a sense of personal mission when she, upon experiencing a family setback, realized that her city was poorly equipped to assist young people at risk. She became determined to help develop civil society in Cheonan, South Korea, for the benefit of various vulnerable local groups. Benjamin Abadiano, who works to improve the conditions of life of indigenous peoples in the Philippines, was inspired by mentors in his schools to serve others. Sheila Coronel and other Asian journalists have been outraged by abuses they encountered in the exercise of their journalism profession, and as a result they worked to correct these abuses and improve life for all.

2. *Credibility.* The Magsaysay awardees are people who "walk the walk" rather than just "talk the talk." Aruna Roy, who formed the *Mazdoor Kisaan, Shakti Sangathan,* or Organization for the Empowerment of Workers and Peasants, lived simply with a small group in a village. "Living as the poor lived and eating as the poor ate, Roy and her comrades began assisting villagers to assert themselves against the local power structure."[13]

Because many of the leaders work with volunteers, their credibility is important and they inspire others through their example. The experience of Mother Teresa working in India among the destitute is well known, and hence her ability to inspire others to do similar work. In recent times, examples include the work of Oung Chanthol to confront violence against women in Cambodia and the work of Rajendra Singh to organize Rajasthani villagers and secure their voluntary commitment to undertake environmental renewal.

3. *Caring.* The Magsaysay Award winners have worked tirelessly with disadvantaged groups such as the blind, individuals with Hansen's disease (formerly known as leprosy), refugees, rural peoples, urban slum and squatter dwellers, the disabled and the sick, the illiterate, and indigenous peoples. One example among recent winners is Cynthia Maung. Cynthia Maung worked courageously and consistently with staff and volunteers to address the urgent medical needs of thousands of refugees along the Thailand-Burma border. Dr. Maung herself was a Burmese refugee, and she started with a makeshift clinic, almost no equipment, and few supplies. Through her example, she attracted volunteer medical practitioners who helped run the clinic and expand its services, started training health workers; midwives, and "backpack medics"; and sought the support of international non-governmental organizations (NGOs) to build up infrastructure and facilities. Another example is Benjamin Abadiano, who set up ILAWAN, a Center for Peace and Sustainable Development, and TUGDAAN, a Center for Human Environmental Development. Both organizations were established to provide education and social development support for different indigenous groups in the Philippines.

4. *Humility.* Another hallmark of the leaders, which follows from the three attributes just discussed, is a genuine sense of humility. Many of the foreigners who have been given awards for their long-time work in Asia are religious persons. Others come from the world of business. A good example is Henning Holck-Larsen, a Danish industrialist, who has been described as "the most humble and accessible executive in the organization."

5. *Courageous Action.* The causes that the leaders have undertaken involve personal sacrifices and much risk. These were described vividly during one award ceremony: "Often the work that must

be done is tedious, discouraging, and awesome in its proportion. Often, too, loneliness is its terrifying test of character. Danger to health is a constant threat."[14]

Early awards were given to freedom fighters and nation builders. One example is the leadership of Tunku Abdul Rahman Putra in "guiding a multiracial society through its constitutional struggle for independence, toward communal alliance and national identity." Many leaders recognized during the early years of the awards program were people who had been imprisoned, harassed, or censured as freedom fighters or for their outspoken championship of causes and peoples. And indeed, more recent awardees have often had similarly to defend freedom and rights courageously despite threats. Aniceto Guterres Lopes, for example, established a foundation to fight for human rights and justice in Timor Leste during the turbulent times of the mid 1990s, and subsequently, with independence, he was unanimously chosen to lead the Commission for Reception, Truth, and Reconciliation. Dita Indah Sari has been detained, beaten, and imprisoned in Indonesia on charges of subversion because she led workers' strikes for better pay and conditions.

Other leaders speak up against corruption, establish monitoring groups, or work to eliminate criminal acts. One example is Teten Masduke, who was head of the Indonesian Corruption Watch when he received an award in 2005, and who faced repeated threats to his life, while knowing that a colleague was actually murdered. Matiur Rahman, a journalist whose work to expose hideous crimes such as acid throwing in Bangladesh, has been harassed, threatened, and sued. Despite the treatment they have been subjected to, all have persevered and have expanded their spheres of influence even further.

The leaders have risked personal and professional security to sound alarms in the interest of public welfare. Magsaysay awardee Jiang Yanyong courageously and strategically challenged Chinese officials who were not adequately addressing the threat from early cases of severe acute respiratory syndrome (SARS), forcing government to act on the emergency and to manage it. Gao Yaojie, likewise, has sometimes felt as though her work to alert government and society to the urgency of addressing the AIDS epidemic is "like flipping spoonfuls of water onto a roaring fire."[15] Other awardees have also spoken out on environmental (desertification, deforestation, and industrial pollution), political, cultural, economic, and social problems.

LEADERSHIP STRATEGIES

The strategies applied by these leaders can be grouped into three categories: (1) strategic thinking that includes short-term action and long-term planning in a dynamic region, (2) cultural sensitivity to work effectively in collective societies, and (3) ability to maintain a balance between progress and stability. Figure 1 shows the elements of leadership discussed in this section.

Figure 1 Effective Transformative Leadership

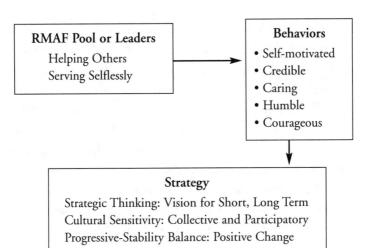

The leaders use their skills and behaviors to accomplish their public-welfare goals. This section presents some of the skills that they have in common and offers some examples. These include the ability to do strategic thinking and set long-term visions, the ability to work with all participants in ways that are culturally sensitive, and the ability to manage the change process effectively.

Strategic Thinking

All the leaders who have received Magsaysay awards have been able to widen their impact through their ability to translate concern and vision into a strategy that works. Reviewing their experience reveals that they excelled in two main areas of strategic thinking. Specifically, they were able to balance short-term action with long-term vision and to expand their programs through empowerment. Immediate action and longer-term visioning are explored in the following paragraphs. Approaches to getting support and mobilizing resources are discussed in the next section.

Short-Term Action and Long-Term Vision. Magsaysay awards have gone to successful leaders who have seized the moment, whether that moment be a crisis, an urgent problem, or an opportunity to better serve public needs. The examples given earlier show that the leaders have addressed problems of poverty and disease such as leprosy, health crises such SARS and HIV/AIDS, and urgent problems related to human rights and press freedoms; no less important, many have seized opportunities to deliver basic urban services more effectively. They have used their skills and insights in health care, journalism, public policy, engineering, agriculture, and business to address these diverse problems.

While offering their help and working with people, however, they provide a vision for a better future and often a channel for working together in the attainment of that better future. The attributes and behaviors discussed in the earlier section help them to establish their credibility and win the acceptance necessary for expanding their influence.

For some leaders, the vision is their craft, and leadership in different art forms has also been recognized. This is important because culture shapes perceptions, influences societal values and norms, and shapes local and world views. Many of the awardees indicate how they have been influenced by role models, and then many became role models who could attract others to join in their causes. Ela Bhatt goes further and states that the real task for achieving true development is the rehabilitation of "hearts and minds."

Most of the awards featuring the expression of arts and culture have gone to pioneering leaders concerned with the preservation and celebration of native music, literature, dance, visual art, and other art forms that build in people a sense of identity, pride, and dignity. There was one award given in 1962, within the first seven-year period, to Francisca Reyes Aquino, whose leadership in preserving and promoting native songs and dance in the Philippines inspired millions to appreciate their culture. Over succeeding years, the number of awards given for leadership in various art and literary forms (including film, theater, dance, religious art, museums, and literature) greatly increased. For the first time, after the first seven years of the award program, a film maker, Akira Kurosawa, was recognized for his pioneering leadership in "the perceptive use of film to probe the moral dilemma of man."[16] Other examples abound in recent years. Choreographer Lim Hwai Min was recognized for "revitalizing the theatrical arts in Taiwan with modern dance that is at once eloquently universal and authentically Chinese."[17] Ikuo Hirayama was honored as an artist and UNESCO Goodwill Ambassador working for cultural preservation in Cambodia and Afghanistan, and Wannakuwatta Amaradeva for bringing "dazzling creativity in expression of the rich heritage of Sri Lankan music."[18]

Expansion and Empowerment. One strategy of Asian leaders is to strengthen the voice of marginalized peoples. Awardees have done this in several ways, such as taking actions to monitor the public sector, provide information and educate the citizenry, and build up citizens' capacity to participate effectively in their own development.

- *Monitoring conditions of life and service provision.* One approach taken by leaders is to organize citizens to monitor government provision of services, and the public stewardship of assets such as natural resources, and protection of people's rights. This is important in view of the high levels of poverty, disadvantage, and corruption and the low levels of accountability in many Asian countries. If (in Sen's words) "development is freedom,"[19] then it is important in Asia to root out the "cancer" of corruption that cripples freedoms and development. "A less corrupt Asia would mean its countries are likely to have more growth, improved foreign investments, higher per capita income, lower infant mortality, increased literacy, stronger property rights, increased business growth, and many additional benefits." The challenge for leaders is finding ways of achieving these goals by "(1) building coalitions of anticorruption champions, (2) creating effective management and leadership structures, and (3) supporting regular monitoring and reporting on corruption."[20]
- *Providing information and opening communication channels.* Another leadership approach is to focus on the provision of independent and accurate information and communication with the belief that an informed citizenry is a strong citizenry. There is much tension in this kind of reporting. Yet, as Amitabha Chowdhury discussed several decades ago, "Investigative reporting can fulfill special needs in a country which on the one hand is in the grip of a tremendous development and on the other [is] also beset with problems of maladministration and corruption."[21] Sheila Coronel of the Philippines underscored the need for accurate and thorough investigative journalism that leads to official action.

Increasingly, in many parts of the world, democracy does not bring an end to corruption, cronyism, or environmental devastation. Abuses merely take new forms. Corruption, for example, becomes more decentralized, no longer concentrated in the head of state and his family. Many more snouts feast [at] the public trough and it becomes ever more important to guard it. The criminal waste of public resources continues in scandalous proportions and very often, unless the media expose these crimes and unmask the criminals, reforms do not take place. Investigative reports must make an impact in terms of policy reversals or personnel changes, or at least the initiation of official investigations of the wrongdoing that they have exposed. Otherwise, citizens will think that nothing can be done, and they will view exposé as yet another distraction proffered by the media.[22]

According to Matiur Rahman, in addition to investigating and analyzing data, the challenge that a leader faces as "navigator of positive social and cultural change"[23] is to communicate in various ways, such as in research reports, report cards, study groups, newspapers, and the traditional and electronic media. The awardees have addressed this in a variety of ways over the years, and the award program has included more and more space for innovative expressions to be recognized. Oung Chanthol, for example, and her Cambodian Women's Crisis Center have painstakingly documented hundreds of cases of rape, human trafficking, and domestic abuse. CWCC broadcasts its campaigns on radio and TV and provides authoritative data to journalists, provoking the wrath of brothel owners, angry husbands, police, and politicians.

The Venerable Pomnyun Sumin surveyed refugees from North Korea in 1997 and 1998, calculated that some 3 million people had died from famine, and alerted South Korean society, the government, and international relief organizations, which then sent massive amounts of aid. His followers built a factory in North Korea to supply essential nutrients for some 11,000 children. Bharat Koirala established the Nepal Press Institute. To reach Nepal's remote rural world, he pioneered in setting up "wall newspapers," established an FM radio station, and promoted locally owned and operated radio stations. Abdullah Abu Sayeed helped establish and promoted nationwide enrichment study circles in Bangladesh with a mobile library system. Some other examples in past decades are Dato Zakiah Hanum binti Abdul Hamid, a Malaysian public official who set up the national archives that "illuminate the country's past and play a vital role in its present"[24] and awardees who used satire, humor, and political cartoons to underscore their messages and reach bigger audiences.

• *Actively participating in government service.* Leadership within the government service has been consistently recognized in the awards program. By 2005, forty-seven people had received awards for government service, and for strengthening the credibility of the government agencies and their success in achieving their missions. Some awardees enter the political arena to give more voice to their concerns. Jon Ungphakorn, for example, ran for the senate in Thailand and won a seat, stating as his rationale, "No one listens to NGO's, but if you are elected senator . . . everyone is interested."[25] He used this platform to fight for the disadvantaged—to subsidize drugs for HIV/AIDs patients, expose government discrimination against Muslims, defend the rights of rural people against mega-projects that threaten their livelihoods, and to gain media support for health and social development programs. Wu Qing won a seat in a Chinese local district People's Congress to represent a university; Prayong Ronnarong of Thailand helped form a community-based council of leaders that crafted a master plan for self-reliant local enterprises and community learning, and Dita Sari helped found the People's Democratic Union (later renamed the People's Democratic Party) that acts on behalf of working people in Indonesia.

As city and local governments become increasingly important in Asia, more of the Magsaysay awards go to local leaders—for example, Jesse Robredo for leadership in participatory and effective city government, and Tasneen Siddiqui and Jockin Arputham for working with slum dwellers in the main cities of Pakistan and India. Arputham initiated slum-to-slum learning exchanges in India that sparked the development of a federation and has inspired others to promote approaches tried in India's National Slum Dwellers Federation in South Africa, Cambodia, Sri Lanka, Nepal, Laos, Indonesia, and several other countries in Africa.

Cultural Sensitivity—Collective Societies and Participatory Leadership

Many studies have been done on the relationship between leadership styles and culture. The GLOBE study referred to by Rondinelli in Chapter 2 of this volume found that although there are universally accepted attributes of leaders, there are also important cultural differences. One study of Southeast Asian countries points out that because of the widespread influence of the Confucian culture, some Asian societies tend to be collectivist and favor a participatory leadership style. Others, however, observe leadership styles that range from directive to participatory in East Asia (depending on the difficulty or ease of the task) and the tendency for leaders to be modest but paternalistic in Southern Asia and to be authoritarian in Southeast Asia.[26]

The selection criteria used by the Ramon Magsaysay Award Foundation for its awardees, therefore, fit very much into the nature of both universal and culture-bound attributes of leadership. Leadership is recognized among people who demonstrate their concern and care for others based on their core beliefs, who establish their credibility with sincerity and in a modest manner, and who show courage in the pursuit of noble goals. In the words of a Magsaysay Award Foundation official, "The people of Asia are looking and hoping for leaders with the capacity to shoulder responsibility—to help the group, society or movement reach wise decisions and to cooperate in implementing them, rather than imposing their own designs. The search is for leaders who stand in a special relation to their fellow citizens, recognized by their people's respect for them, their sympathy for the people and their power or response to the people's thoughts and aspirations."[27]

A common feature of the leaders recognized by the Magsaysay awards is their exercise of leadership through a collective approach—the establishment of councils, organizations, movements, or foundations. Leaders in government often cannot establish organizations; they work instead to strengthen the credibility and service of the agency and government they represent. For example, awardees Haydee Yorac and James Michael Lyngdoh have worked, often under heavy opposing pressure, to make elections free and fair. Yorac improved government accountability first as a national election commissioner and then as chair of the Presidential Commission on Good Government in the Philippines, and Lyngdoh as a chief election commissioner in India.

Most of the Asian leader-awardees, however, did not start from a position of authority. Early on, they try to gain a small consensus and form an organization, movement, or foundation that will provide them with an identity and an umbrella to expand their activities. This strategy has been consistently used by Asian leaders receiving the Magsaysay awards. For example, two of the first awardees set up their own civil society organizations, the Lanka Mahila Samiti women's institutes set up by Mary Rutnam in Sri Lanka (then Ceylon) and the Bhoodan Movement for "land for the landless" set up by Vinoba Bhave in India. Twenty-first-century leadership awardees have helped set up or lead a whole range of organizations, including a Thai Volunteer Service, Indonesia Corruption Watch, the Cancer Institute (WIA) in India, the Participatory Development Center in Laos, Citizens Opening the World for Welfare in South Korea, the Cambodian Women's Crisis Center, the Women's Studies Forum in China, the Mazdoor Kisaan, Shakti Sangathan (Organization for the Empowerment of Workers and Peasants) in India, the Yayasan HAK (Human Rights and Justice) in Timor Leste, the Bishwo Shahitto Kendro (World Literature Centre) in Bangladesh, and India's National Slum Dwellers Federation. The forms of organization differed depending on the socio-politico-cultural context, the time period, and the mission of the organization.

Often leaders helped found organizations to offer each other support, continuing education, and professional development. One example is the Philippine Center for Investigative Journalism, which, in the words of 2003 awardee Sheila Coronel, "has realized that if reforms are to be sustained, there must be a conscious effort to develop a community of journalists who can trade techniques and sources as well as provide each other support when they are being hounded by the powerful . . . The role of press journalists is also important. These groups can act as lobbyists for journalists' rights and for greater access to information. They can monitor infringements on press freedom and develop mechanisms to assist and protect journalists."[28] In Southeast Asia an independent organization to expose corruption, the Indonesia Corruption Watch, was established with the support of volunteers with specialized skills and a network of regional partner organizations.

This pattern of leadership indicates that soon after leaders have started to tackle the issue at hand, they tend to create a consensus and proceed to help establish an NGO, civic group, or movement. Over time, however, and with continuing leadership, the organization tends to take on related activities and larger social concerns, expand from service provision to include advocacy and policy making, or expand in geographical focus to improve its effectiveness and responsiveness to people's needs. A good example is the case of Hye-Ran Yoon, who, after establishing the YMCA in Cheonan, South Korea, became its manager and helped develop a program of activities ranging from recreational activities to concerts and study clubs. She then transferred leadership to a successor and developed another organization, Citizens Opening the World for Welfare (COWW), to address other social welfare issues, such as services to the elderly, the handicapped, and the mentally troubled. The approach used by Yoon through COWW was to "incubate" new organizations to address these concerns and then to spin them off as independent community NGOs. In the case of Sheila Coronel and the Philippine Center for Investigative Journalism, this leader helped form a watchdog and support group for the region, the Southeast Asian Press

Alliance, with colleagues from Indonesia and Thailand and also helped found a support group, the Freedom Fund for Filipino Journalists, to aid the families of journalists killed or injured in the line of duty. Oung Chanthol of Cambodia lists networking, reliable information, and transparency as essential factors to put causes on the agenda.

Asian leaders have found it important to develop and maintain links internationally and within the region. From the early years of the Magsaysay awards, there has been an appreciation of the roles of the various stakeholders in development. In the words of 1958 awardee Dr. Chiang Mon-Lin of the Joint Commission on Rural Reconstruction, who thought that rural reconstruction should involve the people: "Use aid as yeast. Let the people or government have a chance of supplying as much flour as possible for the dough. Experts or technicians should act as bakers."[29] Decades later, Tasneem Ahmad Siddiqui, director general of the Sindh Katchi Abadi, a government agency established to address the squatter problem in the Sindh Province in Pakistan, reconfirmed the importance of partnerships and the need for rapport among government officials, NGOs, and the slum dwellers themselves to improve their conditions.

Networking in recent years has been facilitated with Internet technology, the development of global awareness, opportunities for networking among international organizations or linking like-minded local organizations, recognition and more cooperation from some governments, and the affordability of international travel. Networks of professionals and NGO leaders were formed in South Korea to press for public sector reforms and an ombudsman group in one locality to monitor the city's social services. International foundations have provided technical support, facilitated the exchange of information, and provided valuable resources in cash and kind. The Magsaysay awardees, for example, encouraged the award foundation and the Rockefeller Brothers Fund to support opportunities for them to develop stronger links through conferences, more impact through projects assistance, and more learning through technical and other forms of assistance.

Maintaining a Balance Between Progress and Stability

Tensions arise as leaders try to promote change and yet realize that they need to maintain some stability during the process of change. In the example of Aruna Roy, who worked with local villagers for fair treatment in wages and public works, the strategy involved building up credibility and living with local people before establishing small groups and using traditional forms of protest. After achieving some success in solving the land-grabbing issue, the group held open-air hearings, undertook research, and organized mass rallies in the capital. Resistance from public officials who were "loathe to open their books . . . prompted Roy and Organization for the Empowerment of Workers and Peasants to launch a series of rallies culminating in a fifty-three-day protest in Jaipur, the capital of Rajasthan, to compel the state to make its development-fund records public. The movement soon took on India-wide dimensions as the media and prominent intellectuals and political reformers joined in. As a result, right-to-information laws have now been passed in Rajasthan and three other states. A comprehensive national law is pending before the government of India."[30]

Leaders also must address urgent concerns in the twenty-first century, and they have to develop new strategies to do so. Awardees have had to take these actions in a well-informed and skillful manner—and to develop solutions as they went along. Some of the concerns include conflict resolution and peace building in the region, addressing environmental concerns, and technology change.

Conflict Resolution and Peace Building in the Region. Three succeeding conferences of the awardees from 2002 to 2004 focused on ways to achieve peace. Many awardees themselves have devoted their lives to resolving conflicts and exploring paths to peace. The perspectives of the awardees, reflecting their philosophies and realities, have differed widely from meditative approaches (Nakamura: "The key to peace . . . a spirit that must be built in our hearts.") to activism. For many, the pathway to peace lies in addressing the mind of the individual; for others it is removing the sources and conditions of conflict. Some of the awardees directly attribute the conflicts to adverse economic conditions. Sandeep Pandey, for example, found that

> India is going through very troubled times. We have primarily been a culture of tolerance. Today, fueled by the onslaught of new economic policy and aggressive campaign of multinational companies, a belligerent ideology is being imposed on the nation. Violence is being glorified on one hand in the name of religious intolerance and on the other [in the form of] nuclear weapons. The former is creating bloody internal conflicts whereas the latter has created a continuous war like situation on the border.[31]

Others point to the increasing demands on natural resource bases that are creating conflict among people, loss of productive assets, and negative externalities. The awardees promote peace as an offshoot of their medical, legal, or other missions, or they do so directly through strategies to reduce conflict and promote peace. Laxminarayan Ramdas and Ibn Abdur Rehman, for example, co-founded a Pakistan-India People's Forum for Peace and Democracy to work for popular support for peace in the two countries.

The awardees at the 2004 conference on "Social Conflicts and Cultures of Peace: Rethinking Roadmaps" considered that the best approach to peace was to establish and strengthen connectivity, and this was done even visually in an exercise creating a web as a symbol of the importance of "a strong ethical force in creating ripples of transformation" in a community. They found strength, for example, in sharing their ideas—"that as leaders they shared passion, patience, and perseverance in doing service to others, in addition to respect for human dignity and certitude in the capacity of humanity to do good."[32] Leaders from this conference identified the elements they considered for a new paradigm for peace: developing transformative leaders, education for living with diversity, respect for basic rights, advocacy for justice and equity, promoting religious tolerance, cultivating individual peace and compassion, working for cultural transformation and change, finding and using local solutions, and providing for a healing process.

Environmental Stress and Degradation. The Asian landscape is increasingly degraded because of greater demands on natural resources. More awardees are recognized for their leadership in environmental causes ranging from promotion of eco-friendly activities such as rehabilitating the degraded habitat and renewing the vitality of rivers in India (Rajendra Singh and his group of Rajasthani villagers), greening Chinese deserts (Seiei Toyama and the Japan Association for Greening Deserts and Project Green Hope volunteers), other nature protection activities undertaken by Liang Congjie working in China with the Friends of Nature, and activities to raise environmental consciousness through the media (Bharat Koirala and the Nepal Forum for Environmental Journalists). These leaders use various approaches to gain the awareness and trust of volunteers and to use appropriate technologies. One imaginative way was the use of landmines in Afghanistan by villagers who were former guerillas working with Tetsu Nakamura to excavate wells for clean water.

Technology and Innovation. Awardee M. S. Swaminathan emphasized the need for leaders in Asia to develop technologies that make a difference in such areas as education and science or new seeds, crops, or village technologies. Many leaders and organizations that were recognized by the award program do this both at the local level and on a bigger scale. Leaders help determine the pace of progress in relation to their society's culture and values. The Dalai Lama, for example, has "desired radical changes in land tenure, but said such reforms 'must conform with the dignity, needs and peculiar conditions of my own people.'"[33]

Capacity Building for
Sustained Improvement to Public Welfare

Much of the focus of leadership is on building the enabling environment that will sustain development for the benefit of all groups in society. This has involved institutionalizing changes in systems of law or practice that ensure fairness for all, measures to distribute power more equitably, programs to educate all in society about people's rights and responsibilities, and the use of technologies that will promote accountability and transparency.

These examples of the Magsaysay awardees' leadership are testaments to their ability to inspire others and their commitment to develop other leaders. Many of the awardees themselves speak of the inspiration they derived from someone in their family or from reading something that made them commit themselves to lives of service for the public good. In some cases this led people to seek similar paths or professions, and in other cases it led them to use their talents and energies for a variety of causes. Leaders working on health issues, for example, almost immediately start training village health nurses, medics, midwives, and other volunteers. Other leaders train youth groups, journalists, budding scientists, and others for service in particular fields. Many end up working for bigger causes and energizing others to do so. Hye-Ran Yoon started with an interest in developing youth services in her city in Korea and ended with a bigger dream, "a city energized by the actions of many small healthy organizations."

THE MAGSAYSAY AWARD PROGRAM IN THE NEXT FIFTY YEARS

The Magsaysay Award Program has almost five decades of experience in identifying and supporting Asian leaders—a remarkable feat and a treasure of valuable knowledge in development experience. The awards program has underscored the importance of recognizing leaders and holding them up as role models. It has also increased the visibility of the issues and causes they espouse.

The award foundation has remained a stable organization that is high in prestige and integrity. Its activities evolve with changes in technology (for example, developing an e-newsletter and e-conversations on the website, and sponsoring essay contests for youth to learn from the role models) and as its officials find other ways to optimize the impacts of the program.

In a region marked with diversity and lack of trust, the Magsaysay awards highlight strategies for peace and improved welfare that have created goodwill within the region. The challenge for the Magsaysay Foundation in the years to come will be to build on and expand the valuable network of leaders and to explore new ways of sharing and widening their experience. The award program has continued to spawn new activities such as conferences and other projects to support social change promoted by a growing network of awardees. Increasingly, the Magsaysay Foundation is working to disseminate information about the awards and to create enthusiasm among Asian youth for the role models the awardees exemplify.[34]

NOTES

1. Asian Development Bank, "Review of the Asian Development Bank's Poverty Reduction Strategy" (Manila: Asian Development Bank, 2004).

2. United Nations Development Programme, *Human Development Report 2005* (New York: Oxford University Press, 2005).

3. Tore Frangsmyr, "Life and Philosophy of Alfred Nobel" http://nobel prize.org/nobel/alfred-nobel/biographical/frangsmyr/index.html.

4. David Bornstein, *How to Change the World: Social Entrepreneurs and the Power of New Ideas* (New York: Oxford University Press, 2004).

5. Lorna Kalaw-Tirol (ed.), *Great Men and Women of Asia: Ramon Magsaysay Awardees 1958–1967* (Manila: Anvil Publishing, 2004).

6. Ibid.

7. http://www.rmaf.org.ph. To a limited extent, the Ramon Magsaysay Award Foundation also gives awards to organizations.

8. *The Ramon Magsaysay Awards 1958–1962* (Manila: Ramon Magsaysay Award Foundation, 1977).

9. http://www.rmaf.org.ph.

10. Ibid.

11. Ibid.

12. Ibid.

13. Ibid.

14. General Jesus Vargas, *The Ramon Magsaysay Awards 1963–1965* (Manila: Ramon Magsaysay Award Foundation, 1980).

15. http://www. rmaf.org.ph.

16. Ibid.

17. Ibid.

18. Ibid.

19. Amartya Sen, *Development as Freedom* (Oxford: Oxford University Press, 1999).

20. Vinay Bhargava and Emil Bolongaita, *Challenging Corruption in Asia: Case Studies and a Framework for Action* (Washington, DC: World Bank, 2004).

21. *The Ramon Magsaysay Awards 1958–1962,* op. cit.

22. Ibid.

23. Ibid.

24. Ibid.

25. Ibid.

26. Robert J. Taormina and Christopher Selvarajah, "Perceptions of Leadership Excellence in ASEAN Nations," *Leadership* 1, 3 (2005): 299–322.

27. Vargas, op. cit.

28. http://www. rmaf.org.ph.

29. *The Ramon Magsaysay Awards 1958–1962,* op. cit.

30. Ibid.

31. Ibid.

32. Ibid.

33. *The Ramon Magsaysay Awards 1958–1962,* op. cit.

34. I would like to thank the following people and their institutions for their generous help during my research: Carmencita T. Abella and the staff at the RMAF, William F. McCalpin at the RBF, Darwin H. Stapleton at the Rockefeller Archives Center, and Dennis A. Rondinelli and John M. Heffron at PBRC.

Part III

Imperatives of Globalization:
Leadership and the Problem of Change

10

GLOBALIZATION, LEADERSHIP, AND DEVELOPMENT:
EMERGING PATTERNS AND CHALLENGES

Dennis A. Rondinelli and John M. Heffron

All of the chapters in this book reinforce a consistent conclusion: development requires change, and change requires leadership. Bringing about political, economic, and social changes for peaceful human development is not likely to occur at any level—internationally, nationally, or locally—without individuals and organizations exercising leadership. The concepts of development, change, and leadership converge if we accept James MacGregor Burns's definition of leadership as "leaders inducing followers to act for certain goals that represent the values and motivations—the wants and needs, the aspirations and expectations—of both leaders and followers."[1] Globalization compounds those needs and aspirations and so places special demands on leaders seeking change.

The chapters in this volume offer ample evidence of the challenges a diversified yet interconnected world poses to leadership and of its role in improving people's lives, which ultimately is what development is all about. They also effectively rule out the search for one best way, testifying to the fact that no single style or approach to leadership is universally applicable in all cultures, countries, or organizations. Effective leadership is both culturally influenced and situationally defined; the values, needs, wants, and aspirations of people seeking a better life not only shape the motivations of development leaders and followers, but also influence the efficacy of leadership attributes, styles, and approaches. As Dennis A. Rondinelli notes in Chapter 2 of this volume, numerous studies conclude that leadership styles that are effective at one time and place may be less so at another time or under different circumstances. Our studies of individual and organizational leadership in the Pacific Basin also reinforce several widely known but sometimes forgotten lessons: not all of those in positions of authority are really leaders, all leaders are developmental in their intent, and not all of those who aspire to promote development are successful. The contributors to this volume highlight the fact that globalization—increasing political, economic, social, and technological interaction across national borders—has not only redefined the tasks of development but also made the challenges that leaders face in promoting change more diverse and complex. Globalization imposes new tasks and mounts new challenges for leaders who promote development, creating the need to balance those styles of leadership that are most effective in their own cultures and societies with international expectations of what effective development leaders should do and how they should do it.

In this book we explored five research questions. First, how does global interdependence among governments and organizations in Pacific Basin nations—primarily in Asia and South America—affect approaches to and practices of leadership around important development issues? Second, how do political, business, and social leaders in the Pacific Basin exercise leadership to achieve development goals? Third, are transformational or transactional leadership styles more effective in bringing about developmental change in Pacific Basin countries? Fourth, what differences and similarities in leadership styles, approaches, concepts, and methods within and across Asian, Latin American, and North American cultures and societies influence development decisions? Fifth, what lessons can be learned from recent experience with economic, social, and human development in Pacific Basin countries about the styles, traits, and attributes of leadership that could be used to develop future leaders?

GLOBALIZATION AND DEVELOPMENT LEADERSHIP

The contributors to this volume find that globalization is influencing the roles and styles of development leadership in at least three ways. First, globalization is increasing the complexity and diversity of tasks and challenges that development leaders face in the twenty-first century. Second, globalization is shaping expectations of development leaders' roles and behaviors. Third, globalization influences expectations about the attributes of effective development leadership in bringing about economic, social, and political changes. The forces driving globalization and expanding interaction among political, economic, and social organizations across national borders both have had direct impacts on leadership tasks and challenges and have indirectly shaped the environment in which effective development leaders must perform their tasks.

Globalization's Impacts on Issues
and Challenges of Development Leadership

With the inception of the Marshall Plan, the creation of the United Nations and Bretton Woods institutions, and the expansion of bilateral foreign assistance programs of governments in North America and Europe in the 1950s, the tasks of promoting development in poor countries became everyone's responsibility. Promoting development also became a more complex task for leaders in both aid-giving and aid-receiving countries. Economic globalization shaped the way governments and businesses in developing countries responded to rapidly changing patterns of trade and investment, technological advances in transportation and communications, and increasing economic interdependence. As Rondinelli points out, globalization changed perceptions of effective leadership in the private sector, at least in North America. The complexities of coping with international competition accelerated the shift in corporations from hierarchical, directive leadership to more participative and consultative cooperation through inter- and intra-organizational teams.

But long before the acceleration of economic globalization in the early 1980s, government leaders of both aid-providing and aid-receiving countries discovered that decisions about the flows of financial and technical assistance from richer to poorer countries were inevitably affected by a political calculus. That is, aid-giving countries saw development assistance not only as a way of promoting economic and social progress in poor countries but also as an instrument for enhancing their own political influence internationally and enhancing their competitiveness in a globalizing economy.

The Truman administration's Marshall Plan clearly sought to help devastated European economies stabilize and grow, but its justification for stimulating economic recovery in Europe was inextricably linked to American foreign-policy goals of containing the spread of Communism and protecting American security. The leadership that President Truman and his brain trust of diplomats, academics, and former military leaders brought to the creation, enactment, and implementation of the Marshall Plan was as much intended to enhance the influence of the United States in a world of political turmoil as to help former allies and developing countries shore up their economies and rebuild their societies.

In Chapter 3, John M. Heffron notes Truman's commitment—at a time when technological innovation was driving a new era of economic globalization—to shifting United States foreign aid beyond simply providing financial assistance to sharing America's growing technological expertise and know-how with the rest of the world. By 1957, as Heffron points out, the Senate Foreign Relations Committee was arguing that technical assistance was "the basic program," with economic aid viewed as "temporary" and "an adjunct." What was implied in sharing America's technical knowledge, of course, was the use of foreign aid to forge ties with developing countries in which the acceleration of economic growth would open opportunities for American corporations to provide them with new products, services, and technologies and to create political goodwill that the United States government could call upon in its fight to contain Communism.

The international political and economic interests of the United States were no less important to President Kennedy as he used his personal leadership, buttressed by his own brain trust, to redefine and expand the American approach to foreign assistance in the 1960s. Although never entirely divorced from American Cold War policies, Kennedy's vision was to separate US foreign aid from "America's immediate military interests." Heffron notes that America's global image so deeply influenced Kennedy as a young senator from Massachusetts that he sent each of his fellow senators a copy of Eugene Burdick and William Lederer's blistering critique of US foreign policy in their 1958 novel *The Ugly American.* Kennedy's leadership in promoting a "Decade of Development," while seeking to help underdeveloped countries escape from the devastation of human poverty, also aimed to recast the United States in a more favorable light around the world and to strengthen American political influence in a still highly contentious international setting.

Globalization also changed the roles of and challenges for leaders in countries receiving foreign assistance for development. The need to respond to economic crises resulting from rapid changes in a globalizing economy, as Judith Teichman emphasizes in Chapter 7, drove the calls in Mexico and Chile for broad market reforms during the 1970s and 1980s. But few of those reforms took hold in either country until strong leaders advocated or imposed them. Teichman contends that reforms initiated in Mexico in 1984 did not really get under way until the government of Carlos Salinas responded to recurrent economic crises in the early 1990s by pushing hard for trade liberalization and privatization. She points out that a small coterie of highly trained technocrats, led by the president himself, was able to insulate economic reform decisions from opposing technocrats and from congress, largely thanks to the combination of *caudillismo* (manifested in the Mexican case in the intense loyalty of political cliques, or *camarillas*) and the influence of the Institutionalized Revolutionary Party (PRI), which concentrated political power in the presidency. As in the Chilean case, economic reforms were pushed through in Mexico by powerful economic groups who were the major beneficiaries of the changes.

Teichman explains that in Chile, market reform, which occurred in two phases, arose from the economic crisis of 1981 to 1983. The first phase involved "shock treatment": rapid trade liberalization and the privatization of companies nationalized by the previous government. Much of the leadership for these reforms came from the close personal relationships among a small cadre of technocrats and the owners of three industrial-financial conglomerates. Subsequent market reforms characterized by the expanded role of the state in promoting export-led economic growth involved a more pragmatic approach that incorporated a wider cross section of the business community in decision making. The programmatic (though highly polarized) political leadership of the previous period, Teichman argues, was a key factor in this economic success. President Allende's land reforms in the early 1970s broke down the power of the old unproductive land owners and opened the way for the emergence of a new, dynamic agricultural entrepreneurial class.

One of the strongest drivers of globalization—the creation of worldwide communications systems—enabled information to be disseminated quickly across international borders. As Ian Smillie emphasizes in Chapter 8, the spreading access to communications dramatically changed the roles of nongovernmental organizations (NGOs) and their leaders. Most of what are now the largest international NGOs began as small relief organizations responding to news of international emergencies. The technological innovations in communications made possible the almost instantaneous worldwide dissemination of information about international disasters. Smillie argues that this not only gave relief organizations new and expanded tasks but also motivated many of them to evolve into development assistance organizations that sought to prevent disasters as well as to provide relief.

Many leaders of the largest international NGOs were thrust into roles not of their own making. Smillie points out that because of its widespread poverty and the willingness of international donors to support poverty reduction programs, Bangladesh has spawned more NGOs, and more large NGOs, than any country in Asia. Building Resources

Across Communities (BRAC) grew to operate more than 30,000 primary schools and a university; it took on huge rural dairy and poultry projects, a major health program, and a chartered bank as large as Grameen. It has seconded staff as consultants to UN agencies and the government of Vietnam and has operated a large rural development project in Afghanistan. With an annual income in 2003 of US$148 million (about 25 percent of it supplied by international donors), BRAC became one of the largest NGOs in the developing world.

Because their organizations often did not deliberately seek to become as large as they eventually became, the founders and their successors had to manage unexpected growth, coordinate and cooperate with international development organizations and with each other, and deal with a broader array of challenges that often required new or different leadership styles. The communications innovations accompanying globalization enabled NGO leaders to challenge some of the largest bilateral and multilateral development projects in their countries—the Narmada Dam project in India and the Three Gorges project in China. Although they did not always succeed in stopping these projects, they sometimes pressured governments and international donors into reappraising and redesigning them.

Globalization and the Reshaping of Leadership Roles and Behaviors

By imposing new tasks and challenges on development leaders, globalization also required them to take on new roles and reshaped international standards of acceptable and appropriate behavior. Although some political and organizational leaders use authoritarian or highly directive approaches to bringing about change, worldwide systems of communication now make it difficult for most "toxic leaders" to hide or cover up violations of human rights, corruption, or use of force in imposing their will on citizens. The world now learns quite quickly which political leaders are developmental and which are simply exploiting their country's resources for their own political and economic gain.

In Chapter 4, G. Shabbir Cheema reviewss the pressures that globalization exerts on political leaders to be more open, transparent, accountable, and inclusive in governance. Numerous United Nations conferences and summits have created new development demands on political leaders. The strong pursuit of the Millennium Development Goals by the United Nations, the World Bank, and other international organizations assisting poor countries refocused government leaders' attention on their critical roles in reducing poverty and human suffering and on enhancing people's living conditions and capacities to earn a decent living. Cheema sees a growing international consensus that "good" political leaders promote human development through democratic and decentralized governments that "combat exclusion, protect public goods, actively engage civil society and the private sector, use the power of information and communications technology (ICT) to promote e-government, and strengthen partnerships among different economic sectors, societal groups, and levels of government."

Economic globalization and the growing international concern about poverty and inequality require political, business, and social leaders to deal in one way or another with rising economic expectations of citizens. In an increasingly interconnected world, few political or social leaders can completely ignore the exclusion or marginalization of the poor from growth-oriented policies without adequate safety nets or the increasing need to accommodate diverse and often conflicting ethnic and religious minorities in political decisions. In one way or another, they must come to grips with the gradual weakening of state capacity to resolve internal conflicts or to control external political and economic pressures that can constrain or limit their options.

The economic, technical, and political complexities arising from globalization require leaders in government, business, and civil society organizations to act in new ways to promote development. Hierarchical, directive, command-and-control approaches are becoming less effective in solving the diverse and complex problems that accompany globalization. Yet cultural traditions and political legacies favoring more authoritarian

styles of leadership in some Asian and Latin American countries continue to create tensions between leaders' own pursuit of political power
and the need for them to act in more democratic and participative ways
to mobilize support for sustainable change.

In China and Japan, contrasting leadership styles have led to dramatically different approaches to globalization and change, with profound consequences for the economies of these two countries. In Chapter
6, William H. Overholt attributes Japan's reversal of fortune—its precip-
itous economic decline from the heyday of the 1970s and 1980s, when
Japan's GDP was second only to that of the United States, to the spectacular collapse of its economy in 1990 and its ongoing doldrums—
to a recondite bureaucratic apparatus that discourages innovation and
change, as well as to an anachronistic leadership style sunk in hierarchy,
shrouded in secrecy and obscurantism, and aimed at protecting the status quo. Although conditions today in Japan are ripe for change, the
apathy of the voting public, the continuing dominance of the Liberal
Democratic Party and its system of patronage, and an inveterate con-
servativism in policy-making circles have blocked the emergence of bold,
effective, and visionary leadership. Though quick to grasp the advantages of globalization, and moving aggressively into international markets while creating wildly lopsided trade deficits with its partners, Japan
has nevertheless been slow to accept its responsibilities, barricading itself
behind a wall of protectionism and failing to practice good governance
at home.

China, on the other hand, in moving toward a market-oriented system, has disarmed its critics by instituting economic reforms that would
have been politically impossible as little as ten years ago. Facing an even
deeper financial crisis than Japan in the 1990s, a crisis made more in-
tractable by the predominance of large state-owned banks and enterprises,
China's leaders took an entirely different tack than their Japanese counterparts, presiding over a massive restructuring of the economy. State
enterprises in the thousands were either "absorbed, devolved to local governments, privatized, or sold to foreigners." Under the leadership team of

Premier Zhu Rongji and President Jiang Zemin, banks and state en-terprises were freed from centralized political control and held to new and higher performance standards in their management and adminis-tration—something Japanese leaders were either too timid or too po-litical to do themselves. In contrast to Japan's protectionist policies, China not only opened its doors to foreign financial institutions but also offered them a stake in the management and a share in the profits of its increasingly privatized, slimmed-down industrial sector. It im-paneled foreign experts on the China Securities Regulatory Commission, where they could play a direct role in reforming China's financial system, in most cases along liberal, democratic, capitalist lines.

These changes, vast in size and scope, were not effected without some bloodletting. Scores of central and provincial-level government jobs were eliminated in the process; new civilian controls were imposed on the military and its political influence sharply curtailed; and key min-isterial industrial bureaus, once dispersed, unaccountable, and rife with corruption, were consolidated into one. These were "politically diffi-cult" measures for Chinese leadership, but they were essential to restor-ing confidence in the country's future. Japan, Overholt argues, "allowed a similar but somewhat less severe problem to stagnate the economy, demoralize the citizenry, and leave the country without a vision for the future." In the end, the differences between the economic fates of Japan and China have come down to the kind and degree of leadership exercised by the people in charge.

In Latin America, as Teichman points out, strong international pressures have forced political leaders to move away from paternalistic authoritarianism to electoral democracy. Leaders' behaviors now differ in important ways from those of a quarter century ago, she argues, al-though some continuities remain. Chile's political leadership—the left-center Concertación coalition of the Christian Democratic Party and two socialist parties—reflects these tensions between authoritarian and dem-ocratic leadership. Although the nature of the country's political transi-tion and the institutional legacy of military rule have guaranteed its adherence to the neoliberal model, Teichman argues, Chilean leaders continue to be heavily influenced by the country's past military rule. This legacy has resurrected issues of social justice and equity, which have increased markedly in recent years, along with tensions between the political leadership and the private sector. Despite progress in the reduction of poverty, largely through job expansion, Chile remains a highly unequal society. Consensus building on this issue is essential, Teichman argues, but many political leaders remain highly resistant to opening up the policy process to multiparty and civil society influence.

In the Mexican case, Teichman notes, the emergence of democracy and the election of Vicente Fox in 2000 were generally seen as an important change in the institutional distribution of political power and, presumably, in the way political leaders behaved. Congress became much more important when it was freed of control by the PRI leadership, but one of the consequences was stronger opposition to further economic or governance reforms. The Fox administration, taking its cues from governments in other countries seeking to gain competitiveness in the global economy, focused on economic issues but largely ignored social equity. Economic policy making remained in the hands of many of the same technocrats who held power under the PRI, joined by members of the private sector, many of whom were appointed by Fox to top government positions. The Fox administration appeared reluctant to compromise, and the opposition parties remained highly distrustful of the presidency. Like Chilean political leaders, those in Mexico resisted opening up the policy process to wider participation. At the same time, multilateral lending agencies were able to more deeply influence policy discussions in Mexico because of its periodic economic crises and the country's high level of poverty.

The tensions arising from changing international perceptions of appropriate leadership roles and behavior are also reflected in the strategies of international assistance organizations and bilateral aid agencies. William Ascher points out in Chapter 5 that over the years, US and Japanese aid agencies have tried both directive leadership (by attaching conditions to financial assistance) and more indirect forms of "modeling" or "giving orientation." Although it is difficult to demonstrate definitively, Ascher asserts that interactions with Japanese and US foreign aid organizations have influenced the behavior of developing nations' leaders. Both foreign aid organizations sought to "give orientation" by (1) targeting specific groups of "followers" in the selection of foreign assistance recipients; (2) using assistance to convey desirable leadership styles and roles in development; (3) attaching conditions and constraints on recipients' discretion or by channeling recipient-country leaders into desired paths of action; (4) supporting the education and training of recipient-country leaders by instilling new ways of thinking and expanding their cross-cultural awareness, as well as by providing training in leadership development; (5) using technical assistance as a form of modeling to influence the priorities, practices, and behavior of recipient-country counterparts; (6) embedding development assistance in broader models of development philosophy and strategy; and (7) using the interaction of international experts and recipient-country counterparts in political, technical, and managerial practices considered effective by aid providers.

Both foreign aid programs suggested values and goals that leaders in developing countries should espouse—the United States program through its priority on assistance to social betterment and through education and training in American colleges and universities, and the Japanese program through its focus on assistance for projects that would promote rapid economic growth and increase trade and investment, presumably with Japan. But both countries also sought to influence behavior in developing countries by attaching conditions and restrictions on the use of aid. The United States often placed conditions on aid that required policy changes within recipient countries to promote democracy, free markets, capitalism, and the use of NGOs in pursuing social and economic development.

In some instances, government leaders adopted financial and managerial practices that were suggested by the aid agencies or were embedded in their "conditionalities" for foreign assistance. Sometimes, however, political leaders and government officials in other countries learned less desirable lessons, such as how to take advantage of geopolitical consid- erations by engaging in international brinksmanship. (For example, during the Cold War period, Egypt's Gamal Abdel Nasser tried playing the United States off against the Soviet Union, and more recently, po- litical leaders in Iran and North Korea developed or threatened to de- velop nuclear weapons to offset the power of the United States.) It remains open to question whether organizational modeling has been an effective means of exercising leadership or of influencing counterparts' behavior. Ascher concludes that there is little evidence that US develop- ment doctrines have been adopted through emulation of American pre- scriptions for using foreign assistance. Indeed, for officials of recipient countries, US foreign assistance may appear to be imperious, self-serv- ing, and politicized. The adoption of market-oriented reforms seems likely to be the result of more indirect means of "giving orientation"— that is, through the growth of cadres of technically trained economic pol- icymakers attending US universities, although even the funding of this program constituted a rather small proportion of US foreign assistance.

Perhaps a more successful approach to international modeling of leadership behavior came through the award system that the Rockefeller Brothers Fund sponsored at the Ramon Magsaysay Award Foundation in the Philippines. By recognizing and awarding leaders who demonstrated "good" leadership behaviors in government service, public service, lit- erature, creative and communicative arts, and peace and international understanding, the Magsaysay awards gave orientation for admired at- tributes and behaviors of development leadership. As Rosemary Fernholz concludes in Chapter 9, "the awards program has raised the importance of recognizing leaders and holding them up as role models. It has also in- creased the visibility of issues and causes they espouse."

DEVELOPMENT LEADERSHIP ATTRIBUTES AND STYLES

Globalization is reshaping international expectations not only of the tasks that development leaders should pursue, but also of desirable leadership attributes. As Fernholz notes, those Asian leaders who have received awards from the Magsaysay Award Foundation over the past half century demonstrated attributes valued both in their own societies and by the international community. Increasingly, some attributes have come to be associated with good leadership around the world; these include credibility, courage, persistence, self-motivation, caring, and humility.

Courage and persistence seem to reinforce each other as attributes of development leaders. Even those leaders who advocated peaceful means of development and change have had to muster enormous courage to persist in the face of personal threats of violence and death against themselves and their families. Fernholz notes that many of the Magsaysay Award winners in Asia were people who had the courage and persistence to challenge political authorities on development issues. Aniceto Guterres Lopes fought for human rights during turbulent times in East Timor, and Dita Indah Sari was imprisoned in Indonesia for advocating workers' rights. Jiang Yanyong's persistence in publicizing the threats to public health forced the government of China to face up to the SARS problem, and Gao Yaojie risked retribution for publicizing its failure to deal with the AIDS crisis.

Other examples in this book highlight the importance of persistence as an attribute of development leadership. In the United States, those responsible for adoption of the Marshall Plan drew on a strong commitment to their vision of achieving a more stable world. They had to overcome the reluctance of a war-weary and skeptical public and the efforts of many in Congress to pull the United States back into a comfortable isolationism after World War II. Heffron recounts President Kennedy's persistence in changing the American public's and Congress's view of foreign aid from that of a Cold War weapon to an instrument of peace and human development.

Fernholz's description of those receiving Magsaysay awards emphasizes that those recognized as strong leaders also shared other attributes. They all had a strong sense of vision; they led through empowerment, public service, and collective action; they balanced the drive for change with maintaining an appropriate degree of stability; they networked internally within their countries and internationally; and they relied heavily on building the capacity of development organizations and of other development leaders to extend and sustain their influence. Cheema argues that the United Nations' focus on reinventing government has led to widely shared international perceptions how effective leaders bring about development: they should have the capacity to communicate a vision to followers; reconcile long-term goals with short-term pressures; forge partnerships with public, private, and civil society organizations; and exhibit personal integrity and commitment to reform.

All of the successful development leaders discussed in this book were able to influence the behavior of others because they had a strong vision of a better future that they were able to articulate in order to mobilize followers. George C. Marshall, Harry Truman, and the brain trust that shaped the European Recovery Plan mobilized support for US foreign assistance to Europe because they foresaw the potential of using American resources and know-how to bring about a more peaceful and stable world. Mahathir Mohammad, the long-time prime minister of Malaysia (and a man more comfortable with command and control than with participative decision making) remained in power and moved his country toward faster economic development because he could transform his vision into a feasible strategy and then into policies for which he could mobilize support.

Successful development leaders had the knack of combining seemingly contradictory leadership attributes to influence the thinking, behavior, and actions of others. Even the most idealistic development leaders, for example, had to be pragmatists in order to succeed. They could balance the drive for change with the need to maintain an appropriate degree of stability. Pragmatism was the hallmark of President Kennedy's leadership in restructuring the US foreign aid program. Heffron points out that in leading the fight for a new development policy, Kennedy's political instincts told him he had to balance his appeals to the public and to Congress by highlighting both the altruism underlying the new foreign aid doctrine and its benefits in reshaping the world's image of the United States and in protecting national security. Shifting the argument too drastically or too quickly to foreign aid as altruistic development would, he concluded, be seen as an uncertain departure from more than twenty years of Cold War justifications for expanding American foreign assistance. Kennedy also balanced and selected from a wide variety of sometimes conflicting intellectual ideas about how to change American foreign aid policy. Kennedy's leadership style was to orchestrate, blend, and combine the ideas of leading thinkers in the field of development with his own political instincts about which ideas would attract the political support he needed to push through his policy changes.

Heffron noted that Kennedy considered himself "an idealist without illusions"; he adjusted his vision for change in American foreign aid policies to political realities and adapted the provisions of his proposals to the necessities of amassing sufficient congressional and public support to get new foreign aid legislation enacted. That pragmatism was accompanied by his ability and willingness to be flexible; he used a variety of foreign aid instruments to increase political support for his proposals. Cheema's description of Jaime Lerner's leadership in developing the city of Curitiba also notes his ability to balance the need for action with consensus building, seeking support for change without becoming bogged down in conflict and disagreement, and finding ways of putting his vision in place gradually over time.

Likewise, although he was considered a more directive leader, Mahathir Mohammad combined vision with pragmatism and flexibility in guiding Malaysia through a period of economic and social transition. Cheema refers to his skills in balancing often contradictory forces and conflicting opinions and interests by building public trust in his claim to be acting on behalf of all Malaysia's ethnic and religious groups. As a persistent pragmatist, he adjusted his plans and policies to changing global and national political, economic, and social realities. Mahathir exercised leadership by continuously re-forming coalitions of support and forging partnerships between public sector and private sector organizations.

Some others, who sought to become development leaders without the pragmatism and flexibility that Kennedy and Mahathir demonstrated, were often less effective. Vicente Fox's ambitious vision setting and political commitment to government reform in Mexico were instrumental in bringing about some changes, but his inability to mobilize political support and to overcome resistance among those with vested interests in the status quo disappointed many of his followers by the end of his presidential term. His inability or unwillingness to adapt his goals to the political realities in Mexico, to reach out to civil society organizations by adopting their suggestions for changes in his agenda, and to react flexibly to alternative ways of enacting and implementing reforms undermined his ability to achieve his good intentions. Teichman concludes that Vicente Fox's inability to attain many of the development objectives and policy reforms in Mexico may have been due to overly progressive visions and overly ambitious goals that were politically unrealistic, given his party's lack of a majority in congress and the recalcitrance of opposition parties. She points out that Vicente Fox's leadership attributes as president of Mexico were often contradictory and inconsistent. As a result, he sometimes sent mixed messages and confusing signals to both his followers and his opponents. Because of his unwillingness to compromise, his very commitment to reform often undermined his efficacy in bringing about change. His attempts at participative leadership were often offset by his tendency to ignore or veto proposals that emerged from consultations with civil society organizations.

Because of their increasing dependence on international financial support, leaders of NGOs involved in development, as Smillie discovered, must exhibit leadership characteristics that are effective in their own cultures and societies as well as characteristics that meet the expectations of international funding organizations. Effective development leaders have to satisfy the expectations of both their demand-based constituencies and their supply-side supporters. Cheema points out that national political leaders and government officials seeking to promote development often have to reconcile short-term political necessities with long-term development goals. Successful leaders must be able to forge partnerships among diverse groups, mediate differences, consult with interest groups, and still maintain a commitment to social justice for all.

TRANSACTIONAL AND TRANSFORMATIONAL LEADERSHIP STYLES

Globalization and the internationalization of development assistance also create tensions over leadership styles, and especially between highly directive and highly participative forms of leadership. Although some leaders rely more heavily—or even exclusively—on transactional leadership, many of those profiled in this book achieved their success through transformational leadership. Debates continue, however, over which style of leadership is more conducive to bringing about developmental change. Burns notes that transactional leadership is based on a relationship of exchange between leaders and followers, and the leader's influence depends on the ability to provide rewards that followers desire. Although transforming leaders must also recognize the needs or demands of potential followers, they go beyond that to find potential motives, satisfy higher needs, and elevate followers to pursue change.[2] In the process, Burns argues, both followers and leaders "raise one another to higher levels of motivation and morality."[3]

The analyses in this book discuss both transactional and transformational leadership styles and the wide range of attributes and approaches associated with each. Some leaders were transactional and directive, relying on exchange of rewards through command and control, whereas others were transformational, consultative, and participative in making decisions. The studies confirm Rondinelli's finding, reported in Chapter 2, that in neither Asia nor Latin America has one style or method of leadership been universally adopted by political, business, or social leaders. Yet many of the leaders discussed in this book seem to have been more successful in achieving their objectives and in convincing others to pursue their vision of the future through transformational leadership styles than through transactional approaches.

Many development leaders in Asia and Latin America, and especially those working at local levels, found not only that transformational leadership was more effective but also that it was essential in attracting and guiding followers. Perhaps precisely because they lacked the official positions of authority in government that sometimes make transactional leadership styles more effective, they had to rely on their ability to inspire and motivate followers by appealing to moral principles or strong social values.

As Fernholz points out, Magsaysay Award Foundation leadership award winner Ela Bhatt, who organized and empowered more than a half million women in India to improve their lives through the Self-Employed Women's Association, was a transformational leader driven by the belief that "development is the rehabilitation of 'hearts and minds.'" Taking her inspiration from the philosophy of Gandhi, Bhatt, a lawyer by training, joined the textile labor union that had been formed by Gandhi and was placed in charge of the Women's Wing. Dissatisfied with the welfare approach the union took to women's issues, Bhatt passionately believed that women were capable of being successful entrepreneurs who, with vocational training, small amounts of capital, and strong reinforcement, could play an important role in supporting their families and contributing to India's economic development.[4] Using Gandhi's principles, Bhatt organized the Self-Employed Women's Association, established a Cooperative Bank to provide microfinance, organized vocational training programs, taught women about information technology, developed an insurance cooperative, and helped women set up small businesses.

Bhatt's success as a transformational leader derived from her persistence in inspiring women's empowerment and in attempting to change the mindset of both poor women and government policymakers about the roles and capabilities of women in society. Bhatt summed up the philosophy driving her leadership in women's empowerment: "For the people, development is not a project. It is not institutions. It is not even economics. It is about restoring balance. It is about the well being of the poor woman, her family, her community and her work environment and this world we all live in. This we have learnt from Gandhiji."[5]

Transformational leadership was also at the core of the success of another Magsaysay Award winner. Antonio Meloto, a Fillipino born to humble circumstances, launched a successful business career after receiving a scholarship to Ateneo de Manila University, a Jesuit-run Catholic college. Meloto's encounter years later with a Catholic organization for couples brought him to question the direction of his life. "I was so focused on repackaging, and building up myself that . . . I forgot the poor. I left them behind. I left them like so many others before me," he later told a graduating Ateneo University class. "How could I expect them to love the poor whom they do not know when I grew up poor and yet forgot to help them too."[6] Meloto rededicated his life to helping the poor, convinced by immersing himself in the lives of slum dwellers that, with decent living conditions and the dignity that came with those improvements, they would find the hope to improve their lives.[7]

Meloto believed that if slum dwellers could have access to decent, clean, safe, sturdy houses in viable neighborhoods, it could help them turn their lives around. He mobilized volunteers to begin transforming one of the poorest squatter areas of Manila, Bagong Silang, by building homes that would be distributed to the poorest families. The homes could not be resold, and the recipients had to volunteer to help build them and abide by neighborhood covenants. Meloto formed a foundation, Gawad Kalinga (To Give Care) to build the houses, and inspired a broad network of volunteer organizations, major domestic and international corporations, hundreds of city mayors, and members of congress to contribute the funds and provide other forms of support needed to carry out the foundation's work.

By 2006, Meloto's Gawad Kalinga had built more than 850 villages around the Philippines and had committed itself to building 7,000 new communities by the year 2010. In most of the tidy, clean, and colorfully painted Gawad Kalina villages, Meloto points out, "Crime has virtually disappeared. Former street children are now in school. The idle have been motivated to find employment and are now leading productive lives."[8] Meloto inspired others to transform their own lives and those of the poor through a vision shaped by his Christian beliefs and principles, as well as by four tenets of his own personal philosophy: (1) never stop hoping for our country, (2) don't stop caring for our people, (3) demand greatness of yourself as a Filipino, and (4) inspire greatness in other Filipinos.[9]

Transformational leadership exhibits itself not only at the local level but sometimes in national leaders as well. Although, as a pragmatist, John F. Kennedy used transactional leadership when he needed to build a coalition of support for changes in US foreign aid policy, his push for a fundamental redefinition of the purposes of American foreign aid was embedded in a transformational style that appealed to basic social values and to the altruism of the American people. Kennedy inspired a whole generation of young people who served in the Peace Corps to join the US Agency for International Development and international NGOs upon their return from Peace Corps service and to support American foreign assistance policies that sought to bring about peaceful international development.

Many of the purely transactional and highly directional leaders profiled in this book, however, seem to have fallen short of the mark in inspiring sustainable development. Thaksin Shinawatra's directive and control-oriented leadership in Thailand was temporarily effective in mobilizing the support of those people living in rural areas who benefited from his policies, but it alienated those who saw his leadership as self-serving, authoritarian, and corrupt. The military coup that overthrew his government in 2006 was enthusiastically accepted by those people living in Bangkok and other urban areas who viewed Thaksin's actions merely as the exchange of public largesse for votes, while the rural beneficiaries of Thaksin's policies passively accepted his overthrow.

Teichman documents clearly that the predominant leadership style of those in political power in Latin America has often been directive and transactional, shaped by the *caudillismo* tradition. Much of the political history of Mexico during the twentieth century, she argues, was one of hierarchical, authoritarian, and exclusionary presidential rule under a one-party monopoly or a military regime, with little freedom for the legislatures, the courts, or civil society organizations to exercise checks and balances on the personal power of those occupying the presidency. Pinochet used authoritarianism to consolidate power, putting those loyal to him and his policies in positions of authority and crushing political opposition in both the military and the bureaucracy.

Even as the pressures of globalization and democratization have raised new challenges and required the government to address new issues of social reform in Chile, Teichman points out, the legacy of military rule and of command and control kept Chilean political leadership styles predominantly hierarchical and exclusionary. The economic and political impacts of directive and transactional leadership have been disappointing for many of those who have been excluded from benefits, and those impacts have come under widespread criticism by more populist leaders. As in Chile, the emphasis in Mexico on appointing government officials loyal to the president and his party subordinates ensured a directive and transactional style of leadership throughout the bureaucracy.

CHALLENGES OF DEVELOPMENT LEADERSHIP IN A GLOBALIZING SOCIETY

One of the clearest lessons of our review of experience with leadership for development is that emerging leaders face new and more complex challenges in bringing about sustainable changes in an era of globalization. Twenty-first-century development leaders at both national and local levels must be able, in Smillie's colorful analogy, to "dance backwards and in high heels." In a world widely connected by advanced communications technology, development leaders must appeal, with visions of a better future and appropriate attributes and styles, to followers in their own cultures and societies, while at the same time doing everything that is expected of development leaders internationally. To succeed they must often balance roles and behaviors that are effective in their own cultures and political systems with fulfilling the roles and using leadership styles that meet the expectations of the international development organizations, bilateral foreign aid programs, and international NGOs that increasingly provide external support for their programs.

As Cheema points out in Chapter 4 of this book, the growing international mandate to meet the UN Millennium Development Goals and to reinvent government to promote human development in a rapidly globalizing economy also requires that political and social leaders exhibit new competencies. In the twenty-first century, effective leaders must have a better understanding of the complexity of globalization processes, an ability to adapt to rapid changes over which they may have little or no control, the capacity to foster collaboration and partnerships among those involved in governance, and a firm commitment to building democratic institutions for political legitimacy. By international standards, good leaders must demonstrate commitment to integrity and fairness in the exercise of power, adopt entrepreneurship and risk-taking behavior, provide for the professional and personal development of their staff, and build strategic planning capacity.

The profiles of leaders in this volume also indicate the importance of another lesson for development leaders: the need to prepare followers to adopt new attitudes and behaviors in order to bring about change. Without prepared followers, few leaders can effectively mobilize support for change. In some cultures and political systems, followers must be prepared to accept inclusive or participative leaders as a precondition for achieving development goals. As Teichman points out, the long tradition of *caudillismo* and authoritarian rule made it difficult for civil society groups to participate effectively, negotiate, and reach consensus on social reforms when Chile's President Ricardo Lagos attempted to open up the process of decision making in the early 2000s. Despite his efforts to make policymaking more inclusive, Teichman reports, Lagos "came up against the deeply polarized positions that continue to characterize many policy areas in Chile."

In countries where government is not responsive to the need for change or resists individuals or organizations that seek to promote development, leaders must find ways of creating expanded political space. As Smillie points out, the roles of NGOs in development have expanded in the past because of failed leadership in government. In countries with "toxic" or ineffective political leadership, people must often organize themselves or be organized by those outside of government to provide services or solve problems that governments ignored or addressed inadequately. Enlarging the roles of NGOs in Asian societies—Indonesia, Malaysia, Thailand, and Singapore—required extraordinary leadership to expand the political space for civil society organizations to act at all.

In this sense, development leaders outside of government must find the most appropriate ways of "speaking truth to power" without creating such a strong political backlash from unsympathetic opposition groups or political leaders threatened by influential civil society organizations that it undermines their influence or completely suppresses their programs. Many of the NGO leaders profiled here have had to struggle with the question of how directly they seek to participate in politics in the countries where their governments control or heavily influence the ability of voluntary organizations to operate effectively.

Ultimately, all development leaders face difficult challenges in learning how to "scale up" successful development programs without losing the driving principles, motivations, and methods that made small or focused activities successful. Development leaders, and especially charismatic leaders and founders of new social movements, must find effective ways of transferring their vision, inspiration, and principles to organizations—and to other leaders—who can carry on, expand, and sustain activities that successfully promote human development.

NOTES

1. James MacGregor Burns, *Leadership* (New York: Harper & Row, 1978), 19.

2. Ibid., 3–4.

3. Ibid., 20.

4. *The South Asian,* "Ela Bhatt—In First Person," October 2003. Accessed at http://www.the-south-asian.com/Oct2003/Ela%20Bhatt.htm.

5. Ela R. Bhatt, "Our View of Development," speech given at the Conference on Rethinking Development, Local Pathways to Global Wellbeing, Antigonish, Nova Scotia, Canada: St. Francis Xavier University, June 20, 2005. Accessed at http://www.gpiatlantic.org/conference/proceedings/bhatt.hem.

6. Antonio P. Meloto, "The Eagle Will Not Fly Without the Poor," speech delivered at the Ateneo de Manila University Commencement Exercises, March 25, 2006. Accessed at http://www.adzu.edu.ph/Utls/print/Article.php?id-444.

7. Ramon Magsaysay Award Foundation, "Citation for Antonio Meloto," August 31, 2006. Accessed at http://www.rmaf.org.ph/Awardees/Citation/CitationMelotoAnt.htm.

8. Ibid.

9. Meloto, op. cit.

REFERENCES

Abueva, José. "Administrative Doctrines Diffused in Emerging States: The Filipino Response." In *Political and Administrative Development*, edited by Ralph Braibanti, 536–87. Durham, NC: Duke University Press, 1969.

Adler, Nancy. *International Dimensions of Organizational Behavior.* Cincinnati, OH: Southwestern Publishing Company, 1997.

Arase, David. "Introduction." In *Japan's Foreign Aid: Old Continuities and New Directions*, edited by David Arase. London: Routledge, 2005.

———. "Japan's and the United States' Bilateral ODA Programs." In *Japan's Foreign Aid: Old Continuities and New Directions*, edited by David Arase, 117–32. London: Routledge, 2005.

———. *Buying Power: The Political Economy of Japan's Foreign Aid.* Boulder, CO: Lynne Rienner, 1995.

Badaracco, Joseph. *Leading Quietly: An Unorthodox Guide to Doing the Right Thing.* Boston: HBS Press, 2002.

Bailey, John. *Governing Mexico: The Statecraft of Crisis Management.* London: Macmillan, 1988.

Barnes, John A. *John F. Kennedy on Leadership: The Lessons and Legacy of a President.* New York: American Management Association, 2005.

Barnes, L. B., and M. P. Kriger. "The Hidden Side of Organizational Leadership." *Sloan Management Review* 28, 1 (1986): 15–25.

Bass, Bernard. *Leadership and Performance Beyond Expectations.* New York: The Free Press, 1985.

Bass, B. M., E. R. Valenzi, D. L. Farrow, and R. J. Solomon. "Management Styles Associated with Organizational Task, Personal and Integrative Contingencies." *Journal of Applied Psychology* 60 (1975): 720–29.

Batiwala, Srilatha, and Aruna Rao. "Conversations with Women on Leadership and Social Transformation," 2005, accessed at www .genderatwork.org/updir/ConversationswithWomen.pdf.

Beaudry-Someynsky, Michelle. "Japanese ODA Compared to Canadian ODA. " In *Japan's Foreign Aid: Old Continuities and New Directions,* edited by David Arase, 133–51. London: Routledge, 2005.

Beer, M., R. A. Eisentstat, and B. Spector. "Why Change Programs Don't Produce Change." *Harvard Business Review* 68, 6 (1990): 158–66.

Bennis, Warren. *Organizing Genius.* Reading, MA: Addison-Wesley, 1997.

Bennis, W. "Managing the Dream: Leadership in the 21st Century. Training." *The Magazine of Human Resource Development* 27, 5 (1990): 44–46.

Bennis, W., and B. Nanus. *Leaders: The Strategies for Taking Charge.* New York: Harper & Row, 1985.

Bernard, Chester I. *The Functions of the Executive.* Cambridge, MA: Harvard University Press, 1938.

Brandenburg, Frank. *The Making of Modern Mexico.* Englewood Cliffs: Prentice-Hall, 1964.

Braverman, Harry. *Labor and Monopoly Capital: The Degradation of Work in the Twentieth Century.* New York: Monthly Review Press, 1974.

Burns, James MacGregor. *Leadership.* New York: Harper & Row, 1978.

Cervero, Robert. "Progressive Transport and the Poor: Bogotá's Bold Steps Forward." *Access,* 27 (Fall 2005): 24–30.

Claflin, Edward B. *JFK Wants to Know: Memos from the President's Office 1961–1963*. New York: William Morrow, 1991.

Coates, A. W., ed. *The Post-1945 Internationalization of Economics*. Durham, NC: Duke University Press, 1997.

Comisión Económica para América Latina (CEPAL). *Panorama social en América Latina, 2002–2003: Anexo estadístico*. Santiago: CEPAL, 2003.

Conger, Jay, and Rabindra Kanungo. *Charismatic Leadership in Organizations*. Thousand Oaks, CA: Sage Publications, 1997.

Contreras, Manuel E., and Maria Luisa Talavera Simoni. "The Bolivian Education Reform 1992–2002: Case Studies in Large-Scale Education Reform." Country Studies. Washington, DC: World Bank, 2003.

Constable, Pamela, and Arturo Valenzuela. *A Nation of Enemies*. New York: Norton, 1991.

Dalek, Robert. *An Unfinished Life: John F. Kennedy, 1917–1963*. New York: Little, Brown, 2003.

Dauvergne, Peter. "The Rise of an Environmental Superpower? Evaluating Japanese Environmental Aid to Southeast Asia." Working Paper 1998/3. Canberra: Australian National University, 1998.

De Pree, M. *Leadership Is an Art*. New York: Doubleday, 1989.

Dorfman, Peter W., Paul J. Hanges, and Felix C. Brodbeck. "Leadership and Cultural Variation: The Identification of Culturally Endorsed Leadership Profiles." In *Culture, Leadership and Organizations: The GLOBE Study of 62 Societies*, edited by R. House, P. Hanges, M. Javidan, P. Dorfman and V. Gupta, 669–719. Thousand Oaks, CA: Sage Publications, 2004.

Dower, John W. *Embracing Defeat: Japan in the Wake of World War I*. New York: Norton, 2000.

Drucker, Peter F. *The Essential Drucker*. New York: HarperCollins, 2001.

Duttweiler, P. C., and S. M. Hord. *Dimensions of Effective Leadership*. Austin, TX: Southwest Educational Development Laboratory, 1987.

Faundez, Julio. "In Defense of Presidentialism: The Case of Chile. In *Presidentialism and Democracy in Latin America,* edited by Scott Mainwaring and Matthew Soberg Shugart, 300–20. Cambridge: Cambridge University Press, 1997.

Fiedler, Fred E. *A Theory of Leadership Effectiveness.* New York: McGraw-Hill, 1967.

———. "How Do You Make Leaders More Effective? New Answers to an Old Puzzle." *Organizational Dynamics* 1, 2 (1972): 2–18.

Fu, P. P., T. K. Peng, Jeffrey C. Kennedy, and Gary Yukl. "Examining the Preferences of Influence Tactics in Chinese Societies: A Comparison of Chinese Managers in Hong Kong, Taiwan, and Mainland China. *Organizational Dynamics* 33, 1 (2004): 32–46.

Giglio, James N. *The Presidency of John F. Kennedy.* Lawrence, KS: University Press of Kansas, 2006.

Gilbert, Christopher, and David Vines. "The World Bank: An Overview of Some Major Issues. In *The World Bank: Structure and Policies,* edited by Christopher Gilbert and David Vines, 10–36. Cambridge: Cambridge University Press, 2004.

Goleman, D., R. Boyatzis, and A. McKee. *Primal Leadership: Realizing the Power of Emotional Intelligence.* Cambridge, MA: Harvard Business School Press, 2002.

Grant, Richard. "Reshaping Japanese Aid for the Post-Cold-War Era." *Tijdschrift voor Economische en Sociale Geografie* 86 (1995): 235–48.

Grant, Richard, and Jan Nijman. "Historical Changes in U.S. and Japanese Foreign Aid to the Asia-Pacific Region." *Annals of the Association of American Geographers* 87, 1 (1997): 32–51.

Greenleaf, Robert K. *Servant Leadership: A Journey into the Nature of Legitimate Power and Greatness.* New York: Paulist Press, 1977.

Gutierrez, Ramon Munoz. *Government Innovations: The Good Government Paradigm in the Administration of President Vicente Fox.* Fondo De Cultura Economica, Carretera Picacho-Ajusco, Mexico, 2004.

Gustainis, J. Justin. "Autocratic Leadership." In *Encyclopedia of Leadership*, edited by G. R. Goethals, G. J. Sorenson, and J. M. Burns Vol. 1, 68–72. Thousand Oaks, CA: Sage Publications, 2004.

Gyohten, Toyoo. "Japan and the World Bank." In *The World Bank: Its First Half Century, Volume 2: Perspectives*, edited by Devesh Kapur, John P. Lewis, and Richard Webb, 275–316. Washington, DC: The Brookings Institution, 1997.

Handy, Charles. "The Language of Leadership." In *Frontiers of Leadership*, edited by M. Syrett and C. Hogg, 7–12. Oxford: Blackwell, 1992.

Hastings, Laura A. "Regulatory Revenge: The Politics of Free Market Financial Reforms in Chile." In *The Politics of Finance in Developing Countries*, edited by Stephan Haggard, Chung H. Lee, and Sylvia Maxfield, 210–29. Ithaca: Cornell University Press, 1993.

Hermes, Niels. "New Explanations of the Economic Success of East Asia: Lessons for Developing and East European Countries." Centre for Development Studies Working Paper No. 3, University of Groningen, June 1997.

Hicks, Douglas A. "Globalization." In *Encyclopedia of Leadership*, edited by G. R. Goethals, G. J. Sorenson, and J. M. Burns, 570–77. Thousand Oaks, CA: Sage Publications, 2004.

Hirata, Keiko. *Civil Society in Japan: The Growing Role of NGOs in Tokyo's Aid and Development Policy.* New York: Palgrave Macmillan, 2002.

House, Robert, and Mansour Javidan. "Overview of GLOBE." In *Culture, Leadership and Organizations: The GLOBE Study of 62 Societies*, edited by R. House, P. Hanges, M. Javidan, P. Dorfman, and V. Gupta, 9–28. Thousand Oaks, CA: Sage Publications, 2004.

Institute of International Education. *Open Doors 2005.* Washington, DC: Institute of International Education, 2005.

Javidan, Monsour, Robert J. House, and Peter W. Dorfman. "A Nontechnical Summary of GLOBE Findings." In *Culture, Leadership and Organizations: The GLOBE Study of 62 Societies*, edited by

R. House, P. Hanges, M. Javidan, P. Dorfman, and V. Gupta, 29–50. Thousand Oaks, CA: Sage Publications, 2004.

Jolly, Richard, Louis Emmerij, Dharam Ghai, and Frederic Lapeyre. *UN Contributions to Development Thinking and Practice.* Bloomington: Indiana University Press, 2004.

Kanter, Rosabeth M. *The Change Masters.* New York: Simon & Schuster, 1983.

Kapur, Devesh, John P. Lewis, and Richard Webb. *The World Bank: Its First Half Century, Volume 1: History.* Washington, DC: The Brookings Institution, 1997.

Katada, Saori. "Japan's Two-track Aid Approach." *Asian Survey* 42, 2 (2002): 320–42.

Katz, Richard. *Japan: The System That Soured.* New York: M.E. Sharpe, 1998.

Kennedy, John F. *The Strategy of Peace.* New York: Harper, 1960.

Kerr, Alex. *Dogs and Demons: Tales from the Dark Side of Japan.* New York: Hill & Wang, 2001.

Kirkpatrick, S. A. and E. A. Locke. "Leadership: Do Traits Matter?" *Academy of Management Executive* 5, 2 (1991): 48–60.

Koppel, Bruce, and Robert Orr Jr., eds. *Japan's Foreign Aid: Power and Policy in a New Era.* Boulder, CO: Westview Press, 1993.

Labouisse, Henry R. *An Act for International Development, A Program for the Decade of Development: Summary Presentation,* June 1961, Department of State Publication 7224, General Foreign Policy Series 174. Washington, DC: US Government Printing Office, 1961.

Lambert, Jacques. *Latin America. Social Structures and Political Institutions.* Berkeley: University of California Press, 1967.

Larrañaga, Osvaldo J., and Jorge R. Marshall. "Ajuste macroeconómico y finanzas públicas, 1982–1988," Programa de post grado de economía, ILADES. Georgetown: Georgetown University, 1990.

Lasswell, Harold D. "Conflict and Leadership: The Process of Decision and the Nature of Authority." In *Conflict in Society,* edited by A. de Rueck and J. Knight, 210–28. Boston: Little, Brown, 1966.

————. "The World Revolution of Our Time. In *World Revolutionary Elites: Studies in Coercive Ideological Movements*, edited by Harold D. Lasswell and Daniel Lerner, 29–95. Cambridge, MA: MIT Press, 1965.

Lederer, William J., and Eugene Burdick. *The Ugly American.* New York: Norton, 1999 reissue.

Lewis, Arthur. *The Theory of Economic Growth.* London: Allen and Unwin, 1955.

Lipman-Bluman, Jean. "The Allure of Toxic Leaders: Why Followers Rarely Escape Their Clutches." *Ivey Business Journal* (January–February, 2005): 1–8.

Llanos, Mariana, and Ana Margheritis. "Why Do Presidents Fail? Political Leadership and the Argentine Crisis (1999–2001)." *Studies in Comparative International Development* 40, 4 (2006): 77–103.

Llosa Mario Vargas quoted in Dan A. Cothran, *Political Stability in Mexico: The Perfect Dictatorship.* Westport, CT: Praeger, 1994.

Locke, Edwin A. "Self-Interest," In *Encyclopedia of Leadership*, Vol. 4, edited by R. Goethals, G. J. Sorenson, and J. M. Burns, 1400–06. Thousand Oaks, CA: Sage Publications, 2004.

Mainwaring, Scott, and Matthew Soberg Shugart, eds. *Presidentialism and Democracy in Latin America,* 300–20. Cambridge: Cambridge University Press, 1997.

Maslow, Abraham H. "The Theory of Human Motivation." *Psychological Review* 50 (1943): 370–96.

Mayer, John Jr. "Curitiba, the Little *Cidade* That Could." *Time,* October 14, 1991.

McGee-Cooper, Ann, and Gary Looper. *The Essentials of Servant-Leadership: Principles and Practice.* Waltham, MA: Pegasus Communications, 2001.

McGregor, Douglas. *The Human Side of Enterprise.* New York: McGraw-Hill, 1960.

Miyashita, Akitoshi. *Limits to Power: Asymmetric Dependence and Japanese Foreign Aid Policy.* New York: Lexington Books, 2003.

Mintzberg, Henry. *The Nature of Managerial Work.* New York: Harper & Row, 1973.

Montgomery, John D. *Foreign Aid in International Politics.* Englewood Cliffs, NJ: Prentice-Hall, 1967.

Montgomery John D., and Dennis A. Rondinelli, eds. *Great Policies: Strategic Innovations in Asia and the Pacific Basin.* Westport, CT: Praeger Publishers, 1995.

Nielsen, Stine. "Improving Japanese Official Development Assistance Quality: Discussing Theories of Bureaucratic Rivalry." *Kontur* 7 (2003): 32–40.

Oishi, Mikio, and Fumitaka Furuoka, "Can Japanese Aid Be an Effective Tool of Influence? Case Studies of Cambodia and Burma." *Asian Survey* 43, 6 (2003): 890–907.

Okazaki, Kumiko. "Banking System Reform in China: The Challenges of Moving Toward a Market-Oriented Economy." Occasional Paper. National Security Research Division. Santa Monica, CA: RAND, 2007.

Okazaki, Tetsuji, and Masahiro Okuno-Fujiwara, eds. *The Japanese Economic System and Its Historical Origins,* translated by Susan Herbert. New York: Oxford University Press, 1993.

Organisation for Economic Co-operation and Development. *2005 Development Co-operation Report,* Vol. 7, No. 1. Paris: OECD, 2006.

Orme, John. "The Original Megapolicy: America's Marshall Plan." In *Great Policies: Strategic Innovations in Asia and the Pacific Basin,* edited by John D. Montgomery and Dennis A. Rondinelli, 41–62. Westport, CT: Praeger Publishers, 1995.

Overholt, William H. "Japan's Economy: At War with Itself." *Foreign Affairs* 81, 1 (2002): 134–47.

Pandian, Sivamurugan. *Legasi Mahathir.* Kuala Lumpur, Malaysia: Utusan Publications, 2005.

Pempel, T. J. *Regime Shift: Comparative Dynamics of the Japanese Political Economy.* Ithaca, NY: Cornell University Press, 1998.

Rabinovitch, Jonas, and John Hoehn. *A Sustainable Urban Transportation System: "The Surface Metro" System in Curitiba, Brazil.* Washington, D.C.: EPAT/MUCIA. May 1995.

Rabinovitch, Jonas, with Josef Leitman. "Urban Planning in Curitiba." *Scientific American* 274, 3 (March 1996): 46–54.

Rafferty, Alannah E., and Mark A. Griffin. "Dimensions of Transformational Leadership: Conceptual and Empirical Extensions." *The Leadership Quarterly* 15 (2004): 329–54.

Rix, Alan. *Japan's Foreign Aid Challenge: Policy Reform and Aid Leadership.* New York: Routledge, 1994.

———. "Japan's Emergence as a Foreign-Aid Superpower." In *Foreign Aid Toward the Millennium,* edited by Steven Hook, 75–90. Boulder, CO: Lynne Rienner, 1996.

———. "Japanese and Australian ODA." In *Japan's Foreign Aid: Old Continuities and New Directions,* edited by David Arase, 104–16. London: Routledge, 2005.

Roberts, Kenneth M. "Neoliberalism and the Transformation of Populism in Latin America: The Peruvian Case" *World Politics* 48, 1 (1996): 82–116.

Rondinelli, Dennis A. *Development Projects as Policy Experiments.* 2nd ed. London, UK: Rutledge, 1993.

———. "Processes of Strategic Innovation: The Dynamics of Decision Making in the Evolution of Great Policies." In *Great Policies: Strategic Innovations in Asia and the Pacific Basin,* edited by John D. Montgomery and Dennis A. Rondinelli, 223–39. Westport, CT: Praeger Publishers, 1995.

Rondinelli, Dennis A., and G. Shabbir Cheema, eds. *Reinventing Government for the Twenty-First Century: State Capacity in a Globalizing Society.* Bloomfield, CT: Kumarian Press, 2003.

Rosen, George. *Western Economists and Eastern Societies.* Baltimore: Johns Hopkins University Press, 1985.

Rosenbaum, Allan. "New Challenges for Senior Leadership Enhancement for Improved Public Management." In *Citizens, Businesses, and*

Governments: Dialogue and Partnerships for Development and Democracy." Background Papers presented to the Third Global Forum on Reinventing Government, held in Marrakech, Morocco, December 10–13, 2002.

Rossiter, Clinton. *The Federalist Papers.* New York: NAL Penguin, 1961.

Rostow, W. W. *The Stages of Economic Growth.* Cambridge: Cambridge University Press, 1960.

———. *The Diffusion of Power: An Essay in Recent History.* New York: Macmillan, 1972.

Rostow, W. W., and Max Millikan. *A Proposal: Key to an Effective Foreign Policy.* New York: Harper, 1957.

Schlesinger, Arthur M. *A Thousand Days: John F. Kennedy in the White House.* Boston: Houghton Mifflin, 1965.

Schraeder, Peter, Steven Hook, and Bruce Taylor. "Clarifying the Foreign Aid Puzzle: A Comparison of American, Japanese, French, and Swedish Aid Flows." *World Politics* 50 (1998): 294–323.

Seddon, David. "Japanese and British Overseas Aid Compared." In *Japan's Foreign Aid: Old Continuities and New Directions,* edited by David Arase, 117–32. London: Routledge, 2005.

Sen, A. K. *Development as Freedom.* New York: Alfred A. Knopf, 1999.

Shifter, Michael. "Latin America's New Political Leaders: Walking on a Wire." *Current History* 102 (February 2003): 51–57.

Sigmund, Paul E. *The Overthrow of Allende and the Politics of Chile, 1964–1976.* Pittsburgh: University of Pittsburgh Press, 1977.

Silva, Eduardo. *The State and Capital in Chile: Business Elites, Technocrats and Market Economics.* Boulder, CO: Westview Press, 1996.

Silva, Patricio. "Intelectuales, tecnócratas y cambio social en Chile: Pasado, presente y perspectivas futuras." *Revista Mexicana de Sociología* 54, 1 (1992): 139–66.

Simon, Herbert A. *The New Science of Management Decision.* New York: Harper & Row, 1960.

Smircich, Linda, and Gareth Morgan. "Leadership: The Management of Meaning." *Journal of Applied Behavioral Science* 18, 3 (1982): 257–73.

Smith, Peter. *Labyrinths of Power.* Princeton, NJ: Princeton University Press, 1979.

Sorensen, Theodore C. *Decision-Making in the White House.* New York: Columbia University Press, 1963.

Spears, Larry C. "Practicing Servant-Leadership." *Leader to Leader* 34 (Fall 2004): 7–11.

Stogdill, Ralph M. "Personal Factors Associated with Leadership: A Survey of the Literature." *The Journal of Psychology* 28 (1948): 35–71.

———. "Leadership, Membership and Organization," *Psychological Bulletin* 47 (1950): 1–14.

Taormina, Robert J., and Christopher Selvarajah. "Perceptions of Leadership Excellence in ASEAN Nations." *Leadership* 1, 3 (2005): 299–322.

Tarnoff, Kurt, and Larry Nowels. *Foreign Aid: An Introductory Overview of U.S. Programs and Policy, Report to Congress.* Washington, DC: Congressional Research Service, January 19, 2005.

Taylor, Frederick W. *The Principles of Scientific Management.* New York: Harper, 1911.

Teichman, Judith A. *The Politics of Freeing Markets in Latin America: Chile, Argentina and Mexico.* Chapel Hill: University of North Carolina Press, 2001.

Teik, Khoo Boo. *Paradoxes of Mahathirism: An Intellectual Biography of Mahathir Mohamad.* Kuala Lumpur: Oxford University Press, 1995.

———. *Beyond Mahathir: Malaysian Politics and Its Discontents.* London: ZedBooks, 2003.

Terry, Edith. "The World Bank and Japan." Japan Policy Research Institute Working Paper 70, Tokyo, August 2000.

Todaro, Michael P. *Economic Development in the Third World.* 4th ed. New York: Longman, 1989.

Troy, Tevi. *Intellectuals and the American Presidency: Philosophers, Jesters, or Technicians?* New York: Rowan and Littlefield, 2002.

Tsui, Anne S., Hui Wang, Katherine Xin, Lihua Zhang, and P. P. Fu. "Let a Thousand Flowers Bloom: Variation of Leadership Styles Among Chinese CEOs." *Organizational Dynamics* 33, 1 (2004): 5–20.

United Nations, *Report of the United Nations Expert Group Meeting on New Challenges for Senior Leadership Enhancement for Improved Public Management in a Globalizing World,* Turin, Italy, September 19-20, 2002.

————. *Unlocking the Human Factor for Public Sector Performance."* Third United Nations Public Sector Report. New York: United Nations, 2005.

————. "Report of the Capacity Development Workshops on Innovation and Quality in the Government of the Twenty-First Century." New York: United Nations, 2004.

————. "Report of the Capacity Development Workshops on Citizens, Businesses and Governments: Dialogue and Partnerships for Development and Democracy. New York: United Nations, 2003.

United Nations Development Programme. *Human Development Report, 1990.* New York: Oxford University Press, 1990.

————. *Human Development Report 2004: Cultural Diversity in Today's Diverse World.* New York: UNDP, 2004.

Vera, Dusya, and Antonio Rodriguez-Lopez. "Strategic Virtues: Humility as a Source of Competitive Advantage." *Organizational Dynamics* 33, 4 (2004): 393–408.

Wade, Robert. "East Asia's Economic Success, Conflicting Perspectives, Partial Insights, Shaky Evidence. *World Politics* 44, 2 (1991): 270–320.

Watson, Thomas J. Jr. "Reorganization." In *The Book of Leadership Wisdom*, edited by Peter Krass, 427–35. New York: Wiley, 1998.

Weber, Max. *Economy and Society*, translated and edited by Guenther Roth and Claus Wittich. New York: Bedminster Press, 1921/1968.

Weldon, Jeffery. "Political Sources of *Presidencialismo* in Mexico." In *Presidentialism and Democracy in Latin America*, edited by Scott Mainwaring and Matthew Soberg Shugart, 225–58. Cambridge: Cambridge University Press, 1997.

Westley, F., and H. Mintzberg. "Visionary Leadership and Strategic Management," *Strategic Management Journal* 10 (1989): 17–32.

World Bank. *The East Asian Miracle: Economic Growth and Public Policy*. New York: Oxford University Press, 1993.

Yukl, Gary, and J. Bruce Tracey. "Consequences of Influence Tactics Used with Subordinates, Peers and the Boss." *Journal of Applied Psychology* 77, 4 (1992): 525–35.

CONTRIBUTORS

William Ascher is the Donald C. McKenna Professor of Government and Economics at Claremont McKenna College, and director of the Pacific Basin Research Center of Soka University of America. Previously he directed Duke University's Center for International Development (1985–2000) and was the academic vice president of Claremont McKenna. His research focuses primarily on Latin America, East Asia, and South Asia. His work on policymaking, forecasting, natural resource management, and environmental policy includes *Forecasting: An Appraisal for Policymakers and Planners, Natural Resource Policymaking in Developing Countries, Why Governments Waste Natural Resources, Guide to Sustainable Development and Environmental Policy, The Caspian Sea: Quest for Environmental Security,* and *Bringing in the Future: Strategies for Promoting Farsightedness and Sustainability.* Other research focuses on the operations of international development organizations, as well as on the role of science in US environmental policymaking.

G. Shabbir Cheema is director of the Asia-Pacific Governance and Democracy Initiative, East-West Center, Honolulu. Previously he was director of the Division for Management Development and Governance, UNDP, New York. As a senior UN official for fifteen years, he provided leadership in crafting democratic governance and public administration programs at the country level, and in designing global research and training programs in electoral and parliamentary systems, human rights, transparency and accountability of government, urban management, and decentralization. He received his PhD in political science in 1973 from the University of Hawaii. He has taught at University Sains Malaysia, University of Hawaii, and New York University. He has been a visiting fellow at Harvard University's Ash Institute for Democratic Governance and Innovation. From 1980 to 1988, he worked as development administration planner at the United Nations Center for Regional Development, Nagoya, Japan. His publications include *Building Democratic Institutions* and *Decentralizing Governance.*

Rosemary Morales Fernholz is a senior research scholar and lecturer at the Duke Center for International Development, Sanford Institute of Public Policy of Duke University. She does research on participatory and innovative approaches to development with particular focus on social sector issues, infrastructure and indigenous peoples, environment and development, and empowerment of disadvantaged groups. She has recently codirected policy studies on school feeding and child nutrition programs in selected countries of Latin America and the Caribbean. She is currently teaching graduate courses on policy analysis for development, innovative policies, indigenous peoples and human rights, and culture and policy in the Program in International Development Policy at Duke University. She has a PhD in political economy and government from Harvard University, as well as MPA and MBA degrees.

John M. Heffron is professor of history and dean of students at Soka University of America, Aliso Viejo, California. He also serves as associate director of the Pacific Basin Research Center, a research unit of the university. Prior to joining Soka University of America, Heffron taught at the University of Hawaii at Manoa, Montana State University, and the State University of New York system at both Fredonia and Buffalo. Heffron has a PhD and an MA in history from the University of Rochester and a BA in history from Princeton University. He has also held research and teaching fellowships from the Rockefeller Archive

Center, the Newberry Institute for Quantitative Methods in History, and the National Endowment for the Humanities. Professor Heffron has published research and commentary in *Science & Education, Educational Theory, History of Education Quarterly, Teachers College Record, American Studies,* and *Religion and American Culture: A Journal of Interpretation.* With Rondinelli, he is most recently the author and editor of *Globalization & Change in Asia* (Lynne Rienner, 2007).

William H. Overholt holds the Asia Policy Research Chair at RAND and is director of its Center for Asia Pacific Policy Center. Currently, Overholt is Senior Research Fellow at the John F. Kennedy School of Government at Harvard. He was distinguished visiting professor at Yonsei University in South Korea for 2003–2005 and is visiting professor at Shanghai Jiaotung University for 2008–2010. He served as head of strategy and economics at Nomura's regional headquarters in Hong Kong from 1998 to 2001 and as managing director and head of research at Bank Boston's regional headquarters in Singapore. During eighteen years at Bankers Trust, he ran a country risk team in New York from 1980 to 1984; then he was regional strategist and Asia research head based in Hong Kong from 1985 to 1998. Overholt is the author of six books, including *Asia, America and the Transformation of Geopolitics* (New York: Cambridge University Press, 2008). His previous book, *The Rise of China* (W.W. Norton, 1993), won the Mainichi News/Asian Affairs Research Center Special Book Prize. He has served as political advisor to several of Asia's major political figures and has done consulting projects for the Korea Development Institute, Korea's National Defense College, the Philippine Ministry of Agrarian Reform, and Thailand's Ministry of Universities. Dr. Overholt received his BA (1968) from Harvard and his Master of Philosophy (1970) and PhD (1972) from Yale.

Dennis A. Rondinelli (1943–2007) was director of the Pacific Basin Research Center at Soka University of America. He was a senior research scholar at the Duke Center for International Development, Duke University, Durham, North Carolina, and the Glaxo Distinguished International Professor Emeritus of Management at the University of North Carolina-Chapel Hill. Dr. Rondinelli's research spans the United States, Asia, Central Europe, Latin America, and Africa. He authored or edited eighteen books and published more than 250 articles in scholarly and professional journals and book chapters. He served as an expert, consultant, or adviser to the US State Department's Agency for International Development, the World Bank, the Asian Development Bank, the Canadian International Development Agency, the International Labor Office, the United Nations Development Programme, and private corporations. In 2002 he was appointed to a four-year term as the member from the United States of the United Nations Expert Committee on Public Administration, and he was reappointed in 2005 for a second four-year term. Dr. Rondinelli received his undergraduate degree from Rutgers University and his PhD from Cornell University. He passed away in March 2007.

Ian Smillie was a founder of the Canadian NGO Inter Pares and was executive director of CUSO. He has worked on projects with the Humanitarianism and War Project at Tufts University (now the Feinstein International Center) since 1997, and he was an adjunct professor at Tulane University from 1998 to 2001. As a development consultant he has worked for many Canadian, American, and European organizations. His latest books are *The Charity of Nations: Humanitarian Action in a Calculating World* (with Larry Minear, 2004) and *Freedom From Want: The Remarkable Success Story of BRAC, the Global Grassroots Organization That's Winning the Fight Against Poverty* (Kumarian, 2009). Ian Smillie is research coordinator on Partnership Africa Canada's "Diamonds and Human Security Project and is a participant in the 45-government Kimberley Process, which has developed and is managing a global certification system to halt the traffic in "blood diamonds. He was appointed to the Order of Canada in 2003.

Judith Teichman is professor of political science at the University of Toronto. She is coauthor of *Social Democracy in the Global Periphery: Origins, Challenges, Prospects* (2006) and is the author of *The Politics of Freeing Markets in Latin America: Chile, Argentina and Mexico* (2001); *Privatization and Political Change in Mexico* (1995); and *Policymaking in Mexico: From Boom to Crisis* (1988). She has also published articles on Mexico, Argentina, and Chile in scholarly journals such as *Comparative Politics, Third World Quarterly, Comparative Studies in International Development*, and *Latin American Perspectives* and in numerous edited volumes. Her research has focused on economic policymaking in Latin America. She is currently completing a comparative project on issues of poverty reduction and inequality in Mexico, Chile, and South Korea.

INDEX

Guangdong International Trust and
    Investment Company (GITIC),
    161
Guomindang, 158
guru syndrome. *See also* nongovernmental
    organizations
    charisma of leaders and, 214, 215–216
    NGO's organizational culture and,
        214–217
    outsider-imagined fiction of, 214–215
Guterres Lopes, Aniceto, 247, 280

Haiti, 4
Hamilton, Fowler, 11
Hammarskjöld, Dag, 73
Handy, Charles, 36
Hansen's disease, 246
Hanum, Zakiah, 253
hartal (strike), 220
Harvard University, 56, 57, 121
Heffron, John M., 1, 10–11, 22, 23, 49,
    267, 270, 271, 280, 281–282
Hegel, Friedrich, 209
Hicks, Douglas, 28
Hilhorst, Dorothea, 211
Hirayama, Ikuo, 250
Hitler, Adolf, 155
HIV/AIDS, 82, 248, 249, 253, 280
Holck-Larsen, Henning, 246
Hong Kong, 42, 43, 169
House, Robert, 27
Hu Jintao, 174
Human Development Report
    (United Nations), 30
human rights, 84–85, 196–197
humility, 39, 245, 246
Hyderabad, India, 99

IBM, 32
ICA. *See* International Cooperation
    Administration
ICT. *See* information and communications
    technology
IDA. *See* International Development
    Association
ILAWAN. *See* Center for Peace and
    Sustainable Development
IMSS. *See* Mexican Institute of Social
    Security

India, 57, 63, 70, 171, 216. *See also* Asia
    as emerging economic superpower, 107,
        139–141
    feudal structures in, 218–219
    foreign assistance and, 137–139
    foreign assistance to Myanmar, 140–141
    future actions of economic superpowers
        and, 137–139
    grant awardees in, 243
    international leadership roles by China
        and, 141–143
    leadership case study with Naidu and,
        99–101
    leadership in emerging economic
        superpowers and, 137–145
    NGOs in, 213, 217, 218
Indonesia, 3–4, 5, 19, 41, 150n39, 159,
    205, 215, 254
    Berkeley Boys and, 126
    fear of Communism in, 211
    grant awardees in, 243
    NGOs and, 219
Indonesia Corruption Watch, 247, 255, 256
Indonesian Consumer Foundation, 4
influence(s)
    advocacy of development models and,
        131–132
    conditionalities and, 128–129
    conveying sense of donor-country
        motives and, 127–128
    direct pedagogy and, 129–130
    Japan, U.S., and potential channels of,
        125–132
    leadership as, 33–35
    lessons from interaction and, 132
    modeling and, 131
    selection of foreign-assistance recipients
        and, 125–127
information and communications
    technology (ICT), 83
information technology (IT), 99–100
integrity, 34, 84
    awards, selection process and, 238, 261
    personal, 89, 91, 96, 281
    of purpose, 225, 238
International Cooperation Administration
    (ICA), 67
International Development Association
    (IDA), 119–120

Also from Kumarian Press...

Foreign Aid and Development:

The World Bank and the Gods of Lending
Steve Berkman

Development Brokers and Translators:
The Ethnography of Aid and Agencies
Edited by David Lewis and David Mosse

Everywhere/Nowhere: Gender Mainstreaming
in Development Agencies
Rebecca Tiessen

Development and Management:
Experiences in Value-Based Conflict
Edited by Deborah Eade, Tom Hewitt, and Hazel Johnson

New and Forthcoming:

How the Aid Industry Works:
An Introduction to International Development
Arjan de Haan

Freedom From Want: The Remarkable Success Story
of BRAC, the Global Grassroots Organization That's
Winning the Fight Against Poverty
Ian Smillie

Rights-Based Approaches to Development:
Exploring the Potential and Pitfalls
Edited by Diana Mitlin and Sam Hickey

Coping with Facts: A Skeptic's Guide to the
Problem of Development
Adam Fforde

Visit Kumarian Press at **www.kpbooks.com** or call **toll-free**
800.232.0223 for a complete catalog.

Kumarian Press, located in Sterling, Virginia, is a forward-looking, scholarly press that promotes active international engagement and an awareness of global connectedness.